# OLD-FASHIONED MODERNISM

# OLD-FASHIONED MODERNISM

## Rural Masculinity and Midwestern Literature

ANDY OLER

LOUISIANA STATE UNIVERSITY PRESS
BATON ROUGE

Published by Louisiana State University Press

Manufactured in the United States of America
First printing

Designer: *Mandy McDonald Scallan*
Typeface: *Sentinel*
Printer and binder: *Sheridan Books*

Early versions of chapter 1 appeared as "'Accentuated by the Wavering Uncertain Light': Sherwood Anderson's Construction of Rural Modernity," *MidAmerica,* 37 (2010): 24–34, and as "Sherwood Anderson's 'Shadowy Figure': Rural Masculinity in the Modernizing Midwest," in *Queering the Countryside: New Frontiers in Rural Queer Studies,* ed. Mary L. Gray, Colin R. Johnson, and Brian J. Gilley (NewYork: New York University Press, 2016), 69–87. Part of chapter 4 was first published as "'Their Song Filled the Whole Night': *Not Without Laughter,* Hinterlands Jazz, and Rural Modernity" in *College Literature* 41, no. 4 (2014): 94–110.



Library of Congress Cataloging-in-Publication Data

Names: Oler, Andy, author.
Title: Old-fashioned modernism : rural masculinity and Midwestern literature / Andy Oler.
Description: Baton Rouge : Louisiana State University Press, [2019] | Includes bibliographical references and index.
Identifiers: LCCN 2018050916| ISBN 978-0-8071-7078-6 (cloth : alk. paper) | ISBN 978-0-8071-7160-8 (pdf) | ISBN 978-0-8071-7161-5 (epub)
Subjects: LCSH: American literature—Middle West—History and criticism. | Masculinity in literature. | Middle West—In literature. | Middle West—Intellectual life—20th century.
Classification: LCC PS273 .O44 2019 | DDC 810.9/92860977—dc23
LC record available at https://lccn.loc.gov/2018050916

The paper in this book meets the guidelines for permanence and durability of the Committee on Production Guidelines for Book Longevity of the Council on Library Resources. ♾

For my parents, Steve and Cindy Oler,

who taught me to fix fence and also to dance.

# CONTENTS

# ACKNOWLEDGMENTS

I couldn't possibly count the kindnesses that have come my way in the course of writing this book. I'll try to account for some of them, and I'll apologize in advance for the ones I've left out.

I wrote most of this book sitting across from Erin Pryor Ackerman, Harmony Jankowski, Cat Ozment, or Matt Sharp. I thank them for their good humor, insightfulness, and constancy and for indulging some boisterous contrarianism from the other side of the table. These four have offered a great deal of feedback along the way, and so have many others. Your attention is a gift, and so is your time—I hope I've done it justice. Thank you to Janet Casey, Ed Comentale, Jonathan Elmer, Jen Fleissner, John Han, Emily Houlik-Ritchey, George Hutchinson, Sara Kosiba, John Lamothe, Ashley Lear, Heather Love, Pat Maley, Annika Mann, Jessica McKee, Taylor Mitchell, Carter Neal, Marcia Noe, Rebecca Peters Golden, Lynnette Porter, Margaret Ronda, Doug Sheldon, Jenny Smith, Maura Smyth, Ross Tangedal, Taryne Taylor, and Sarah Withers. Near the end of the process, Douglas Reichert Powell provided an important perspective and asked for just the right revisions. I am especially grateful for the time and attention Scott Herring gave to this project. From the concepts to the everyday, this book wouldn't be what it is without his influence.

Audiences at several conferences have been gracious enough to offer commentary on parts of this project, including those at the Modernist Studies Association in Buffalo and Pittsburgh, Modern Language Association in Boston and Philadelphia, American Literature Association, Agricultural History Society, Midwestern History Association, the Louisville Conference on Literature and Culture since 1900, and the Association of Literary Scholars, Critics, and Writers. Special thanks to Mary Gray, Colin Johnson, and Gabe Rosenberg at the Queering the Countryside symposium and to Aimee Bahng and Stephanie Farrar at the Futures of American Studies Institute. I could list everyone in the Society for the Study of Midwestern Literature, but I'll at least mention Tricia Oman, Marilyn Atlas, and Jeff Swenson.

I couldn't have completed this book without the help of many librarians and archivists, including those at Indiana University, Embry-Riddle Aeronautical University, Wayne County Museum, Cleveland Art Museum, the Smithsonian, US Census Bureau, National Archives, National Postal Museum, and the Historical Societies of Indiana and Oklahoma. Thanks to Kris Himelein for making two trips to the National Archives for nothing more than the promise of whiskey, and to Jenny Penberthy and R. Douglas Hurt for answering key questions on Niedecker and cabbage planters, respectively. I owe a special debt to Liz Sterthaus and Sue Burkhart on the Embry-Riddle ILL staff for tracking down all my weird hyperspecific requests. The people of Wauseon have been extremely helpful, especially Samantha Sorge at the public library, April Stidham at the post office, Jo Michelson at Red Rambler, and John Swearingen, John Myles, and Jerry Rupp at the Fulton County Historical Museum. Thanks especially to Bob Krumm for taking me around town and giving me the chance to do some sleuthing at the local feed mill.

This project has been supported by fellowships and grants from Indiana University, the Modernist Studies Association, and both the College of Arts and Sciences and the Faculty Research Development Program at Embry-Riddle Aeronautical University. Among my colleagues at Embry-Riddle, special thanks to Donna Barbie, Sally Blomstrom, and Sarah Fogle for always running a tight ship and to Tanya Rice and J. R. Anderson for making my life easier in so many ways. I also want to thank the staff at LSU Press, especially James W. Long and Catherine Kadair, for being attentive and responsive throughout the entire publishing process.

This book is dedicated to my parents, Cindy and Steve Oler. They have supported me, demanded of me, and answered my questions. Between the cattle, the corn, the dancing, and the work ethic, they are my models for what it means to be Midwestern, and not always in the expected ways.

Elin Grimes deserves the most thanks of all. We have covered a lot of ground these past seventeen years, and it has always felt like we were doing it together. I am lucky to be making a life with you, one that lets us settle in when we can and stand up when we need to. Those decisions feel more urgent now than they did in 2001, not least because we've managed to make three pretty terrific children. Ada, Silas, and Miriam, you make each day better. I am proud that you are gentle, caring, and curious kids. Your daddy loves you.

# OLD-FASHIONED MODERNISM

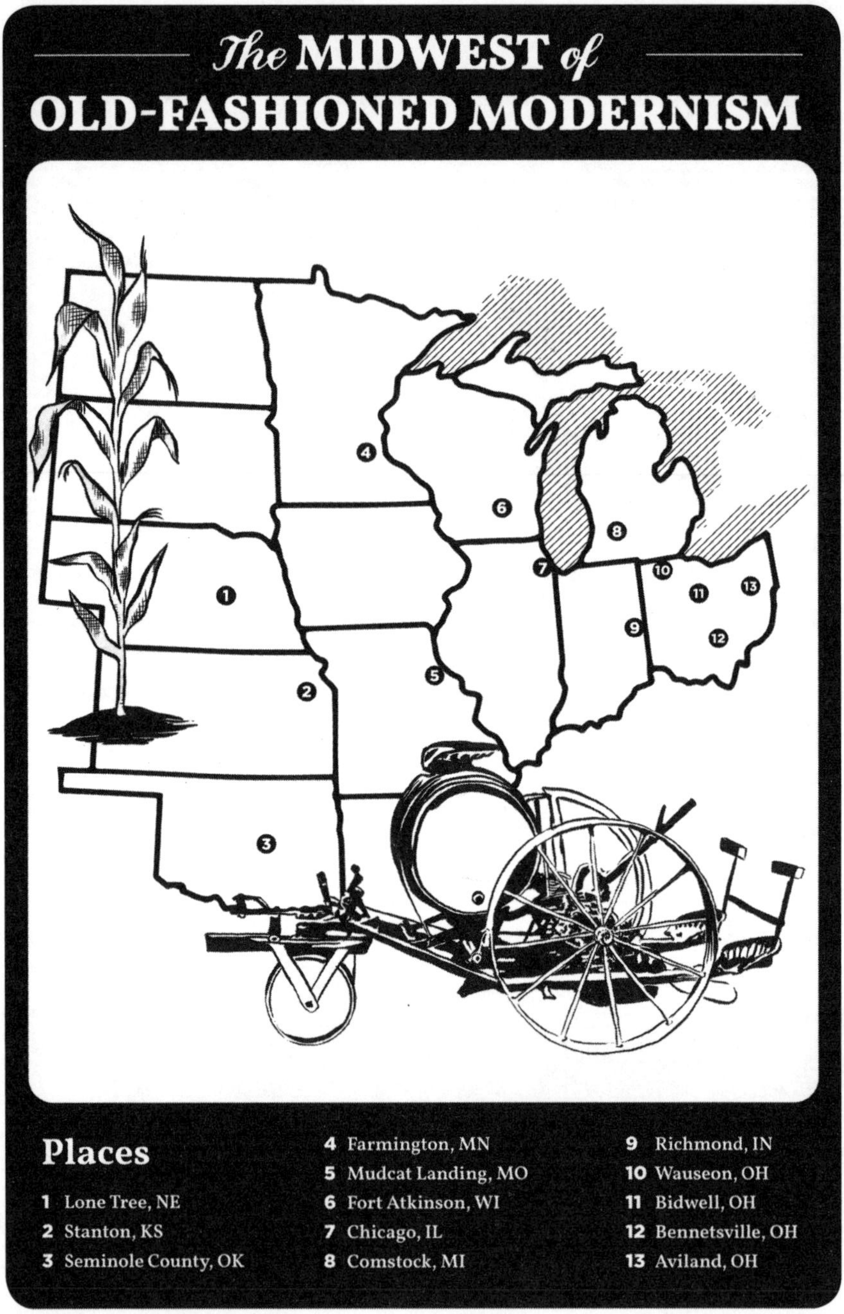


Map by Izzy Jarvis, 2018

# INTRODUCTION

## *Masculinity and Midwestern Modernism*

> Many improvements have been offered to the town of Wauseon. Never has any, which promised progress and development, been turned down by its citizens. The spirit of its founding fathers still persists. At the end of its first century, in which a swampy wilderness has been transformed into a flourishing community of homes which caters the farm community around it and still withal recognizes the advantages of industrial development, the town looks forward to its second century with high hope, courage, and the confidence born in and nourished through long experience.
>
> —*Official Publication of the Wauseon Centennial,* 1954

Wauseon, Ohio, was originally carved from the Great Black Swamp, which stretched from Lake Erie almost all the way to Fort Wayne, Indiana.[1] Early settlers lived off the land, "draining it acre by acre and putting its rich black soil to good use" (Reighard 66). By the late 1860s, partly because of the arrival of the railroad, the town had grown enough to become the seat of government in Fulton County. In the late nineteenth and early twentieth centuries, Wauseon developed much like many towns across the Midwest, adding electricity, telephone lines, and rural free delivery. Residents were proud of its wide boulevards as well as its thriving dairy industry. By the time of the Great Depression, the US Census reports that Wauseon was home to about three thousand people, who worked in agriculture, industry, and services that sprang up around the railroad. As seen in the epigraph, Wauseon city leaders promoted the town's growth, which they attribute to "the spirit of its founding fathers" and, elsewhere, to a "vigorous and ambitious" citizenry (*Official* 31, 19). When the new post office was built during the Depression, the US Treasury Department commissioned Cleveland artist Jack J. Greitzer to paint a mural

for the lobby. In 1938, Greitzer's *Cooperative Planning and Development of Wauseon* (fig. 1) was hung on the west wall, where it remains today, above a stamp display and the door to the postmaster's office.

Greitzer's mural tells a story that is consistent with Wauseon boosters' account of a "flourishing community" that supports both agricultural and industrial pursuits (*Official* 31).[2] The background is filled with houses and a church, and there are hills in the distance. A grass field dappled in sunlight sits between the houses and a railroad depot, which matches the historic Wauseon depot down to the placement of a railroad crossing sign and the logo of the Detroit, Toledo, & Ironton Railroad.[3] Rays of sun shine directly on the depot, which is in the center of the painting, surrounded by a water tower, railroad tracks, and electric wires.[4] A mid-1920s Model T Ford

Fig. 1. Jack J. Greitzer, *Cooperative Planning and Development of Wauseon,* 1938. Photograph © 2018 United States Postal Service.

Touring Car has been parked next to it. In the foreground, Greitzer depicts four men working—three white and one African American. On the right, a farmer tends cabbages. On the left, facing the farmer, three men appear to be building something. The leftmost figure, a white man in a gray suit and fedora, looks at plans. In front of him are two laborers. The central figure, a white man whose pose mirrors the farmer's, shovels dirt while an African American man pushes a wheelbarrow full of concrete from the cement mixer just behind them. The two construction workers are heavily muscled. The farmer is less so, though his forearms and jawline imply a comfort with physical labor not shared by the businessman in the rear.

This painting yokes Midwestern masculinity to manual labor. It suggests that productivity is necessary for Midwestern men, and it links agricultural, industrial, and capitalistic yields to community identity and ideals. In this way, it offers up an idealistic image of heroic Midwestern masculinity.[5] But this is also a story in conflict, full of uncertainties and anxieties, simultaneously providing alternatives to the dominant narrative. Certainly, this mural represents agricultural communities being overwhelmed by industrial development—the lone farmer appears about to lose his field to some kind of concrete structure, and the painting displays the resulting anxieties over changes to Wauseon and similar communities across the Midwest. Wauseon's history bears out this concern, as Fulton County cabbage production declined by two-thirds during the 1930s.[6] The painting's title, however, tweaks this story by emphasizing that these developments are *cooperative.* From this perspective, the mural's composition, in which the laborers are facing each other, becomes more prominent. Their bodies also frame the railroad depot, suggesting one of the main ways that Midwestern farmers and industrialists joined together. Indeed, this painting represents a concrete connection between agriculture and industry, for "cooperative" is also a noun.[7] Like many farm communities across the Midwest, Wauseon's farm cooperative sat along the railroad tracks, increasing local farmers' market power and allowing them to ship grain and other agricultural products more easily.[8] In this respect, Greitzer depicts a major development for area farmers—while there may still be concerns about farmers losing their independence, the creation of a cooperative signals the area's investment in agriculture and rural life. Whether "cooperative" is a place or a description, this mural suggests that early twentieth-century Midwestern masculinity, while still entwined with anxieties over the loss of agricultural identities, also requires multiplicity and the cooperation between different groups.

Of course, even within the mural's portrayal of Midwestern diversity, there are exclusions that make this a stereotypical image of the region. For one, the town is clearly rural, with only the suggestion of urban centers through the railroad tracks, the DT&I logo, and the electric lines.[9] In terms of the people themselves, women are completely absent, as are both children and the elderly. And while the mural portrays an African American workman, Greitzer's original sketch for the mural included two—in the finished product, the central construction worker became a white man.[10] In another symptom of the Midwest's pastoral mythmaking, Greitzer paints the businessman as much less a focal point than the heroic workmen in front of him.

Within the frame of this mural, the family farmer and the hired workingman are more conspicuous markers of regional pride than the capitalist and local booster, even though all are key figures in the Midwestern imaginary.[11]

From its setting in a Midwestern small town to its imagination of the tensions between agricultural production and industrial modernity, Greitzer's mural draws together the works I examine in *Old-Fashioned Modernism.* Not only is the protagonist of Sherwood Anderson's *Poor White* a railroad telegraph operator, but he also invents a cabbage transplanting machine and oversees its production in a brand-new factory. In Dawn Powell's *The Story of a Country Boy,* Chris Bennett is a factory boss but imagines himself to remain the country boy of the title. William Cunningham's *The Green Corn Rebellion* represents the capitalist exploitation underlying rural discontent, and Wright Morris's *The Home Place* shows the effects on rural communities of a national economy that has long privileged urban industrialism. Lorine Niedecker crafts poetic links between rural and industrial objects in *Next Year or I Fly My Rounds, Tempestuous,* developing an evocative Midwestern modernity that collapses stereotypical gender roles. In *Not Without Laughter,* Langston Hughes also offers an explicitly regional imaginary, including the railroad alongside fields of golden wheat, small-town Kansas alongside the streets of Chicago. Each chapter of this book concentrates on images of rural Midwestern men and the challenges to them. *Old-Fashioned Modernism* thus tells a story of the modern Midwestern countryside that proceeds from the moment of agricultural mechanization, engages the commercial exploitation of premodern nostalgic pastoralism, explores the effects of the Great Depression, and develops a regional masculinity accounting for the travel of people, commerce, and ideas throughout the Midwest. To flesh out this story, I examine Midwestern literature alongside photographs, film, newspaper articles, manufactured ephemera, race records, and agricultural advertisements. The book closes by extending "old-fashioned modernism" into the present day, attending to the competing socioeconomic and cultural narratives of post–farm crisis Midwestern masculinity.

## THE MIDWEST AND AMERICAN MODERNITY

The Midwest holds two conflicting positions in the American cultural imagination, both of which rob the region of cultural distinctiveness. Often, it is the "heartland," standing in for all of American culture. Alternately, the Midwest is "flyover country," part of the great undifferentiated mass between the coasts.[12] This book challenges both views. It does so by pairing fiction and poetry from the Midwest with a variety of cultural and material texts and by focusing on a time when the region appeared to have become, according to Randolph Bourne, "the apotheosis of American civilization" (480).[13] This book features writing by authors from all over the Midwest, from the Great Lakes to the Great Plains.[14] Sherwood Anderson was born in Camden, Ohio, and famously walked out of a paint factory in Elyria, Ohio, to become a writer in Chicago.[15] Lorine Niedecker was born in Fort Atkinson, Wisconsin, and lived most of her life on nearby Black Hawk Island, on the Rock River. Though Dawn Powell was born in Mount Gilead, Ohio, after graduating college she left the Midwest for New York City, then wrote biting portrayals of New Yorkers and Ohioans throughout her entire career. William Cunningham was born in Okeene, Oklahoma, and grew up twenty miles south of there in Watonga. Wright Morris was born in Central City, Nebraska, and his childhood home is a national historic site. Langston Hughes was born in Joplin, Missouri, raised in Lawrence, Kansas, and spent time all over the Midwest, including Lincoln, Illinois, and Cleveland, Ohio. J. Ryan Stradal was born in Waconia, Minnesota, and raised an hour away in Hastings. Bonnie Jo Campbell grew up on a farm near Kalamazoo, Michigan, and still lives near there, in Comstock.

Novels, poetry, and short fiction by these writers produce specific forms of regional modernity through male protagonists who both fulfill and resist common American narratives of economic advancement, spatial experience, and gender roles. By complicating these stereotypes, Midwestern literature counters the simple binary of progressive urbanity and retrograde rurality that has been perpetuated in literature and criticism about the region. These texts dwell in liminal spaces, imagining the Midwest as a comparatively inclusive middle ground that joins past and future and on which masculinities, spaces, and literatures can be both rural and urban. In so doing, they manage the development of urban industrialism, not to circumvent its influence but to prevent interactions with it from spinning into unachievable futurity or retreating into nostalgic rurality. Partly as a result of these many possibilities, these works do not create the "genial middle ground" that Van Wyck Brooks hoped would unite American life (83).

*Old-Fashioned Modernism* explores Midwestern responses to the shifting discourses of American modernity. In *The Middle West: Its Meaning in American Culture,* James Shortridge claims that "the term Middle West initially was coined to describe a particular pastoral setting," a label that has endured despite the region's growing cities and industrial economy (7). Still, Shortridge finds fractures in that image related to the paths he traces between regional and national identities, which he claims are themselves entwined with the region's socioeconomic history: "The basic pattern is thus something of a paradox—continuity yet change; and this mélange is a key to the cultural confusion that has characterized the region throughout much of its history" (7). In this book I demonstrate how Midwestern literature employed that confusion as a method to define the region and to make claims on the processes of American modernity more generally. As a result, when *Cooperative Planning and Development of Wauseon* combines industry with agriculture, local with national, and past with future, Greitzer does not imply that life in the Midwest is simply confusing. Rather, like many of the texts I study, Greitzer's picture of Midwestern modernity accepts the power of these competing influences but does not capitulate to any one of them.

Similarly, while the spaces in these texts may be primarily rural, I argue that these authors rarely portray them as simply isolated, nostalgic, or parochial. Acknowledging a strong tradition of Midwestern urban literature that highlights cultural and socioeconomic links, I consider how farms and small towns participate in those same interlinked systems. In *The Midwestern Ascendancy in American Writing,* Ronald Weber gestures to the way these networks manifest as key themes in early twentieth-century Midwestern literature: "the loss of a natural pastoral life, village mediocrity, escape to the city in search of the fullness of life, rural returns touched with feelings of nostalgia, guilt, and superiority" (3). While it is debatable whether Midwestern literature reveals, as Weber suggests, "some central truths about American life" (3), I build on his argument to develop a theory of the complicated relations among the village, the rural, the pastoral, and other key concepts of Midwestern culture.

The central texts examined in this book show how the links between these spaces are both structural and individual, and though they were all published after 1920, they represent an enduring strain of Midwestern fiction linking economic mobility to expectations on male characters. As a result, I could have started this book with late nineteenth-century novels about migration to the rural Midwest such as Edward Eggleston's *The Hoosier Schoolmaster* (1871) and E. W. Howe's *The Story of a Country Town* (1883). Or I could have critiqued common narratives of masculinity through texts that return characters to their rural Midwestern origins, including Hamlin Garland's *Main-Travelled Roads* (1891), Willa Cather's *My Ántonia* (1918), and Ernest Hemingway's *In Our Time* (1925), or explored the effects of transnational immigration on the region with *My Ántonia* or O. E. Rølvaag's *Giants in the Earth* (1927). I also could have included several novels featuring the experience of urban spaces, such as Tillie Olsen's *Yonnondio* (1930s/1974) and Richard Wright's *Native Son* (1940) or those that almost entirely remove their Midwestern characters from the region, like F. Scott Fitzgerald's *The Great Gatsby* (1922) and Theodore Dreiser's *An American Tragedy* (1925).

By considering twentieth-century Midwestern literature as an influential participant in forming and understanding modern American life, this book challenges the practice of labeling writers "regionalist" as a "minoritizing gesture" (Duvall 243). In their influential study of regional women writers, feminist scholars Judith Fetterley and Marjorie Pryse maintain that bracketing regional writing results in losses for women and men: "We believe that American culture is impoverished by the imbalance, even the 'surfeit' of heroic stories about men and boys, and that the texts of regionalism provide an alternative vision of what American culture might look like if the stories we chose to pass on to the next generation of readers reflected a broader spectrum of values" (30). Thinking alongside Fetterley and Pryse, I emphasize two ways that these texts offer an "alternative vision." First, I consider rural writing from the Midwest as part of a fuller picture of American modernity. Second, I develop their claim that "masculinities themselves might become more various and fluid than they are in the official story" (30) by calling attention to these texts' particularities and the (mostly) nonurban spaces they represent.

I qualify my interest in the particularities of locality, history, and masculine experience, however, by approaching the Midwest knowing that "region is always a relational term" (Reichert Powell 4). As a result, although the local enters into my discussions of various texts, I do not develop a theory of localism. The present study participates in the growing field of "critical regionalism," which Douglas Reichert Powell describes as "a methodological umbrella for this work that recognizes (in ways more cosmopolitan critical and aesthetic communities sometimes do not) that regionalism is not necessarily parochialism. Critical regionalism thus involves tracing a path across the disciplines as well as the dimensions of the place under consideration" (7).[16] As I demonstrate throughout the following four chapters, many of the communities in these novels—Hughes's Stanton, Anderson's Bidwell, Powell's Aviland, and Morris's Lone Tree—are represented as distinctive localities, but none of them are presented parochially. Instead, these novels highlight each community's relations to socioeconomic narratives and the materials of a broader cultural field. I show how these texts exist and participate in an interconnected field of American modernity, one that includes but is not limited to local (or regional, or national) concerns.

Of course, local, regional, and national—like rural and urban—are flawed descriptive terms, not least in their geographic and cultural imprecision and their varied and conflicting critical histories. Recognizing those flaws, I employ these terms because they also open up meanings and highlight instabilities in constructions of space, community, and character. In *Barnstorming the Prairies: How Aerial Vision Shaped the Midwest,* Jason Weems shows how a shift in perspective causes these concepts to bleed into each other: "For some people, aerial perspectives embodied the promise of modernization on a vast and systematic scale. To others, such views dissolved traditional patterns of rural life into unrecognizable abstraction" (x–xi). While Weems discusses the map-level vision of survey grids, his study of aerial photography—which increased after World War I—provides an example of how people experience rural life when confronted with technology that challenges their assumptions about it. He argues that seeing rural spaces from new perspectives causes people to reconfigure their understandings not only of the family farm but also the relationship between the countryside and the flow of capital in modern America.

Ideas of the Midwest in the early twentieth-century made space for both the old-fashioned and the modern—in both aerial photography and regional literature—that translates to the ability to see Midwestern land as both an individual homestead and a contributor to broader economic systems. Such dualism counters common narratives of US economics in this period, which historians and cultural critics often frame in terms of centralizations and dependencies. Alan Trachtenberg's version of that narrative, which he terms *incorporation,* describes rural spaces as primarily providing raw materials for urban centers. According to Trachtenberg, the impression of an "impoverished" countryside (*Incorporation* 115) results from the city's function as the hub through which wealth and production flows:

> In the 1880's, as much as 40 percent of the population of rural townships seemed to disappear. Images of bustling, frenetic cities arose against a background of abandoned farmhouses and deserted villages, and many Americans pondered the change with regret and lament. But these emptied places and impoverished regions were as much icons of incorporation as factories, railroads, and department stores. It was not that progress had passed them by. The emptying itself represented a kind of integration. (*Incorporation* 114)

In early twentieth-century America there was evidence of incorporation everywhere. All of the texts that I examine include that evidence, from bustling cities to abandoned or impoverished rural sites.[17] Thus when Chris Bennett leaves farm for factory, Dawn Powell acknowledges the powerful draw of urban industrialism, or Sandy Rodgers moves to Chicago and takes a service job, centralized economic incorporation is part of what makes that possible. Still, I argue that these authors generally write against such narratives, using the Midwestern space to carve out greater and more frequent pockets of resistance to incorporation.

Configuring rural spaces as sites of resistance allows these texts to present small-town and farm life as inherently modern even when many aspects of those spaces appear obsolete or antiquated. For instance, in *The Home Place,* the decorations haven't changed in thirty years, and Uncle Harry operates a horse-drawn corn planter in an age of tractor farming. He also uses synthetic rubber tires, however, and sells his grain to a middleman at the grain elevator next to the railroad. Lone Tree, Nebraska, appears to be left behind, recalling the "emptied places and impoverished regions" of incorporation. But the town's modern elements and Harry's and Clara's ability to work and survive there also suggest continued rural vitality. Such liveliness is minimized when the main story of rural life is urban industrialism. In this book I show how Midwestern rural literature counters Trachtenberg's incorporation narrative as well as other versions of this story such as William Cronon's, whose argument that "the urban market concentrated hinterland trade" (357) emphasizes rural economic systems but still examines the city as its central object.

Even in a novel like *Not Without Laughter,* which ends with its protagonist living in a major city, Hughes adopts a tactic similar to other Midwestern authors of this period: Stanton, Kansas, does not simply produce raw materials for Chicago, nor does it conform neatly to tropes of rural deadening. Rather, it does both, and Hughes also includes moments in which the rural is alternately pastoral, modern, and a space of horrific racial violence. In *Poor White,* Anderson's Bidwell similarly absorbs elements of both nostalgic pastoralism and technological modernity. Bidwell and Stanton—like Lone Tree, Bennetsville, and the unnamed town of *The Green Corn Rebellion*—might be understood in terms proposed by Leo Marx: "The distinctive attribute of the new order is its technological power, a power that does not remain confined to the traditional boundaries of the city. It is a centrifugal force that threatens to break down, once and for all, the conventional contrast between these two styles of life" (32). By imagining rural communities in which the train passes next to the wheat fields and the farm exists alongside the factory, Midwestern authors echo Marx's sense of cultural and epistemological breakdown. In so doing, they propose forms of regional modernity that shift the possibilities for rural spaces, literatures, and masculinities.

In historical accounts of this breakdown, the growth of rural consumerism shows the limits of what Marx calls the "conventional contrast" between country and city life. Thomas Schlereth, for example, frames the history of rural consumerism as a shift from production to consumption:

> Throughout the period 1880–1920, the country store, the county fair, and the mail-order catalogue acted as agencies of change where rural Americans made direct contact with the mass production and mass distribution of industrial, commercial America. In each of these contexts, rural folks encountered consumption on their own turf, at the crossroads, at the county seat, or at their mailboxes. Not all country people took to the new ways of buying and selling: some simply did not have the money to do so; others preferred more traditional ways

> of trading. Most, however, eventually joined the spreading consumer revolution. They did so for an assortment of reasons: to ape their urban peers, to mitigate the unremitting domestic toil of most farm wives, to achieve personal convenience and individual comfort, to merit or maintain social and economic status, to vent self-indulgence and acquisitiveness, to have more leisure and recreation time, to delight in the new and the novel, and to achieve a higher standard of living. No matter what their reasons and no matter what institution formed and followed their visions of "the good life," people who prided themselves on being producers increasingly became consumers. In this long process, people who thought of themselves as advocates of the traditional increasingly became participants in the modern. (375)

Schlereth describes this shift in both domestic and public spaces, using turn-of-the-century material experiences to designate the onset of rural modernity for both men and women. The texts that I examine in many ways substantiate this shift, from Niedecker's "bathroom luxuries" (65) to Chris Bennett's impulsive purchases of "the latest farm gadgets" (Powell 3). Nevertheless, I argue that these authors attempt to imagine a middle ground on which production and consumption coexist, and not simply as part of an uneven but totalizing transition to urban consumerism. So while it's certainly true that, as Schlereth claims, "rural folks *encountered* consumption" (375; emphasis added), these Midwestern texts underscore the ways they revise it.

This book does not therefore claim that Midwestern authors outright reject common heartland narratives. Rather, as seen in Greitzer's heroic laborer, Hughes's accumulation of masculine stereotypes, and the material coexistence of Niedecker's pasted palimpsest, they employ those narratives to manage characterological, generic, and historical concerns. Midwestern authors were uniquely situated to both carry out and confront twentieth-century narratives of masculinity, economics, and rural space, not least because the Midwestern economy of this period facilitated such simultaneity. For one, Schlereth's account of rural consumerism registers the multiple and occasionally conflicting experiences of modern life in the countryside, which Deborah Fitzgerald also addresses in her analysis of the impact of farm economics on Midwestern identities. Noting the high percentage of tractors on Midwestern farms in the 1920s, Fitzgerald argues that "these farmers were quite different, however, from farmers in the Plains and far west, whose farms were much larger and more 'industrial' than those in the midwest. Not coincidentally, farmers in the midwest tended to think of themselves as traditional yet progressive and often boasted of their rural genealogy" (15). In Fitzgerald's study, Midwestern farmers identify themselves by combining contradictory temporalities, which can also be seen in the mix of manual agricultural labor and modern railroad distribution in *Poor White, The Home Place,* and Greitzer's mural. That these kinds of complicated identities develop in fictional and nonfictional representations of the rural Midwest suggests how such spaces were vital to the development of American modernity and literary modernism.

*Old-Fashioned Modernism* focuses its attention on texts that resist the prevailing narratives of the early twentieth-century United States—resistances that can take the form of not only rejecting specific narratives but also inclusively adopting multiple, apparently conflicting ones. By showing how the "middle" of Middle West ought to be figured not just geographically but also temporally, I claim that Midwestern authors are primarily interested in negotiating the challenges of their present moment. This approach diverges from some studies of Midwestern literature. For example, David Holman claims that "the Midwestern mind is characterized by its belief in the possibility that the promise of the past can be realized in the future, and the present is thus a constant reminder of the region's and the nation's failure to keep faith with the ideals of the past and with the promise of the future" (17). For Holman, the Midwestern present functions as a "reminder" and a "promise." Jon K. Lauck similarly projects nostalgic values into the Midwestern future, calling for a revival of regional studies predicated on regionalist authors who rejected the "Revolt from the Village," Carl Van Doren's enduring assessment of Midwestern modernism.[18] According to Lauck, these regionalists "promote a culture rooted in the Midwestern soil" through narratives that "recognized the positive aspects of family, farm, church, and school" (*Warm* 41, 42). The literary and cultural texts that I examine also represent rooted regional cultures, but they do not insist upon the authority or intrinsic value of "traditional" institutions and structures. I argue that when Midwestern modernists represent the disruptions of agricultural modernization and the struggles of the Great

Depression, they don't wish for the revival of pastoral masculinity. Their focus, rather, is on how their characters and communities can negotiate the failures, challenges, and promises of their disorderly, modern moment.

## GENDER IN THE HEARTLAND

When confronted with criticism that a laborer's physique was "unduly exaggerated" in the plans for the Wauseon, Ohio, post office mural, Greitzer replied: "I purposely treated the figure in this manner to impart an heroic and idealistic feeling to him and to the work he represents, namely, civic improvement" (Letter to Rowan, 13 Mar. 1938).[19] Greitzer's response highlights the relationship among masculinity, economics, and community. The four men in Greitzer's mural represent different archetypes of Midwestern (and American) masculinity, but this is a limited version of twentieth-century American manhood. Each figure represents a form of heroic masculinity that fits nicely within urban industrialization. Despite their limits as individual figures, however, I argue that in combination they draw on regional possibilities for "more various and fluid" masculinities (Fetterley and Pryse 30). When taken as a tableau, this mural represents some of the key concerns of this book: a community that features both rural and urban elements, as well as the anxieties that go along with the materials and imagined possibilities of modern masculinity. Many Midwestern texts think through the shifts in gender performance that accompany the changes in rural communities across the region. Sometimes they question the sustainability of normative gender roles, as when Lorine Niedecker creates regionalized poetic archives that reveal the fractures in masculine and feminine experiences. At other times, they are more sanguine about the possibilities for modern rural life, as when the railroad in Langston Hughes's *Not Without Laughter* brings a modern jazz band to small-town Kansas and introduces Sandy Rodgers to new ways of acting like a man. And occasionally they focus on how common archetypes combine to challenge masculine expectations, such as in Sherwood Anderson's *Poor White* when Hugh McVey's blend of dreaminess and drive thrives in the confluence of agriculture and industry.

In this period, much of Midwestern literature details socioeconomic shifts that alter expectations and possibilities for men. Several texts explicitly show the limits of allegiance to common narratives and practices of masculinity, such as the critique of rural Iowa's masculinized judicial system built into Susan Glaspell's play *Trifles* (1916), Booth Tarkington's exploration of manufacturing's effects on Indianapolis social hierarchies in *The Magnificent Ambersons* (1918), or how Sinclair Lewis's *Babbitt* (1922) mocks the middlebrow pride of its Ohio protagonist. Modern masculinities' connections to the tensions of socioeconomic and technological modernization in rural spaces can be seen in the small-town ennui of Edgar Lee Masters's *Spoon River Anthology* (1915) and Sherwood Anderson's *Winesburg, Ohio* (1919), as well as in farm novels such as Ruth Suckow's *Country People* (1924) and Marjory Bayley's *In Friends We Trust* (1938). Among more recent literature, Frank Bill's country noir short stories in *Crimes in Southern Indiana* (2011) and John McCarthy's poetry debut, *Ghost County* (2016), depict rural men struggling with the lack of opportunity in the postindustrial Midwest. Midwestern literature has long attempted to imagine rural masculinities that do not simply incorporate or reject common narratives of gender expectations, social change, economic modernization, and urban futurity. *Old-Fashioned Modernism* claims that Midwestern literature engages these narratives through their simultaneity, demonstrating the personal, regional, and national elements that complicate the formation of masculine identities.

In the early twentieth century, definitions of masculinity and femininity were unstable, partly because of parallel processes of urbanization and industrialization, which were themselves linked to the centralization of economic and cultural capital. For instance, as greater numbers of unmarried men and women moved to the city, their concentration gave rise to a number of changes, including increased factory jobs for women, the rise of dating culture, and greater opportunity for (and visibility of) queer sexual practices.[20] In detailing the development of hetero- and homosexuality in early twentieth-century New York, George Chauncey finds that class distinctions cohere with sexual identity: "The predominant class locations of the queer, the fairy, the heterosexual, and trade illuminate the shifting relationship of sex, gender, and sexuality in different class cultures" (126). No matter their preferred sexual partners, Chauncey emphasizes that concepts of sex and sexuality were inseparable from men's economic position. This book extends Chauncey's claim to the Midwest—in other words, showing how this was as true in eastern Kansas as it was on the Lower East Side (or, more precisely, as true in fictional Stanton, Kansas, as on actual Stanton Street).

*Old-Fashioned Modernism* endeavors to demonstrate how the entwined normative and minoritized discourses of twentieth-century masculinity create anxiety over shifting, fluid, or contradictory expectations. Such contradictions were especially acute for African American men. Marlon Ross argues that Jim Crow–era black men were simultaneously excluded from and expected to conform to "social codes established for the conduct of men" (1–2). Ross and Chauncey suggest how conflicting demands on American men manifest in uneasy, pastiched versions of American masculinity. I address this potentially contradictory simultaneity not only through Langston Hughes's accumulation of African American stereotypes but also through Chris Bennett's attempts to be both a businessman and a country boy and, later, through Bonnie Jo Campbell's genre play. Broadly speaking, this book examines attempts to absorb multiple conceptions of twentieth-century masculinity—rural and urban, self-made and corporate, pastoral and modern—into individual male characters. I contend that Midwestern authors' allowance for contradictory masculinities indicates that, in some ways, they forgo steady progress to consider both the limits and benefits of constructing masculinities that function outside or drag on teleological narratives.

Each chapter builds on studies exploring American masculinity's complicated relationship to the period's central cultural and socioeconomic narratives. Gail Bederman demonstrates how the possibilities for middle-class masculinity shifted in the late nineteenth century: "Middle-class Americans had long believed that a man's hard work and talent would inevitably be rewarded with riches and success. Yet by 1880 an increasingly corporate economy, as well as recurring rounds of bankruptcy-spawning depressions, meant fewer middle-class men could achieve manly power as successful, independent entrepreneurs" (30). Bederman provides a narrative that is common within masculinity studies: the nineteenth-century ideal of the "self-made man," in control at work and home, declined as the economy centralized, and the resulting dependencies fundamentally shifted the way that men viewed themselves.[21] In the Midwestern texts discussed here, these economic and cultural shifts are on ample display: Sandy Rodgers in *Not Without Laughter* is subject to the time clock. Chris Bennett in *The*

*Story of a Country Boy* and Hugh McVey in *Poor White* have little control over their factories even though they are, respectively, the general manager and the inventor of the machine being manufactured. I also examine numerous responses to a perceived lack of control, such as Clyde Muncy's attempted return to the farm in *The Home Place* and the way Lorine Niedecker wrests control from corporations through *Next Year*'s cut-and-paste material construction upon a mass-produced pocket calendar.

Beginning with masculinity studies' analysis of socioeconomic change's implications for American masculinities, this book considers how those shifts play in the rural space—and how Midwestern literature engages, resists, and imagines alternatives to national masculine identities. In *Masculine Style: The American West and Literary Modernism,* Daniel Worden examines a frontier masculinity that, he argues, is thought to be representative of American manhood. According to Worden, American modernists such as Willa Cather and Ernest Hemingway are suspicious of interiority and, therefore, "one becomes masculine not through the interior but through external self-fashioning, through bodily discipline" (13). Worden finds ample evidence of this kind of self-control in westerns and frontier literature and describes its contribution to common narratives of American masculinity. Midwestern authors do represent self-made men—as well as versions of what Worden calls "cowboy masculinity"—but they also offer alternative methods of defining and sustaining masculinity. For instance, farmers in Bonnie Jo Campbell's "Boar Taint" have been marginalized by agricultural conglomerates, so they abandon large-scale farming and begin to assert themselves into local, niche economies. And the farmers revolt in *The Green Corn Rebellion* partly because of complaints like Jim Tetley's that he and his wife have to "work like a dog all the time" for no discernible benefit, "just so a bunch of bankers and wheat speculators can make a little more money" (72).

While the rebellion itself focuses on the actions of men, Jim initially objects to the way his wife Jeannie constantly feels compelled to labor on the farm, which indicates how this novel—like others I study—binds women's experience to men's. Though Jim thinks of Jeannie as primarily a mother and secondarily a workmate, they both struggle against capitalist exploitation. By the end of the book, each is further diminished by their shared struggle. This structure has shades of literary naturalism that illuminate not only the rebellion but also Jeannie's position relative both to it and the wider community. According to Jennifer Fleissner, examining men's and women's experiences alongside each other shows "that the very motor that drives the male fall actually helps bring forward, in the women's case, a truly new kind of narrative, one irreducible to the alternatives of sheer triumph or absolute decline" (21–22). In Fleissner's analysis, naturalism creates space for new narratives for women, which illuminates one way that gendered struggle contributes to modernity.[22] Midwestern authors extend this development of gendered modernity into the modernist period. Willa Cather's *My Ántonia* and Sinclair Lewis's *Main Street* are just two of the Midwestern novels that cultivate a kind of blended modernity for women. *Old-Fashioned Modernism,* on the other hand, focuses on texts that foreground male experience and address women's narratives as a related but secondary matter. For instance, after Jim's conscription at the end of *The Green Corn Rebellion,* Jeannie is a single mother with an uncertain future. The book does not continue her story, but it offers a few possibilities: she remains in the country and farms, she moves to town with her son and rents the farm, or she leaves the community entirely. Cunningham implies that Jeannie has multiple options and, with the rent money, the financial wherewithal to take advantage of them.

Similarly, in *Poor White,* Clara Butterworth exemplifies Midwestern literature's construction of modernity for women. Though she grew up on a farm, her college education makes her familiar with modern ideals of "the independent future of women" (190). Like Jeannie, Clara's options combine rural life with cosmopolitan ideals. Marilyn Holt presents an example of that blending in the scrapbooks submitted to the Kansas Wheat Queen competition in the 1930s, in which contestants would provide photos of themselves on the farm alongside those of them with automobiles or dressed up as Hollywood stars: "Placed side by side, the images made a great impact. Here was the New Woman, the Outdoor Girl, living in two worlds. She was part of the farm environment, but she was also familiar with the larger society and its outward trappings of popular culture" (147). As contestants juxtaposed rural and modern, they made claims on their abilities to incorporate both of them into a single personality. There is a hopefulness inherent in such blending. Recalling Fleissner's argument about new, complex narratives for women, however, Clara's story is not a "sheer triumph."

Through her marriage to the inventor Hugh McVey, Anderson shows the limits of blended rural-cosmopolitan identities: she becomes a housewife in her rural hometown even though she is aware of other possibilities for women, and she supports Hugh's factory despite her concern with the costs of industrialization.

*Poor White* demonstrates the ambivalence many Midwestern texts display about gender and modernity. This bears out historical narratives that, corroborating Schlereth, posit rural people's modernity through increased consumerism. For example, Mary Neth claims that rural Midwestern "women and children were no longer agricultural laborers but consumers" (5), and she later expands her claim to include men: "Contrary to historical interpretations that paint farm people as eager to abandon the 'backwardness' of rural life for city living, many farm people blended the modern and the rural and were satisfied with the modified country way of life" (6). The authors I study present widespread dissatisfaction as a feature of modern life for both men and women. Much like the subjects of Neth's study who actively molded their identities and participation in modernity, characters combine modern and pastoral elements in their attempts to overcome such discontent. For instance, Madeleine in *The Story of a Country Boy* is a modern woman with both personal and financial independence. While she remains unmarried and owns a retail store in town, however, she also maintains her rural roots through her store's quaintness and the relationship she has with Chris Bennett, her childhood friend and the "country boy" of the title. Like Clara and Jeannie, Madeleine encounters limits of rural modernity specific to white women of various socioeconomic classes, which differ from the challenges Harriett Williams encounters in *Not Without Laughter*'s small-town black community. Harriett responds to her mother's restrictiveness, her own limited economic possibilities, and their town's racism by becoming an urban-based blues singer, more fully rejecting the rural space than Clara, Jeannie, and Madeleine, or even a contemporary figure like Jill from Bonnie Jo Campbell's "Boar Taint," which I examine in the conclusion.

By attending to gendered experience in these texts, this book illustrates individual, communal, and generic constructions of modernity in the rural Midwest. I find that Midwestern authors often arrange their versions of modern life according to the failures of normative gender roles, a structure also seen in Janet Casey's argument that "the women discussed herein—

real and imaginary—are modern precisely insofar as they refuse to accept the containment of the pastoral category, of the agrarian ideal" (199). In terms of the extent of their resistance to rural stereotypes, some Midwestern authors produce characters and texts that are more overtly modern than others. On one hand, Clara accepts the containment of the rural housewife. On the other, Harriett rejects the limitations of the small town and becomes a modern blueswoman, and Niedecker creates a modernist patchwork of the nostalgic and the avant-garde. Among men, Chris is limited by his allegiance to an erstwhile country boy identity, but Sandy finds rural community in Chicago, and Hugh invents a cabbage transplanter that infuses mechanical modernity into its pastoral setting. By examining these combinations of pastoral and modern, I slightly adjust Casey's claim: Midwestern authors do not only generate modern rural spaces and characters by resisting pastoralism; they also add a critique of futurism. That twinned critique returns them to a messy, modern present in which both male and female characters attempt to balance the unappealing or infeasible expectations placed upon them. Indeed, that they sometimes fail at this balancing act underscores the modernity of these characters and texts. Much like the refusals that Casey sees among rural women, these texts achieve rural modernity by staving off idealized narrative expectations. But when they attempt to formulate regional modernity for men and women, those expanded possibilities become more difficult to balance, which results in continued failures and disruptions to characters, communities, and the texts themselves.

## REGIONAL MODERNITY, OLD-FASHIONED MODERNISM

When Greitzer made the railroad depot the setting of *Cooperative Planning and Development of Wauseon,* he highlighted one of the core symbols of American modernity. For Leo Marx, the locomotive was "the machine in the garden" (229). William Cronon and Jon Teaford present the railroad as an essential technology transporting grain, livestock, and other raw materials from their origins in the countryside to the factories and markets in Chicago, St. Louis, Cleveland, and other Midwestern cities. In Wauseon, the railroad occasioned the town's initial growth as well as civic improvements such as a new reservoir and automated crossing gates. It carried the mail and was the reason for economic developments such as the farmer's cooperative and new freight depots to serve the town's growing industries. Not only were the rails used to ship goods out of town, however, but they also enhanced Wauseon's cultural life—in the late nineteenth and early twentieth centuries, several circuses performed, "occasionally stopping overnight to water and rest the animals" (Krumm 32).[23] The railroad performs similarly in Midwestern literature: it disrupts rural life and folkways as well as providing opportunities for rural people to make their way in the modern world. In both Greitzer's mural and Midwestern modernist literature, one of the railroad's key characteristics is that it links communities to each other much in the way Wauseon residents could ride the Lake Shore east to Toledo or west to Chicago.

The railroad thus forms regional networks, which can be seen in the central texts examined in this book. Greitzer's mural pictures the depot of the Detroit, Toledo & Ironton Railroad, and in Wauseon the DT&I tracks intersect the Lake Shore in the center of town. The Lake Shore appears again in *Poor White* and *The Story of a Country Boy,* which also refers to the Baltimore & Ohio. In later years, B&O was purchased by the Chesapeake & Ohio, the railroad that passed by the Gennett Records studio in Richmond, Indiana.[24] I discuss Gennett's participation in the race record market in chapter 4, along with *Not Without Laughter,* which mentions the Kansas City Southern and the Western & Atlantic. In Hughes's novel, Sandy also rides the train to Chicago. Based on the geography of Lawrence, Kansas (Stanton's inspiration), Sandy was probably on the Atchison, Topeka & Santa Fe, which is mentioned in *The Home Place* along with the Chicago, Burlington & Quincy, which likely owned the trestles that the farmers attacked in *The Green Corn Rebellion* and was probably the line Hugh rode as he left Mudcat Landing near the beginning of *Poor White.* In these novels, railroads transport goods, employ people, and allow characters to move around the region. Serving as both social hubs and sites of protest, railroads are symbolic both for authors and for characters within the novels. In aggregate, the repetitions, mergers, and junctions of these railroads help map the terrain of Midwestern literature—as an interconnected field, linked through economics and migration, with borders based more on cultural flows than precise geographical boundaries.

The railroad exemplifies a regional network that demonstrates how Midwestern literature does not simply depict a conflict between rural and urban experiences. Enduring images of the country and the city do, nonetheless, underwrite these authors' representation of regional modernity. Raymond Williams shows how, when considered together, static images of the country and the city reveal the limits of those representations:

> The common image of the country is now an image of the past, and the common image of the city an image of the future. That leaves, if we isolate them, an undefined present. The pull of the idea of the country is towards old ways, human ways, natural ways. The pull of the idea of the city is towards progress, modernisation, development. In what is then a tension, a present experienced as a tension, we use the contrast of country and city to ratify an unresolved division and conflict of impulses, which it might be better to face in its own terms. (297)

Williams primarily focuses on British literature and history, but he finds evidence that these "common images" remained consistent throughout Greek, Roman, and preclassical writing, as well as in the literature of the English colonies. Much of his argument holds true for American literature from the first half of the twentieth century, in which rural spaces are often characterized as nostalgic or pastoral (or, to counter, old-fashioned and stagnant), while urban life promises new beginnings and socioeconomic modernity (or sin and decay).[25] According to Ed White, however, Williams's claims have limited applicability for American literature due to structural differences between English and early American society. White claims that printing and literary culture became centralized in colonial cities because the "dispersal" of American rural populations resulted in "disintegration, fragmentation, isolation, scattering" (29). In this book, I examine a period of American literature in which those isolated fragments were being reconnected. I argue that Williams's description of "a present experienced as a tension" gestures toward the confusions of socioeconomic modernity as Midwestern authors imagined regional cultures that disrupted long-held stereotypes about rural and urban spaces and the people who live there.

Despite Williams's influence, scholars do not often study regional literature in terms of its modernity. Scott Herring cautions against the assumptions underlying this tendency: "While we should be wary of collapsing metropolitanism with modernism and regionalism with ruralism, this scenario remains commonplace in contemporary literary criticism" ("Regional" 3). Herring's formulation of dual collapse denotes two key concerns for this book. I take issue with the first—defining modern in terms of metropolitan—by considering how social and mechanical innovations facilitate rural and regional forms of modernity. As for the second, given that I discuss both rural and regional modernity, one of this book's challenges is to avoid using them as synonyms. I sidestep this concern by discussing rural modernity in terms of the representation of specific places, such as chapter 1's articulation of the ways Bidwell balances pastoral and industrial characteristics. Regional modernity appears in multiple ways, perhaps most obviously when I include cities as part of Midwestern modernity, as in chapter 4's discussion of Chicago alongside small-town Stanton, Kansas. More often, I develop a concept of regional modernity that foregrounds the links between places and ideas. Both of these appear in chapter 2, in which those links are both literal (when Chris Bennett travels between country, city, and metropolis) and figurative (as with Lorine Niedecker's diverse regional archive).

By imagining modern people and communities outside of stereotypical boundaries, I show how nonurban literatures revise the forms, structures, and available spaces of literary modernism.[26] These works I examine, then, constitute a regional modernism, which departs from much of the available criticism on regional literature. According to John Duvall, "Regionalism was generally seen as an outgrowth of realism and naturalism, playing out in rural settings the same thematic of realist ethics or naturalist determinism that urban writers had already staked out" (243). While comparing regionalist writers from several US regions, Duvall finds "decided modernist tendencies" even in "fiction draw[ing] on the strategies of realism" (248).[27] Throughout this book, I similarly address the cultural ambivalences of twentieth-century Midwestern literature by contextualizing it within its contemporary socioeconomic materials and narratives—in some ways, then, I extend Amy Kaplan's discussion of realism as "an anxious and contradictory mode" (9) to the way regional literatures mobilize modernist techniques. I build on regionalist scholarship, then, by avoiding Herring's sense of terminological collapse as well as by finding value in both Duvall's explication of regionalism's modernity and the relationship to realism and naturalism that he finds outdated.

Here is one way that this book articulates the idea of an *old-fashioned modernism:* each novel I examine develops modern rural masculinities alongside a stylistic tendency toward turn-of-the-century literary modes. For instance, a majority of the writing in each novel could be called realist or naturalist. But I establish each text's modernism through its periodic turns to modern anxieties and modernist techniques. I argue that these regional Midwestern texts provide a new way of looking at literary modernism by showing that modern fragmentation doesn't have to be totalizing. Rather, they propose experiences of modern masculinity and rurality that may feel dated, or residual, but in which key moments foreground the anxieties and fragmentations of American modernity. Such anxieties surface in Greitzer's mural as the cabbage farmer seems about to be overwhelmed by industrial development, and they emerge in *The Story of a Country Boy* when a local businessman "paused with embarrassment" at the "vast emptiness" of a railroad station in small-town Aviland, Ohio (121). Such examples demonstrate Midwestern literary and cultural engagement with the experience of modernity as it "shatters into a multitude of fragments, speaking incommensurable private languages" (Berman 17). Powell's novel represents the fragmented modern experience of many characters, including this unnamed businessman. In the station, it juxtaposes the businessman's unease with the architecture's "modernistic splendor," the station's functionality, and the artistic vitality of the railroad murals on its walls (120). The combination suggests that the past and future exist and inform the experience of the train station but that Powell's attention is squarely on negotiating the challenges of the novel's present moment.

Those confusions mark the starting point from which Midwestern literature attempts to envision regional modernity. These texts' seemingly unceasing attempts to negotiate the modern rural experience leads Edward Comentale to claim that, for Midwestern novels, "regionalism is increasingly bound to issues of resources, production, and potential, and the region finds expression only in a tireless activity of cultivation; traditional modes of representation give way to an inscriptive process, a sort of graphic plowing that links material production to the process of meaning-making itself" (243). In *Old-Fashioned Modernism,* the cultivation of potential happens at multiple levels, from representations of characters and communities to structural links with Midwestern material and social histories to more abstract generic concerns. For example, in *The Home Place,* Clyde Muncy believes that moving to Lone Tree might alleviate his family's New York housing struggles, but he encounters a community that is still recovering from a different aspect of the Great Depression and doesn't accept him as easily as he hoped. Morris conveys Clyde's disappointment by pairing the novel's text with photos of worn and outdated objects from his family's actual Nebraska farm, challenging modernist genre conventions through the disconcerting combination of a semiautobiographical narrative with photographs that occasionally (and only partly) illustrate the text. Thus, while potentiality figures prominently in these texts, my argument turns more fully toward Comentale's description of "middle America" as "underdetermined and inchoate ground" (244). Rather than focus on Midwestern literature's interest in potential—and therefore in the future—I contend that these texts propose that an inchoate lack of order is a key feature of modern life. They suggest a way to negotiate the promises and challenges of modernity, not to imagine a better future or reach back to a nostalgic past but to settle in the middle.

Midwestern modernist texts seek spaces or narrative trajectories that are somewhat outside of, or act as a drag on, urban industrialization. Because they accept the prevalence of certain narratives and historical trends, their resistances are not totalizing. As a result, they do not simply reflect or attempt to realistically represent the processes of Midwestern socioeconomic modernization. Rather, they register and revise it as part of the way they understand their spaces and characters. My thinking here is guided by Fredric Jameson's discussion of the process of mediation, which he expresses in terms of the relationship between modernist literature and the socioeconomic environment of the early twentieth century:

> Modernism and reification are parts of the same immense process which expresses the contradictory inner logic and dynamics of late capitalism. Yet even if our aim, as literary analysts, is rather to demonstrate the ways in which modernism—far from being a mere reflection of the reification of late nineteenth-century social life—is also a revolt against that reification and a symbolic act which involves a whole Utopian compensation for increasing dehumanization on the level of daily life, we are first obliged to establish a continuity between these two regional zones or sectors—the practice of language in the

> literary work, and the experience of *anomie,* standardization, rationalizing desacralization in the *Umwelt* or world of daily life—such that the latter can be grasped as that determinate situation, dilemma, contradiction, or subtext, to which the former comes as a symbolic resolution or solution. (42)

Jameson defines the experience of modernity as the interplay between social standardization and the fragmentation of anomie. For my purposes, his description usefully gestures to the anxieties of Greitzer's mural as well as the twinned accumulations and rejections of Midwestern fiction. The texts I study both resist and absorb the prevailing models of twentieth-century manhood, feature communities that support self-made as well as corporate identities, and generate spaces that meld rural and urban economics, land use, and affective experiences. Therefore, my argument that these authors imagine spaces and experiences outside of incorporated teleologies conforms in some sense to Jameson's description of the modernist literary act as a "Utopian compensation."

But because the resistances I find aren't total, I argue that they are neither utopian nor, precisely, a "symbolic resolution."[28] As I discuss in all four chapters, the language and structure of these texts do not attempt to portray a complete and accurate picture of Midwestern socioeconomic transitions or the experience of them. Rather, building on Jameson's definition of modernism, they use literary techniques and the "determinate situation" of modernity to various ends: among others, to critique the challenges of modern masculinity, to grind against the pastoral, and to find modernity in unexpected places. For this reason, they do not resolve or compensate for the problems of modernity but instead suggest a method for managing modern life. In the spirit of Jameson's comment that literary texts offer an "'imaginary resolution of a real contradiction,' it being understood that an imaginary resolution is no resolution at all" (256n242), I demonstrate how Midwestern modernist literature is bound up with—but not bound by—the experiences and "real contradictions" of Midwestern modernity. *Old-Fashioned Modernism* is an attempt to face that tension on its own terms. The fiction and poetry examined here pair common images of the country and city with the anxieties of modern masculinity, and they imagine spaces and gender roles that do not conform to prevailing narratives of socioeconomic modernization. These tensions, of course, are not uniform. Still, one common feature among these works is that they try to balance a multiplicity of divergent influences, which include socioeconomic trends, gender roles, and the shifting characteristics of rural and urban spaces. In so doing, Midwestern literature creates an *old-fashioned modernism* that blends older forms alongside modernist techniques, pastoral nostalgia with mechanical modernity, and stereotypical stories with disruptive ones.

Chapter 1, "Manufacturing Rural Modernity: The 'Vast Energy' of Midwestern Masculinity," challenges the critical custom of writing American modernity as a story of individual and communal transitions to city life. Critics commonly look to Sherwood Anderson's *Winesburg, Ohio* as the exemplar of regional modernism, but I argue that his 1920 novel *Poor White* more compellingly combines the communal and economic particularities of rural settings with the modern confusions of changing gender and socioeconomic hierarchies. As Anderson works through the implications of urban industrialization, he addresses related shifts in gender roles and expectations. Pairing Anderson's novel with agricultural implement advertisements, this chapter addresses how *Poor White* engages common narratives of Midwestern masculinity such as the self-made man, the independent farmer, and the local booster. Protagonist Hugh McVey, the inventor of a cabbage-planting machine, cannot reconcile his experiences as a lonely inventor and corporate-controlled company man. Bidwell, on the other hand, more functionally combines the agrarian with the industrial as the town's factories develop alongside its cabbage fields. As Anderson merges rural spaces and production with urbanized factory towns, he carves out a modern rural space in Bidwell and develops a counternarrative of dreamy, poor white masculinity that both depends upon and disrupts nominally "old-fashioned" visions of the region.

While chapter 1 demonstrates the challenge of forming workable masculine identities in a space that is also in flux, chapter 2, "'The Rustic Dream': Gender Norms, Rural Time, and the Modern Countryside," extends this analysis to the temporal aspects of modern rural masculinity. Examining two 1934 texts, Dawn Powell's novel *The Story of a Country Boy* and Lorine Niedecker's short book of poetry *Next Year or I Fly My Rounds, Tempestuous,* I show how the gender expectations and material objects within rural spaces contribute to insistently modern forms of rural time.

Niedecker created *Next Year* by pasting over the text of *The Sunlit Road,* a popular pastoral pocket calendar and, in this chapter, I analyze the calendar's cover and homilies alongside Niedecker's poetry. I argue that *Next Year* literalizes the relationship between rural materials and temporalities, which throws into relief fragmentary techniques within Powell's novel, in which collagist incursions of materiality obscure the novel's narrative progression. Despite characters' wishes, rural spaces and normative gender roles function as neither nostalgic salve nor triumphal future. As a result, both texts reject simplistic notions of the heartland, instead offering multiplicity and simultaneity as key features of the modern countryside.

Chapter 3, "'Where People and Things Wear Out': Masculine Fatigue and the Great Plains Farm Novel," examines two novels that show how men cope with inequity and extends chapter 2's temporal analysis by arguing that, on the farm, masculine failure accelerates. In William Cunningham's 1935 *The Green Corn Rebellion,* which dramatizes an actual 1917 uprising, the rebellion fails because it feels more like barnyard drudgery than idealistic liberation. Rather than picturing the moment of crisis, Wright Morris's 1948 photo-text *The Home Place* represents the long-term effects of economic hardship when Clyde Muncy returns to his childhood home in Nebraska and declares, "Out here is where people and things wear out" (19). Morris's photographs in *The Home Place* typify this fatigue, not only in their content—worn out buildings and farm objects—but also in their inconsistent relationship to the prose. Each novel demonstrates an ethic of fatigue that both trades on masculine stereotypes and taps into Depression-era economic decline. As a result, Morris and Cunningham register the modernity of their male characters by depicting modern life on the Great Plains as simultaneously built upon old-fashioned stories and complicated by them.

*Old-Fashioned Modernism* finds that Midwestern fiction and poetry structure modern masculinities around constant attempts at balance. They participate in the "make it new" discourses of literary modernism, but in terms of endless reactions and revisions—of rural and urban, masculine and feminine, economic and literary, and past, present, and future. Chapter 4, "'A Dreamy-Eyed Boy': Chicago, Race Records, and Regional Black Masculinity," mobilizes archival materials from Gennett Records, a prominent jazz label in rural Indiana, to argue that Langston Hughes's 1930 novel *Not Without Laughter* imagines a modern black masculinity incorporating protagonist Sandy Rodgers's travel to Chicago as well as his small-town upbringing. By accumulating these spaces along with the novel's cast of stereotypes, Hughes creates a referential and decentered masculine identity that is comprehensible only through its conflicts. Sandy's identity nonetheless balances rural and urban aspects, as well as the influences of his male and female role models, and Hughes portrays him as a figure of possibility as he develops a regional form of black masculinity.

The conclusion, "Contemporary Manhood and the Entrepreneurial Midwest," explores the twenty-first-century implications of "old-fashioned modernism" as the possibilities of Midwestern farm life have expanded to include local niche markets more commonly associated with Brooklyn hipsters than heartland farmers. I focus on two stories of rural women entrepreneurs in which men are dragged, unwittingly or hesitantly, into new forms of regional economy and social relationships. I begin with J. Ryan Stradal's "Venison," a chapter from the 2015 novel in stories, *Kitchens of the Great Midwest.* While the book tells the story of Eva Thorvald, who becomes a celebrity chef notorious for her over-the-top destination dining events, I focus on Jordy Snelling, a marginal character who briefly becomes part of Thorvald's supply line when he needs to get rid of some excess venison. I then turn to Bonnie Jo Campbell's short story "Boar Taint," from her 2009 collection, *American Salvage.* Examining the opposition between a poor white trash family and two upstanding farmers, I argue that Campbell accesses national imaginaries of rural decline by using the conventions of film's most abject rural genre, hillbilly horror. Campbell rethinks this image of a gutted Midwest by starting with a space and people that appear "tainted." When the story shifts from horror to farm entrepreneurship, however, "Boar Taint" indicates that its rural Midwestern setting is not the abject space it might seem to be. Rather, continuing a story started with the rural literature of the early twentieth century, this story renders a contemporary countryside incorporating conventional narratives of space and masculinity but also attending to the systemic and material challenges of the rural Midwest.

In the end, this book demonstrates how Midwestern authors negotiate the anxieties and dominant narratives of early- and midcentury rural masculinities. Through the concept of "old-fashioned modernism," it shows how these authors engage multiple cultural streams as they seek a workable balance for masculinities, spaces, and the texts themselves. They do so by planting formal innovations in the Midwestern countryside, pitting nostalgic pastoralism against the by-products of industrial modernity. Accordingly, much Midwestern cultural production is preoccupied with questions of middleness. Sometimes, that arises in careful representations of a place—the Middle West—that is geographically central. At other times, it may be linked to the region's image as a cultural backwater (it's "flyover country," after all) or the nation's moral center (it's "the heartland," home of the family farm and the American working class). Depending on the text, those "middles" can be physical or mental, central or transitional. A middle space might be balanced or ambivalent, and it could incorporate both rural and urban elements or develop into something different entirely. *Old-Fashioned Modernism* thus offers a way to think about the uneasy balancing acts of regional literature. While these Midwestern texts avoid overly simple nostalgic pasts or utopian futures, a scene or character might welcome or resist past and future acts, materials, or influences. A community's class structures might privilege middle-class identities or explore uneven transitions or underscore the violences of structural inequality. And a character might negotiate, accumulate, or reject gender stereotypes. All of the texts I study—from murals to poetry, from *Poor White* to "Boar Taint"—engage the cultural and material archives of Midwestern life and seek to manage the complications of shifting economies, gender roles, and cultural narratives. In some ways, this book's claim is quite modest: Midwestern modernist literature offers neither a pastoral past nor a utopian future. But this book also more radically reconsiders the power of coping, managing, negotiating—not as losses, but in terms of the desirability of stasis, of slowing, of middle ground. Not nostalgia, nor simply modernism, but something in between.

CHAPTER ONE

# MANUFACTURING RURAL MODERNITY

## *The "Vast Energy" of Midwestern Masculinity*

> A vast energy seemed to come out of the breast of earth and infect the people. Thousands of the most energetic men of the middle States wore themselves out in forming companies, and when the companies failed, immediately formed others. In the fast-growing towns, men who were engaged in organizing companies representing a capital of millions lived in houses thrown hurriedly together by carpenters who, before the time of the great awakening, were engaged in building barns. It was a time of hideous architecture, a time when thought and learning paused. Without music, without poetry, without beauty in their lives or impulses, a whole people, full of the native energy and strength of lives lived in a new land, rushed pell-mell into a new age.
>
> —Sherwood Anderson, *Poor White*, 1920

In the Midwest, commercial drilling for natural gas began in 1884. Communities across the region built pipelines, installed street lamps, and took pride in what seemed to be a natural expression of the land's bounty.[1] Along with widespread enthusiasm for the many industrial uses of natural gas and the boosterism resulting from regional economic development, a counternarrative also develops. In a 1903 report commissioned by the state geologist of Ohio, John Bownocker warns that "the result is well known" when communities react with "extravagance" to the discovery of natural gas (36). Following a boom, Bownocker cautions, the drilling industry's "capriciousness" (34) inevitably leads to a catastrophic bust. Nevertheless, throughout the late nineteenth and early twentieth centuries, Midwestern communities took every opportunity to develop their industrial capacity. Such growth affected Midwesterners in multiple ways, including the rise of the automobile and the consolidation of rural schools.

It also resulted in farm mechanization and industrial agriculture, which themselves increased economic precarity for both landowning farmers and wage laborers.[2] In short, to borrow Sherwood Anderson's language from the 1920 novel *Poor White,* by harnessing the land's "vast energy" to "a capital of millions," people of the Midwestern countryside "rushed pell-mell into a new age" (128).

In *Poor White,* Anderson portrays the tensions of a rural community and region undergoing processes of modernization. In the passage quoted in this chapter's epigraph, he develops the literal energy of a natural gas boom into a metaphor for the uneven socioeconomic development of the American Midwest. Energy infuses the people, land, and socioeconomic organization. But Anderson does not simply promote the region's "native energy and strength." Rather, echoing Bownocker's sense of the "well known" consequences of extravagant boom-era spending, Anderson juxtaposes that energy with a confusing, "pell-mell" rush into modernity (128). Pairing a sense of heightened regional possibilities with the anxiety-producing aspects of modernization, the novel constructs a modern rurality of ambiguity and contradiction. *Poor White* neither revolts from the village nor presents it nostalgically, and Anderson thereby rethinks the tensions of modernity in terms of their development in the rural Midwest.

The prevailing cultural association of modernity with urbanity influences critical approaches to *Poor White,* which commonly address the novel in terms of Anderson's purported sentimentality for rural and small-town America.[3] Brom Weber, for example, claims that *Poor White* is "the portrait of an unrecoverable past" (*Sherwood* 32) but destabilizes his sense of the novel's nostalgia by suggesting that it also "fuses visions of the past into the present" ("'Essence'" 686). Irving Howe attributes this instability to "the central fact" that Anderson's late nineteenth-century Ohio includes "the temporary coexistence of sharply contrasting types of social organization" (5). According to Howe, this results in "conflicting strands of the past and the future" (6). John Bassett expands on this idea, claiming that Anderson "identified with a country moving forward yet always nostalgically regretted what that progress entailed—industrialization, standardization, conformity" (10). Drawing on this strand of criticism, I argue that Anderson both embraces and subverts nostalgic modes to explore the possibilities of a modernizing Midwest.[4] In this way, *Poor White* exemplifies an "old-fashioned modernism" that attempts to merge conflicting discourses of pastoral agrarianism and urban industrialism, a balance that is complicated by the masculinized socioeconomic experiences of its protagonist and the uneasy combination of rural and urban space in small-town Bidwell, Ohio.

*Poor White* tells the story of Hugh McVey, who wanders through the Midwest, settles in Bidwell, becomes an inventor of farm machinery, marries the college-educated daughter of a local farmer, and eventually loses his job. Hugh's early years are divided between the influences of his poor white father and a railroad station agent's puritanical wife, a combination recalling Midwestern settlement patterns. During US westward expansion in the eighteenth and nineteenth centuries, the two major groups settling the Old Northwest came from northeastern and southern states, creating tension between "migrant Yankees" and "Upland Southerners."[5] The resulting cultural dichotomy created the preconditions for fractured modern identities, which Anderson represents in *Poor White* through the way Hugh's blend of dreaminess and drive complicates his ability to form meaningful social relationships. When Hugh begins to struggle within Bidwell's new corporate hierarchies, *Poor White*'s emphasis shifts to rising tensions between the town's rural agrarian and urban industrial economies. Anderson thus constructs both Hugh and Bidwell as prototypically Midwestern and reflective of the region's cultural and economic history. By paralleling the stories of an Ohio town and a Midwestern man, Anderson demonstrates one way that rural Midwestern people and places participate in a nonnostalgic, ambiguous, and contradictory modernity.

Anderson's version of life in the modern countryside also highlights several shifts in rural masculinity. *Poor White* includes numerous examples of normalized masculinity such as harness maker Joe Wainsworth, farmer Tom Butterworth, and the town's many bankers and shopkeepers. But these residual visions of rural masculinity—self-made family men living long term in one place, working as small farmers or merchant artisans—prove insufficient in a modernizing Midwest that is beginning to privilege, as seen in this chapter's epigraph, a socioeconomic mobility predicated on the "capital of millions" (128). Thus, when Hugh plans to leave his birthplace on the Mississippi River, Anderson introduces many of the issues informing the novel's engagement with rural masculinity: "'Well, I'm going away, I'm going away to be a man among men,' [Hugh] said to himself over and over. The saying became a kind of refrain and he said it unconsciously. As he repeated the words his heart beat high in anticipation of the future he thought lay before him" (22). Hugh assumes not only that he will be successful but also that he will measure himself against other men. These men, however, are unnamed and unknown—an ill-defined abstraction. Coupled with Hugh's excitement and unconscious repetition, this suggests that Anderson both universalizes and idealizes a modern masculinity that relies on homosocial competition, mobility, and future productivity.[6]

Conversely, the way that Hugh universalizes his expectations of manhood may also disturb the process of normalizing them. According to Eve Sedgwick, challenges to normativity must happen within "an entire cultural network of normative definitions" (*Epistemology* 11), and I argue that Anderson's representation of sexual and socioeconomic normativity also reveals their instabilities. Hugh's dreamy yet determined persona reveals an old-fashioned modernism within Midwestern masculinity—while his combination of character traits is determined by his past, these same traits help him forge his future, and all of these are inspired by his connection to the land around him. In the end, this novel uses Midwestern history as well as common narratives of twentieth-century manhood to produce alternate possibilities for Hugh and other rural men, as well as for Bidwell and the Ohio countryside.

Throughout *Poor White,* Anderson invests in Hugh's imagined ideal—a group of men, successful, future, and elsewhere—but also creates a modern rural space in which such a group doesn't have to exist. By locating the novel's action on Ohio farms and in small towns, he suggests the viability of rural spaces and identities that do not depend upon teleologies of urban modernity. Hugh's invention method, for instance, melds rural and urban elements to cultivate modernity in the fields of Bidwell, which shows how the novel both depends upon and undermines future-oriented industrialization narratives. Anderson broadens the novel's comment on national expectations of masculine gender performance by writing Bidwell's men as so many archetypes of Midwestern manhood. Throughout, *Poor White* illustrates the contingencies of masculinity and rural modernity through men's relationship to the land, particularly through questions of geographic and socioeconomic mobility. When Hugh chooses to remain in Bidwell, Anderson struggles to imagine a functional life for him—ultimately, Hugh cannot balance the town's socioeconomic ambiguities and conflicting cultural expectations, and he withdraws from the promising space he helped create. Therefore, while Anderson values the chaotic, "pell-mell" energy of Bidwell's version of rural modernity, he also indicates the challenges of achieving and sustaining modern rural masculinity.

## MECHANIZATION AND THE MODERN COUNTRYSIDE

By presenting Hugh and Bidwell as ambiguous, contradictory, and modern, Anderson challenges the dominant narrative of urban-industrial modernity, which devalues rural people and places. Alan Trachtenberg has called these socioeconomic changes and the accompanying cultural narrative *incorporation,* which he defines as "the emergence of a changed, more tightly structured society with new hierarchies of control, and also changed conceptions of that society, of America itself" (*Incorporation* 3–4). Focusing on urbanization, industrialization, and the rise of corporate capitalism, Trachtenberg explains the centralization of control and power in the late nineteenth- and early twentieth-century United States. Although Trachtenberg notes that "the process proceeded by contradiction and conflict" (7), he tracks how individuals, communities, and the state were expected to become more efficient and consolidated. In short, for Trachtenberg, incorporation provides a narrative of US society and culture in which the value of personal discipline has been displaced by organizational acumen and institutional growth. In *Poor White,* Anderson shares these concerns, suggesting that Hugh's rural-inspired work of invention can go only so far to help him succeed within Bidwell's corporate system. But Anderson does not accept the incorporation narrative's urban teleology. Such hesitation is borne out in histories of the period, such as William Cronon's and Shane Hamilton's, which underscore fractures in Trachtenberg's incorporation and similar totalizing narratives by showing how rural and urban economies develop in relation to each other. Anderson thus imagines a modern rural space that includes elements of industrial development—mechanical innovation, socioeconomic change, modern anxieties—but tempers them with old-fashioned expectations of rural economics and labor.

Accordingly, *Poor White* situates modern mechanics and invention within rural spaces. Hugh's first invention is a cabbage-setting machine that he creates while watching a local farm family plant cabbages at night. Hiding in the corner of Ezra French's field, Hugh uses his body to figure out the machine's movements. He transforms a purely intellectual pursuit into concrete physical action, which indicates the synthetic nature of Anderson's construction of rural modernity: it incorporates the mechanical mind, the human body, and the land. Furthermore, Hugh's appearance lacks tangibility and causes the farmworkers to feel anxious in what should have been a familiar space:

> Hugh arose and stood in the moonlight in the cabbage field, his arms still going stiffly up and down. The great length of his figure and his arms was accentuated by the wavering uncertain light. The laborers, aware of some strange presence, sprang to their feet and stood listening and looking. Hugh advanced toward them, still muttering words and waving his arms. Terror took hold of the workers. One of the woman plant droppers screamed and ran away across the field, and the others ran crying at her heels. "Don't do it. Go away," the older of the French boys shouted, and then he with his brothers also ran. (81)

When Hugh physically mimics the motions of cabbage planting, he develops his plans for the plant setter. As a result, Anderson has the opportunity to present the onset of technological modernity as a positive or negative development. He declines, however, which takes the form of modernist ambiguity. Hugh's twilight combination of action and thought disembody him. In "the wavering uncertain light," his figure is accentuated but his identity obscured, and his humanity becomes complicated by both myth and machine. Notwithstanding its imperative structure, the eldest French boy's command—"Don't do it. Go away"—demonstrates the scene's uncertainty. The imperative seems to be directed at Hugh, which potentially indicates a fear of bodily harm or an order to stop his attempts at industrialization. But, given its lack of a grammatical subject, the command can also be read as an instinctive response to any indicator of change, intended both to arrest the change and banish the changer.

Despite the farmworkers' fear, *Poor White* does not foreclose on rural modernity. According to Beverly Hogue, Anderson "subvert[s] pastoral nostalgia by planting mechanical gardens, suggesting that berries, corn, and cabbages are merely cogs in the vast machine of human culture" (102). While Anderson appears to regret some of the changes of modern society, Hogue maintains that he is not attempting to return to a pastoral ideal. In this scene, Anderson subverts the pastoral via the "mechanical garden" created when Hugh's moonlit mimicry of cabbage planting merges the temporal concerns of mechanized and pastoral life. *Poor White* thus portrays modernization in Bidwell as a combination of old-fashioned and futuristic elements. By presenting the French family working together in their father's field—one of the privileged spaces and values of rural life—alongside a vision for the industrial future, Anderson asserts the possibility of rural modernity that can support not only the urban factory but also rural labor, both manual and intellectual.

The expansiveness of this version of rural modernity is limited by the way *Poor White* addresses racial concerns. For example, Bidwell is a distinctly whitewashed community, and the novel—signaled by its title—also represents further exclusions via fractures within racial homogeneity. Early in the novel, Sarah Shepard tells Hugh that he comes from "poor white trash" (12), which Matt Wray and Annalee Newitz have argued "is not just a classist slur—it's also a racial epithet" (2). Wray goes on to explain that the term "names a kind of disturbing liminality: a monstrous, transgressive identity of mutually violating boundary terms, a dangerous threshold state of being neither one nor the other" (2).[7] Hugh's poor white background helps account for his monstrous appearance to the farmworkers: despite their racial and economic similarities—Hugh is a white man formerly employed as a hired hand—they perceive him as "some strange presence" (81). Hugh's appearance is almost completely unreadable, and they react in terror. Later, they mythologize the moment by describing Hugh as a "gigantic Indian, dancing and singing a funeral dirge in the moonlight" (82). The farmworkers do not look closely enough to recognize Hugh. In place of precise identification, they use a common frontier myth to impose a primitive racial otherness that is temporally displaced but connected to the land.[8]

The way that the farmworkers mythologize Hugh obscures his race and class, which may suggest that this scene expresses a desire to preserve homogenous, preindustrial rural communities. But *Poor White* also presents a variety of the workers' complaints, which indicates that Anderson offers a picture of rural modernity incorporating residual labor practices as well as individual and communal responses to the historical shifts at hand. Not all of these are tinged with the rosy glow of nostalgia, including representations of the physical difficulty of plant setting and the complaint of one of the youngest of the French family: "I'd rather be a horse or a cow than what I am. . . . What's the good being alive if you have to work like this?" (78). Hugh thinks his invention will improve working conditions, and the way he wants to "share in their labor" (78) recalls their racial and socioeconomic similarities. According to Maria Farland, depictions of rural life became more complex when modernist authors "departed from pastoral's characteristic elision of class differences and conflicts" (930). In this passage, the French family's uneasiness with Hugh's sudden appearance in the cabbage field doesn't indicate nostalgia for a life of manual labor. Rather, as *Poor White* develops a story of the modern countryside that challenges both nostalgic rurality and urban futurity, Anderson explores how rural men can learn more effectively how to participate in the processes of modernization.

Much like this novel's interest in making rural modernity comprehensible to local cabbage farmers, early twentieth-century industrial capitalists trained country people to understand the benefits of modern, mechanized farming methods. For instance, a 1908 advertisement for the Bemis Transplanter (see fig. 2), the most popular cabbage setter on the market, promotes the machine's "money making methods" and refers to "boys or girls" operating it.[9] Each of those appeals might attract figures such as *Poor White*'s skeptical farmer Ezra French, whose children both do the farmwork and complain about its difficulty. Beginning with the prominent placement of "SAVE TIME, SAVE LABOR, SAVE MONEY" and the assurance of "Profitable Crops," each element in the advertisement encourages rural users to believe that industrial products will improve life on the farm. The ad's genre—text mixed with image, varied typefaces, brevity of language—is suited to the educational project. Beyond the promises made in the headlines, the smaller type very explicitly explains the machine's function and benefits as well as the various crops it can transplant. The ad concludes with the promise of a free booklet on "money making methods in soil cultivation," available to anyone willing to write to company headquarters. In the bottom left corner, next to Fuller and Johnson's address, is an illustration of the machine, contrasted in white. Not only does this image correspond to Hugh's ghostly appearance, it also forecasts the result of Hugh's "mechanical calculations"

Fig. 2. Advertisement for Bemis Transplanter, *Dun's Review*, 1908.

(*PW* 81): the machine is directed outside of the ad's boundaries, presumably into some lucky farmer's field.

Although it functions similarly to the Bemis Transplanter, Hugh's machine is so advanced that it would be essentially incomprehensible to the French family and other Bidwell cabbage farmers. Fully mechanized transplanters like Hugh's were not actually produced until long after the novel's setting around the turn of the century. The Bemis Transplanter, for exam-

# The Tiger Automatic Plant Setter

An implement which has by past performance created not only a remarkable demand for itself, but which today sets the standard of excellence for transplanters.

*A Planter Handled, Sold and used for Profit*

**OHIO RAKE COMPANY, DAYTON, OHIO**

**Tractor Attachments for Automobiles.**

40 Champion Corp., Hammond, Ind.
55 Cutaway Harrow Co., Higganum, Conn.
85 Fond du Lac Tractor Corporation, Fond du Lac, Wis.
98 Gould Balance Valve Co., Kellogg, Ia.
125 Knickerbocker Motors, Inc., Poughkeepsie, N. Y.
165 Pullford Co., Walton Heights, Quincy, Ill.
225 Three P Auto Tractor Co., Davenport, Ia.

**Tractor Lawn Mowers (Special Golf Course).**

10 Berry-Roseman Co., 234 South La Salle St., Chicago.
20 Shawnee Mower Co., Shawnee-On-Delaware, Pa.

Roseman 10 Shawnee 20 Worthington 20

**Transplanters (Sweet Potato—Horse).**

10 Ohio Rake Co., Dayton, O.
20 Rawlings Implement Co., Baltimore, Md.

Red Star 20 Tiger 10

**Transplanters (Tobacco, Cabbage, Etc.—Hand).**

5 Harriman Mfg. Co., Harriman, Tenn.
10 Masters Planter Co., 229 N. State St., Chicago, Ill.

Harriman 5 Masters Rapid Plant Setter 10

**Transplanters (Tobacco, Cabbage, Etc.—Horse).**

2 Babcock Mfg. Co., Leonardsville, N. Y.
4 J. I. Case Plow Works Co., Racine, Wis.
8 Homer Laughlin Engineers Corporation, Los Angeles, Cal.
10 Madison Plow Co., Madison, Wis.

Fig. 3. Advertisement for Tiger Plant Setter, *Farm Implement News Buyer's Guide*, 1920.

ple, was exhibited at the 1893 Columbian Exposition in Chicago (Ardrey 145), and Wisconsin native Fred H. Bemis received his patent the following year (Seymour 643). Hugh's invention would have been advanced even at the time of *Poor White*'s 1920 publication. Charles Wendel does not document the existence of a "self-setting machine" until the 1920s (429), though Liberty Hyde Bailey notes in 1917 that "the feasibility of handling cabbage by machinery is attracting the attention of growers" (148).

As seen in a 1920 advertisement for the Tiger Plant Setter (fig. 3), transplanters of this period share several characteristics with Hugh's machine: they open the furrow, water the seedling, and close the furrow. But someone must sit at the rear of the machine, manually dropping plants into the furrows. Hugh's machine is different, particularly in its setting motion. Hugh's description illustrates the completely mechanical process of transplanting the seedlings: "'The down stroke will go so,' he muttered, and bringing up his arm swung it above his head. His fist descended into the soft ground" (80). Anderson could have had Hugh create a realistic transitional invention combining manual and mechanical labor, but instead he introduces a machine that was several years ahead of its time. Through the transplanter's fully mechanized setting motion, *Poor White* underscores the disorientation and disruption of industrialization's entrance into farming communities.

Despite the French family's initial hesitation, the economic promise of manufacturing still proves powerfully attractive to many citizens of Bidwell.[10] Across the United States as well as in *Poor White,* farmworkers come to accept production-oriented social structures as well as narratives of compulsory urban industrialization, evidencing Antonio Gramsci's claim that hegemony "is born in the factory" (285).[11] The community's transformation into "a busy manufacturing town" (*PW* 41), then, reflects Gramsci's argument that "the whole life of the nation revolve[s] around production" (285). After Hugh invents the cabbage setter, life in Bidwell revolves around manufacturing. Anderson underscores the townspeople's relationships to capital and corporations as they discuss the machine, take factory jobs, and read about "the talk of new times . . . in the pages of American newspapers and magazines" (51).

Undeniably, Bidwell grows after Hugh's invention. Even so, Anderson privileges rural products and locations within *Poor White*'s version of the early twentieth-century Midwestern economic system. When Hugh explains that "the machine must be built close to the ground" (80), Anderson suggests both the cabbage setter's low-slung physical presence as well as its production near the cabbage fields. Anderson thereby limits the extent to which *Poor White* represents a totalizing national turn to urban industrialism. Not only is Hugh's cabbage-setting machine produced in a rural setting, but its invention is also inspired by rural needs and values. As a way for Hugh to "share in [farmworkers'] labor" (78), the machine is both labor saving and community oriented. Even the book's modern and modernist elements originate in the rural space: the speculators financing the machine's production are from Bidwell, while Anderson stylistically emphasizes the "fluttering, dreamy state" (78) that Hugh feels at twilight in the cabbage fields. In this way, the novel engages alternate narratives of both rural masculinity and industrial modernity—in *Poor White,* rural spaces, people, and products participate equally in a broad-based, shifting network of economic influences and social formations.

This novel offers a way to read modernization and modernity in both national and regional terms: a Gramscian sense of the factory's national importance combined with a more optimistic regional iteration in which Anderson incorporates actual and metaphorical Midwestern energy and rural production. Bidwell modernizes, after all, because "a vast energy seemed to come out of the breast of earth and infect the people" (128). Through Hugh's invention and the subsequent growth of Bidwell's factories, *Poor White* demonstrates regional complicity in national socioeconomic narratives but also asserts an increased local role in capitalist production. By emphasizing the land's energy, Anderson submits that this economic transition does not rely entirely on the "force . . . and persuasion" of workers (Gramsci 285). *Poor White,* then, functions as a rural challenge to Gramscian hegemony as well as a vision of Midwestern modernity. Countering critics who read his attachment to the land as nostalgic, I argue that Anderson does not attempt to displace modern society with an older vision. Rather, he suggests that rural modernity forms as a combination of local needs and modern discourses, and he naturalizes this style of modernization by drawing energy and inspiration from the land.

In many ways, *Poor White* is an optimistic rejoinder to national narratives of urban industrialization. It also shows, however, that rural modernity is never easily created or maintained. For example, when Hugh is swept up in "the flood of new inventions" (79), the novel appears to promote the development of modern industrial capitalism. But Hugh's "impulse to try to invent a plant-setting machine" (80) originates with an interest in mechanical innovation and local labor saving rather than capitalist entrepreneurship. Furthermore, at the end of the novel, Hugh resists undertaking the reverse engineering and patent avoidance tasks assigned to him by factory boss Steve Hunter. Hugh's transition from unwitting servant of economic modernization to unwilling participant in the machinations of corporate capitalism illustrates the inherent difficulty of balancing new demands with old strengths. As this novel manufactures rural modernity, then, it both privileges that attempt at balance and marks it as a potentially insurmountable challenge for Hugh and Bidwell's other men.

## ARCHETYPES OF MIDWESTERN MASCULINITY

Because Hugh is written as a composite Midwesterner, he is positioned at the intersection of multiple, frequently conflicting, historical and cultural streams: rural and urban; agrarian and industrial; manual and mechanical; past, present, and future; corporate, communal, and individual; self-made and incorporated masculinity; Upland Southerner and migrant Yankee. Hugh negotiates a broad range of experiential and socioeconomic discourses by attempting to find balance or stability. In *Poor White*'s version of rural modernity, individuals and communities must be highly and immediately reactive, lest they be pushed aside by any among a variety of forces. Anderson thus submits that Midwestern masculinity may resist the assumed endings of both urban industrial incorporation and nostalgic, bygone rurality. Fittingly, for a character and region in the midst of a messy and contradictory process of modernization, Hugh is beset by several models of masculinity, many of which exemplify national masculine archetypes. While Anderson uses Hugh to bridge the poor white, the self-made man, and the incorporated company man, none of these examples proves sufficient for Hugh's continued success in the modern rural space.

The competing values represented by these different models of masculinity are rooted in Midwestern historical dichotomies. In her study of farmers in southern Illinois, Jane Adams found that "people locally recollect the distinction between the 'wide-awake' farmers and the 'backward' ones as between migrant Yankees and the old settlers from the southern hills. However, the contrast was also between entrepreneurially oriented commercial farmers and the established farming community" (81). Union County, Illinois, is located on the Mississippi River much like Hugh's fictional birthplace of Mudcat Landing, Missouri, and in *Poor White,* Anderson represents the same conflicts that Adams does. In the first chapter of the novel, Anderson glosses the history of Upland Southerners moving into the area around Mudcat Landing. He explains that some Southerners, who had "a deep aversion to physical labor" (18) because they would not compete with slaves, "pushed north along the rivers and settled in Southern Indiana and Illinois and in Eastern Missouri and Arkansas" (19). Upon arrival, Anderson writes, "They seemed to have exhausted their energy in making the voyage and slipped quickly back into their old slothful way of life" (19). Hugh's father John McVey comes from Southern stock, and he represents the indolence associated with both fictional and historical Upland Southerners. When he loses his job at a tannery, Adams's subjects might have portrayed him the same way as *Poor White*'s narrator: "John McVey stayed in town. He also became a drunkard. It was the easy obvious thing for him to do" (*PW* 4).

Notably, McVey's slothfulness arises after he left a job as a farmhand to move to the tannery in Mudcat Landing. As a result, he loses some of the virtues ascribed to rural men. Bidwell farmer Tom Butterworth, for instance, is known as a man who "knew how to make and handle money" (98). His farmhand Jim Priest is similarly capable, though Tom Butterworth's daughter Clara imagines Priest to have a more concrete industriousness: "'The farm hand works,' she thought, 'and the corn grows. This man sticks to his task in his shop and makes a town grow'" (262). Clara is comparing Jim Priest working in the fields to Hugh working on his inventions. She could have been describing another key figure in the novel, the "vastly independent" harness maker Joe Wainsworth, who is described as "tradesman of the old school" (51).

Each of these men is described in terms of their capability and self-control, which also mark discourses of self-made manhood. Anthony Rotundo finds that, in the nineteenth century, "a man defined his manhood not by his ability to moderate the passions but by his ability to channel them effectively" (3). According to Rotundo, men in American culture are expected to discipline themselves and to channel that self-control into individual economic achievement. Anderson represents nineteenth-century ideals of self-made manhood by imbuing his male characters with varying types and levels of self-discipline. Wainsworth, for example, is an independent craftsman. Priest is a longtime hired hand. Butterworth most clearly represents the self-made man, for his success as a farmer has allowed him to amass wealth and gain the respect of the townspeople. *Poor White,* however, takes place at a transitional moment for American masculinity in which nineteenth-century forms began to merge and adapt for new social and economic realities.[12] Hugh thus combines several of these traits: he labors independently to create the cabbage setter, but its production, which will give Hugh both money and acclaim, is financed by speculators, and then Hugh becomes an employee of the factory under Steve Hunter.

As Bidwell incorporates and Hugh enters (then leaves) the corporate economy, *Poor White* does not simply predicate modern masculinity on economic self-determination. Joe Wainsworth, for instance, is skeptical of factory-produced goods and resentful of the changes that accompany Hugh's cabbage setter and the growth of Bidwell's factories. After being humiliated by his employee Jim Gibson, who makes him order and sell factory-made harnesses, Wainsworth strikes out against several figures of Bidwell's modernizing economy—he stabs Gibson, shoots Steve Hunter, and attacks Hugh "with claws and teeth" (360). Befitting his name, Wainsworth represents a declining cultural moment and all the struggles therein. After Wainsworth bites Hugh, Anderson labels him an "insane" representative of a "dead past" (359, 360). In the rural Midwest of *Poor White,* Wainsworth becomes a by-product of modernity in part because he refuses to adapt to the modern economy, especially as it threatens the way he has traditionally conceived of his labor.

While masculinity studies scholars have emphasized the relationship between economic dependency and growing urban centers, Anderson places industrial manufacturing in a farming community and thereby confronts rural men—like their urban counterparts—with a newly hierarchical form of management and economic competition. This shift can be seen in the novel's uneven responses to economic modernization, including not only Wainsworth's resistance but also the way Hugh counters the region's "vast energy" (128) with a tendency toward "weariness and loneliness"

(37). The most enthusiastic participants in the new rural economy are Steve Hunter and his (all male) investors. Hunter wants the townspeople to be confident in the cabbage setter, and he is so invested in the matter that he fraudulently promotes the machine: "Steve took no chances. He engaged Ed Hall to go at night and replace the plants that did not live. 'It's fair enough. . . . A hundred things can cause the plants to die, but if they die it'll be blamed on the machine. What will become of the town if we don't believe in the thing we're going to manufacture here?'" (126–127). By secretly replacing the plants, Hunter attempts to satisfy both "skeptical farmers" and "town enthusiasts" (126) about the machine's performance. The transplanter's failure is immaterial to Hunter, as he is more concerned with positive reception than successful performance. While he pays lip service to the town's future, Hunter is clearly focused on potential profits. But Anderson also indicates that producing wealth is not the sole marker of masculine identity in Bidwell. Specifically, Hunter must balance expectations of monetary success with the needs of multiple social groups.

Still, those groups are almost exclusively composed of white men, which constitutes a distilled example of the masculinity studies argument that modern men form their gender identities through homosocial competition. Historian George Chauncey argues that men in the early twentieth century did not define themselves solely by attempting to obtain power over women but rather expressed masculine anxiety by concerning themselves with their "relative virility compared to other men's" (80). Hugh and Clara's marriage helps drive the novel's plot and, leading up to it, several men attempt to court her, a fairly literal competition among male characters seeking to prove their virility. I contend, however, that Clara's courtship is secondary to Anderson's metaphorical treatment of "relative virility": competition for socioeconomic place in a changing economy. Notably, Anderson leaves out women's factory labor, limiting the social complexity that would have attended a more historically accurate rendering.

In terms of masculine experience, Chauncey's theory of competitive virility neatly matches Hunter's behavior throughout the novel. Hunter justifies replacing the cabbage plants because of the complex possibilities for their death, so he eliminates organic instability and takes control of every element of the machine's production and reception. Taking control in such a way insinuates that Hunter is vitally concerned with advancing his position relative to the other men in Bidwell, and it indicates two key concerns for this chapter: first, that Anderson does not present a unified theory of the land's place in rural modernity and, second, that this novel tracks a transitional moment of gender definition. In this period, the gendering of labor was unstable, particularly in terms of masculinity, which transitioned from a "self-made" ideal into other forms. Self-made manhood valued control—especially self-control—and developed within the context of relative autonomy in the workplace. Along with the growth of centralized industrial capitalism, however, that control became less attainable for most men.

Hunter's attempt to eliminate the land's effect on the cabbage plants, then, demonstrates the residual value and increasing elusiveness of the concept of control, especially in terms of relationships between men, their community, and the social and geographical environment. In this situation, even the soil becomes embroiled in the corporate economy, as Anderson represents a more fragmentary, sometimes oppositional, relationship between man and land. Prior to the cabbage plants' replacement, Hugh told Hunter that the machine was "too heavy to be handled by one team," "would not work when the soil was either too wet or too dry," and "worked perfectly in both wet and dry sand but would do nothing in clay" (121). While rural people and products are essential to this conception of modern rurality, this is not a pastoral idyll. Rather, in this situation, rural production relies upon industrial production, but the land is occasionally at odds with the factory.

Bidwell fits this model of rural modernity in its land use and growth patterns, as well as in the economic practices of its male industrialists. As the socioeconomic structures and normative gender identities of a smaller, ruralized community conflict with the new ones developed in the process of industrial urbanization, Bidwell and its residents experience modern social and identity fragmentation. These manifest in several ways, from the farmworkers' terror to the myths that circulate about Hugh to Clara's disappointment in returning to Bidwell. This alienation shows a still-rural community that also corresponds to characteristic descriptions of modernity. The difference between Bidwell and standard definitions of modernity, of course, stems from its comparatively rural location and economic structure. The very representation of this community, then, may be seen as an act of modernist fragmentation that upends urban-oriented definitions of modernity and removes a single assumed narrative in favor of plurality. Anderson writes Bidwell, in particular, as an exemplar of rural modernity, as the people "rush[ing] pell-mell into a new age" (128) are Steve Hunter, Hugh McVey, and the residents of farms and small towns across the Midwest.

In comparison, Anderson primarily places women either in the home or, as with milliner Fanny Twist, in domestically oriented industries, which implicates him in the same processes of representation that kept small-town Midwestern women "obscured in the historical record" (Murphy 39). Several scholars have found that women's self-representation follows similar trends, arguing that women tend not to create "unifying myths" (Hampsten 40) or otherwise "generalize about their experiences" (Fink xx) even though they saw their work as "central to their identities" (Adams 3). Anderson's treatment of Clara Butterworth exemplifies the limits that he places on his women characters. She is forced to return to Bidwell because her aunt and uncle, with whom she was staying while attending college, find her on their porch in the arms of a young man. When she refuses to explain that he had embraced her against her will, her aunt and uncle decide not to invite her back for the following school year. By sending Clara to college in Columbus and introducing Kate Chanceller, a lesbian love interest, Anderson offers Clara diverse opportunities for her career, her sexuality, and where she might live. Then he removes all three when Clara is sent back to Bidwell, decides to stay, enters a heterosexual marriage, and does not work outside the home. Such limitations illustrate a larger pattern of obscuring women's participation in Midwestern society, which results in a masculinist depiction of social and economic life in Bidwell.

Clara's shifted ambitions also demonstrate one way that turn-of-the-century Midwestern women manage the transitions and processes of modernization. Disinterested by her suitor Alfred Buckley, who is also her father's business associate, she becomes infatuated with tales of Hugh's heroic masculinity: "Hugh was what she wanted to be. He was a creative force. In his hands dead inanimate things became creative forces. He was what she wanted not herself but perhaps a son, to be" (247). The turn from the first to the last sentences of this passage clarifies the position of women in this novel. Though Clara is "startled" (247) by the thought that her ambitions are not for herself, her focus shifts for the remainder of the novel to marrying Hugh and her eventual pregnancy. While Clara has limited access to the structures of self-making that are available to white men in

Bidwell, acknowledging those limits in *Poor White* has led critics such as Jackson Lears to suggest that Anderson's writing aligns "(albeit obliquely and ambivalently) with feminist critiques of modernity" (15).[13] To be sure, this is a generous reading of *Poor White.* But if this novel enables a (oblique, ambivalent) feminist reading, such claims must center on Clara's ability to withdraw from complicated possibilities that are, for whatever reason, unsatisfactory to her.

Though Clara does not become the prototypical New Woman, the possibilities available to her in this novel exist because Bidwell is a modern space. Clara's educational achievements and geographic mobility are both arrested in the narrative, but their existence links gendered experience in the Ohio countryside with a broad range of socioeconomic pressures. In *A New Heartland: Women, Modernity, and the Agrarian Ideal in America,* Janet Galligani Casey identifies some of the ways that masculinity and femininity were in transition in rural spaces in the early twentieth century, arguing that "inherited modes of representation and inherited models of gendered labor were equally threatened in the early twentieth century" (9). Casey shows how women actively constructed a modern rural society, which was particularly visible in their resistance to old-fashioned expectations for women. In *Poor White,* Anderson addresses similar concerns of representational difficulty and shifts in labor expectations but focuses on men's experiences. For instance, Steve Hunter lies about Hugh's background so that the Cleveland newspaper will turn him into "a strikingly romantic figure" (222), but Hugh does not easily fit the stereotype of the self-made industrialist. Despite Hugh's "keen hunger for recognition" (250), the newspaper reporter finds him "embarrassed and uncommunicative" (222). Anderson writes that "the broad, rich land demanded gigantic figures, and the minds of men had created the figures" (246), and while Hugh's achievements facilitate such a story, notions of heroic masculinity insufficiently account for his feelings and experience.

Because we know of Hugh's insecurities and awkwardness, when he is turned into a mythical figure—whether by farmworkers in twilight or on a brochure created by the factory's advertising manager—*Poor White* confirms that one of Anderson's main concerns is to explore how the chaos of the region's changing socioeconomic structures affects rural men. Hugh's struggle to create a balanced modern identity becomes apparent early in the novel, when "the study of mathematical problems, taken up to relieve his loneliness and to cure his inclination to dreams, was beginning to have an effect on his character" (55). Retreating to the measured, solitary study of mechanics indicates how Hugh negotiates the rapid development of Bidwell's manufacturing economy. Hugh's tireless study is an example of what Alan Derickson calls "manly wakefulness" (8). According to Derickson, American industrialists felt that sleeping less helped men increase efficiency and develop self-control. Still, while Hugh is encouraged that "he did his work more quickly and accurately," he feels "hesitating" and "awkward" (55). Hugh's decision to withdraw does not help him develop a balanced modern identity. Instead, his hesitation and loneliness, which Anderson offers as markers of social modernity, lead him to outdated forms of masculinity. This is an old-fashioned modernism that highlights the ambivalence of the concept. From Hunter and Wainsworth to Hugh McVey and his father, the stories of *Poor White*'s men indicate Anderson's strategy for representing the difficulty of this historical moment. Liesl Olson writes that "no American writer explores masculinity better" (143), and in this novel, Anderson attempts to balance elements associated with the past such as nostalgically represented rural land use and the self-control of the self-made man alongside industrial capitalist desires for growth and increased wealth. As a result, both Hugh and Bidwell resist exclusive definition as rural or urban, nostalgic or modern, independent or corporate, which demonstrates how the novel retains a nostalgic vision of independent rural masculinity while also investigating the possibilities of a modern corporate version.

## "A PROBLEM THAT COULD NOT BE SOLVED IN WOOD AND STEEL"

In *Poor White,* the economic and affective transitions exemplified by Hugh McVey are linked to his travels throughout the Midwest. Hugh's identity is not fixed, and Anderson suggests that rural masculinity requires not only balance and flexibility but also a willingness to change perspective. For Hugh changing perspective takes multiple meanings, including his migration from Mudcat Landing to Bidwell, his career shift from telegraph operator to inventor, and his tendency to wander when puzzled. For Bidwell, the major spatial and socioeconomic shifts are due to the effects of industrialization on both the community and its individuals. For the novel,

"Hugh's first inventive effort stirred the town of Bidwell deeply" (70), creating slippage between Hugh and Bidwell, as both the individual and the community are constructing modern identities in the Ohio countryside. Despite Hugh's willingness to revise his social and spatial position, however, Anderson ultimately writes him as failing to sustain a masculine identity that integrates both economic productivity and modern affective experience. Similar to Lorine Niedecker's development of a modern rurality predicated on the failure of normative gender roles and Langston Hughes's creation of a regional black masculinity, which I examine in chapters 2 and 4, Hugh's successes are always contingent. He incorporates multiple models of gendered behavior that reveal conflicting expectations on rural men, showing how creating and sustaining modern masculinity remains challenging even in light of a regional environment conducive to it.

Throughout the novel, Hugh's personal challenges are frequently mental obstacles of some sort—related to work, relationships, or his past. His response to those challenges is to wander, changing his position by walking the roads and countryside in an attempt to better comprehend his situation. In the following passage, Anderson presents Hugh attempting to think through the difficulties in his marriage to Clara, which suggests how the spatial experience of rural modernity affects and is informed by modern gender experiences:

> For hours he walked blindly, but it did not occur to him that as he waited, hating the waiting, Clara also waited; that for her also it was a time of trial and uncertainty. To him it seemed her course was simple and easy. She was a white pure thing—waiting—for what? for courage to come in to him in order that an assault be made upon her whiteness and purity.
>
> That was the only answer to the question Hugh could find within himself. The destruction of what was white and pure was a necessary thing in life. It was a thing men must do in order that life go on. As for women, they must be white and pure—and wait. (316)

Anderson marginalizes the novel's women characters, but in this case Hugh's and Clara's experiences posit a fundamental similarity between masculine and feminine experiences of modernity: they wait impatiently to consummate their marriage, which they both experience as "a time of trial and uncertainty." They experience this moment similarly, as Hugh rejects the normatively (and nostalgically) defined expectation of courageous masculinity and submissive femininity. That relative equality does not enhance their relationship, however, as Hugh's outmoded gender role expectations cause him to assume that Clara is a figure of purity rather than an educated participant in modernity.

While Hugh and Clara have similar relational anxieties and temporal experiences, Hugh walks to help him think, while Clara sits at home. His comparative mobility underlines how expectations for gender-specific behavior also shape this novel's hierarchies of capital and power. When Hugh walks about the countryside in an attempt to better understand his marriage, Anderson also shows Hugh changing his position and his relationship to those discourses. In other words, Hugh alters the spatial component of his experience. Walking helps Hugh sort out the various influences on his personal identity and prescribed social role, but Anderson undercuts Hugh's potential success through his blindness. Because Hugh "walked blindly," he cannot see how those discourses interact, suggesting the attempt will end in failure.

Much as Hugh engages in some stereotypical masculine behaviors while resisting others, his travels throughout the novel do not proceed to the incorporation narrative's expected endpoint. Rather, his blind walking, his travels throughout the Midwest, and his choice to settle in Bidwell reveal a more circuitous route reincorporating rural elements as part of modern life. In different parts of *Poor White,* Hugh walks to stimulate his thoughts, but his walking mobility fails to generate any sustained thought. Instead, it results in a formless musing. Another passage in which Hugh "left his shop and went for a walk" (352) demonstrates how Hugh's economic rise limits his ability to resist the demands of urban industrialism. In this passage, Hugh wanders because he is struggling with his latest task from Steve Hunter, to get around a patent on a mechanical hay baler held by an inventor in Iowa. Instead of focusing on this task, Hugh's thoughts are drawn to the time "when he was striving to come out of the filth, the flies, the poverty, the fishy smells, the shadowy dreams of his life by the river" (352). Here, Anderson taps into the Horatio Alger myth of a young man made good through hard work, assisted by a successful man's altruistic act to remove him from the slums. Drawn into the world of commerce and modern industry by stationmaster Shepard and his wife Sarah, Hugh largely is separated from his father and the filthy, shadowy culture of his birth, eventually working up to—in his unconscious, dreaming way—a more lucrative and powerful economic position. But his thoughts drift, which seems to equalize his concrete tasks of the present with various influences on his upbringing. Hugh finds this perplexing, "a problem that could not be solved in wood and steel" (352).

Consequently, Anderson does not end Hugh's story on an Alger-ian economic up note, as this passage indicates his engagement with another prevalent literary narrative of the late nineteenth century, the fall of the great man. Characters whose ethical or moral failings cause them to fall from a successful socioeconomic position inhabit much of American literary realism, including the patriarchs of Ohio-born W. D. Howells's *The Rise of Silas Lapham* (1885) and Hoosier Booth Tarkington's *The Magnificent Ambersons* (1918). This trope falls in line with a broader concern in the late nineteenth and early twentieth centuries over the effects of increasing wealth on individuals and the moral challenges of a changing socioeconomic order. Amy Kaplan argues that such challenges are central to the form and structure of literary realism. *Poor White* is preoccupied with such social change, and the way Anderson narrates the public and private lives of Hugh McVey and Clara Butterworth indicates the novel's relationship to realist forms. But unlike the characters of Howells, Tarkington, or Theodore Dreiser, Hugh does not fall prey to greed or overextension. Rather, he gets caught up in a modern corporate economy that has begun to ask him to approach his work differently—this is a modernist novel, after all, though its debts to realism show how it is an old-fashioned one.

Hugh's inventions are inspired by local farmworkers, not by profit-oriented machinations of the corporate economy, and Hugh struggles when he is forced from his chosen developmental track. Hugh's dreaminess has merged with the Shepards' work ethic to create a working style that synthesizes many elements of his background and current environment. Early in *Poor White,* Steve Hunter capitalizes on Hugh's inventive talents. At this point, however, Hunter has asked Hugh to shift his work into reverse engineering in an attempt to get around the Iowa man's patent. But because Anderson has written Hugh's creativity as a synthesis of the materials and people around him, Hugh's talents are unsuited to Hunter's profit motive. Indeed, Hugh believes that "he had lived but little in the life of the imagination, had been afraid to live that life, had been warned and re-warned against living it" (352), suggesting that he is so limited in regard to abstraction that he is unable to be productive in his new economic position. If Hugh's imaginative productivity is predicated on his ability to assimilate many different influences, however, then Anderson might be seen in this passage as actually criticizing Hugh's passivity in accepting the task. As Anderson's prototype of modern Midwestern masculinity, Hugh must reincorporate rural influences and inspirations into his work; this profit-oriented reverse engineering job means that he loses part of the synthesis that originally enabled his success.

Hugh's apparent passivity and modified economic position demonstrate the tensions within normalized masculine roles. As Hugh wanders, while "he should have been making new parts for the hay-loading apparatus," his thoughts turn toward "the shadowy figure of the unknown inventor in the state of Iowa, who had been brother to himself, who had worked on the same problems and had come to the same conclusions" (352–353). Describing the Iowa inventor as "shadowy" recalls Hugh's birth culture as well as the "wavering uncertain light" of the cabbage field (81), and it also emphasizes the tension within the Iowa man's position as both brother and competitor to Hugh. As his rurality-inspired brother, the Iowa man evokes Hugh's greatest personal and professional successes—seeing some problem in the life or work of people around him and addressing that issue, thereby tapping into the communal life in which he desires to take part. As a competitor, however, the Iowa man's invention of the hay-loading machine suggests that he has beaten Hugh and, according to Chauncey's argument about masculine competition, positioned himself as more masculine and capable. But their parallel problems of comprehension—Hugh's inability to clearly envision the Iowa man just as, earlier, the farmworkers in the cabbage field could not comprehend Hugh's appearance—indicate a certain level of solidarity, suggesting that their relationship is not so clearly a competition.

In this way, Anderson seems to be critiquing the boundaries of masculinity even as he reinscribes their effects on the individual. Throughout the novel, when Hugh struggles with the expectations of normative masculinity, he isolates himself. Anthony Rotundo argues that such behavior develops during boyhood, during which an American boy must learn "to assert himself and to stand emotionally alone" (46). Whether leaving the house to puzzle over his marriage or fleeing Mudcat Landing to get away from childhood poverty, Hugh tries to break free from normative expectations, but in his detachment, he performs another type of stereotypically masculine behavior. As a result, these attempted escapes rarely provide the clear direction Hugh hopes they will. For example, when "thinking of the Iowa man, Hugh began to think of other men. He thought of his father and of himself" (352). Despite his attempt to negotiate the novel's complex network of thoughts and emotions, Hugh appears unprepared to balance the various historical influences and present demands on him: "Hugh tried to think of himself and his own life. For a time that seemed a simple and easy way out of the new and intricate task he had set for his mind. His own life was a matter of history. He knew about himself" (353). Hugh's literal and figurative meandering causes a retreat to personal history. Here and elsewhere, Hugh resists normative definitions of American masculinity, but he cannot perform the balancing act that this novel requires for modern rural men—in other words, because this problem "could not be solved in wood and steel," Hugh doesn't solve it.

## "THE TOWN WAS REALLY THE HERO OF THE BOOK"

Compared to Hugh, Bidwell more successfully balances rural products and people with the socioeconomic changes accompanying the town's new factories. As a result, the town retains some of its purportedly old-fashioned elements while still functioning as a modern community. This combination is clear from Bidwell's first appearance. Hugh is sent to Bidwell by a former resident, a railroad worker who knows of an opening for a telegraph operator. He assumes that Hugh is an alcoholic and sends him to settle in an area outside of town called "Pickleville." According to the railroad man, this is because "there used to be a saloon there and a factory for putting up cucumber pickles, but they've both gone now. You won't be tempted to slip in that place" (59). In some ways, Pickleville refers to a rural past—it is a mile outside a small town, its factory was agricultural, and it is a place where Hugh can embody nineteenth-century definitions of masculine self-control. But it is also a site of modernity, albeit in many ways a modern ruin—though

Pickleville has a railroad station housing a telegraph operator, its industrialism is in the form of failed corporations, which likely also caused the saloon to go out of business. It appears to exemplify what Jani Scandura describes as "a modernity that idles" (11), though I argue that Bidwell and Pickleville do not, in the end, represent modern life lying fallow.

As Hugh's inventions become more successful, Pickleville grows from the site of Hugh's workshop; several houses are built, as well as factories that produce the cabbage setter, bicycles, and a corn cutter. These machines, much like the name "Pickleville," denote local pride in rural products. According to Anderson's biographer Walter Rideout, the name "Pickleville" likely is patterned after "Sauerkrautville," a nickname for Anderson's hometown of Clyde, Ohio (*Writer* 1:135). Such nicknames are widespread throughout Ohio, which also has towns named Celeryville, Wheat Ridge, Wheatville, and Farmersville. This combination shows how Bidwell challenges two of the central narratives of rural life in the twentieth century. In Bidwell, modern economics join with rural pride, suggesting how Midwestern towns can function as modern rural places that neither grow into large urban centers nor decline as residents and businesses leave for the city.

At the end of *Poor White,* Hugh returns home to Clara and they stand "by the fence" (363) outside their farmhouse, surrounded by the sounds of farm and factory. This passage has received a good deal of critical attention, much of it addressing the novel's moral and narratological ambiguities. Irving Howe, for example, finds the novel's ending "most unsatisfactory" because of Anderson's "curious aversion to dramatic conflict" (82). Robert Morss Lovett also criticizes the ending, noting that "*Poor White* does not end—it merely stops" (37), but he places fewer demands on the novel: "No ending is better than a false one, and perhaps any emphasis would be misplaced in Mr. Anderson's cosmos—or chaos" (37). This chapter intervenes in the middle ground between Howe's criticisms and Lovett's sense of the novel's universality (benevolent or malignant, depending on "cosmos—or chaos"). I read the novel's ending as shadowy, indeterminate in how it resists reduction to a single defining element of masculine, economic, or spatial experience. Moreover, I contend that the ending's ambiguity, and the reason Howe points out a lack of conflict between the characters, is due to the intensified importance of Bidwell as a modern rural space that juxtaposes the urban futurity of a factory whistle with the gently nostalgic "sounds of farm animals stirring" (363).

Such indeterminacy demonstrates the difficulty of creating—or even imagining—modern rural spaces that incorporate both rural and urban elements. Leo Marx reframes this challenge in political terms: "The inability of our writers to create a surrogate for the ideal of the middle landscape can hardly be accounted artistic failure" (364–365). By middle landscape, Marx refers to a Jeffersonian ideal of mechanically improved agrarianism, "a happy balance of art and nature" (226). He suggests that nineteenth- and twentieth-century American writers have failed to update that ideal but attributes their failure to the displacement to the literary realm of what is primarily a sociopolitical problem. Building on Marx's point, I'll accept Anderson's failure in creating a "happy balance" but resist the attribution of utopian ideals to *Poor White.* Rather, I argue that Anderson's engagement with modern rural masculinity requires reincorporating nostalgic, ruralized values alongside the future-oriented vision of economic modernization, of rural spaces and production alongside urban factory towns. In this reading, the novel's ambiguity is a solution in itself, albeit imperfect, an attempt to imagine a modern rural space that does not rely exclusively on one temporal, spatial, or generic element.

As a result, *Poor White*'s clearest version of old-fashioned modernism is not Hugh McVey, Clara Butterworth, or modernized gender roles but the community of Bidwell and its potential to function as a drag on the expected pace of urban industrialization. Throughout the novel, Anderson provides broad sociocultural descriptions of Bidwell that would not be out of place in sociological studies of the period. Indeed, Anderson fancied his novel to be a sociological document, and the novel's broad strokes contribute to a generic confusion typifying widespread anxiety about the social experience of modernity.[14] In a 1934 letter, he claimed that *Poor White* was "'a kind of classic' illustrating 'the destructive influence of present-day uncontrolled industrialism'" (qtd. in Rideout, *Writer* 2:193). Anderson theorizes the artist's relationship to society as revelatory, even prophetic; the Great Depression seems only to have emboldened his claims on the descriptive and predictive powers of the novel. But coupled with Anderson's description of *Poor White* in his introduction to the 1926 Modern Library edition, in which "the town was really the hero of the book" (vi), a theory emerges of rural geographic and social spaces as intimately incorporated into the novel's conception of socioeconomic order.

For Anderson, the space of Bidwell and the collectivity of the town's socioeconomic structure inform each other and the lives of its characters. Throughout the novel, Anderson highlights the land's activity, exemplified by a period of growth in which "new houses seemed to spring out of the ground like mushrooms" (283). In his initial description of Bidwell, Anderson naturalizes certain aspects of the town's activity, describing it as "from the beginning . . . a prosperous place" (41). This passage emphasizes Bidwell's location in a river valley among fertile plains, yet another way in which "a vast energy seemed to come out of the breast of earth and infect the people" (128). While this passage describes the discovery and exploitation of natural gas, it also refers to the land's fecundity. Anderson briefly narrates the shift: "In the days before the factories came the land immediately about town was cut up into small farms devoted to fruit and berry raising, and beyond the area of small farms lay larger tracts that were immensely productive and that raised huge crops of wheat, corn, and cabbage" (41). Thus the "vast energy" of natural gas creates wealth and supports the establishment of factories, while the earlier energy of the river and land creates the conditions for agricultural uses of the land. The land's prosperity, however, requires human intervention. Whether in the form of husbandry, property ownership, or manufacturing, *Poor White*'s land and people are mutually constitutive.

But Anderson doesn't present these shifts in land use and the land's energy as a painless and inevitable process of incorporation. Rather, immediately following his description of Bidwell's river valley, farms, and factories, he spends several pages cataloging the town's residents, including tradesman harness maker Joe Wainsworth and Steve Hunter, who "when he went into a factory, would go into the office, not into the shop" (51). In this catalog of peripheral characters, Anderson begins to arrange the novel's tensions, as the town's prophet/philosopher Judge Horace Hanby foresees a time when "almost everything now done by hand'll be done by machinery. Some'll grow rich and some poor" (50). The land's energy that formerly encouraged a kind of deliberate agrarianism has now altered the terms of the relationship, adding a level of uncertainty to Bidwell's traditional forms of prosperity and value.

*Poor White* signals those uncertainties through the complicated relationship between local pride and production, as a fraudulent sales pitch, unstable communal memory, and a desire to participate in modern capitalism alter the relationship between Bidwell's lands and people. For example, as part of his sales pitch, Hunter challenges potential investors' willingness to change the way they use their land and resources, charging that Bidwell will never develop "because a man like me who was raised here has to go to a city to get money to back his plans" (88). While Hunter manipulates the investors to go along with his scheme through fairly rudimentary reverse psychology and, just after this passage, by playing on their knowledge of his boyhood, the uncertainties he expresses are real. At this point, his entire approach is a bluff—he doesn't know whether Hugh is actually an inventor and has a factory-producible machine. To Hunter's benefit, it turns out that Hugh is working on the cabbage-setting machine, which has the potential to industrialize Bidwell and change farmers' interaction with the land from a manual to a mechanical enterprise. Even then, as discussed earlier, "the machine must be built close to the ground" (80), which indicates how this novel's version of industrial development is not strictly an urban enterprise. Hunter's vision for Hugh's machine departs from standard, urban-oriented incorporation narratives, generating Hunter's anxiety because of the uncertainties of carving out an alternate, ruralized industrial space. In *Poor White,* the connection between characters and the land is not simply a preordained harnessing and directing of the land's power by those characters, nor is it a Marxist abstraction of the fall of capitalism. Rather, reading the town as the novel's main character signals that it has a potentially unpredictable narrative arc much as any other character, indicating how Anderson represents geography and collectivity as spatially oriented but not ultimately fixed to an outcome generated by the area's past.

The novel's closing scene suggests that, despite earlier uncertainties, Bidwell achieves an uneasy balance between the rural and the urban, between agrarian and industrial uses of the rural space. But this relative success also evokes Anderson's failure in doing the same for his protagonist. In the final passage, as Hugh and Clara listen to the sounds of a modernizing Bidwell, they invest her pregnancy with hope for the future and eventually turn into the house as a couple. Regarding this final scene, Susan Hegeman argues that "instead of a resolution to modern alienation, what Anderson leaves us with (besides the allegorical family of Clara, Hugh, and unborn baby), is the nostalgically drawn location of the Midwest. Indeed, as we begin to think of the locale itself as yet another (non-)resolution to the central conflicts Anderson puts into play, we begin to see that the Midwest as a region contains multitudes" (124). Where Hegeman finds an unsatisfactory multiplicity, I propose Anderson's Midwest is a nonresolution precisely because it attempts to balance a complex network of spatial, temporal, cultural, and socioeconomic positions. I therefore consider the novel's ambiguity as a solution in itself—rather than resolving these conflicts, Anderson suggests that the Midwest and Midwesterners absorb them.

The final passage of *Poor White* illustrates Bidwell's juxtaposition of rural and urban elements. While this scene rejects the assumed endpoints of both nostalgia and modernization, it also indicates Hugh's challenges in developing a similarly balanced rural masculinity:

> As they went past the barns and the bunkhouse where several men now slept they heard, as though coming out of the past, the loud snoring of the rapidly ageing farm hand, Jim Priest, and then above that sound and above the sound of the animals stirring in the barns arose another sound, a sound shrill and intense, greetings perhaps to an unborn Hugh McVey. For some reason, perhaps to announce a shift in crews, the factories of Bidwell that were engaged in night work set up a great whistling and screaming. The sound ran up the hillside and rang in the ears of Hugh as, with his arm about Clara's shoulders, he went up the steps and in at the farmhouse door. (363)

There is no definitive return to the rural past here. Hugh and Clara stand together amid a variety of agrarian and industrial elements, objects and sounds that represent past, present, and future. This scene's presentation of multiple possibilities for modern rurality recalls Mary Neth's findings that "farm people continued to resist total reliance on a commercialized economy" and attempted to solve the problem of a modernizing rural society through isolation and also by "creat[ing] alternative organizations rooted in the values of farm neighborhoods" (139). Much like Neth's history of actual Midwestern farmers, this scene cannot entirely reconcile the divergent realistic possibilities for rural life. Critics have generally focused on one of two aspects in this scene, emphasizing either Hugh and Clara's stasis within the present moment or, alternately, their decision to retreat into the farmhouse, a symbol of the rural past. That indeterminacy indicates how they fail to balance the multiple discourses of rural modernity: Anderson presents a hopefulness for the unborn child but less for the adults. One reason for that failure seems to be Hugh's inability to remain productive within Bidwell's industrial economy. While Anderson indicates that the farm sounds can exist alongside the factories, Hugh loses his position and must return to the house. While this echoes his wandering from earlier in the novel and presages the aimless masculinity I explore in the conclusion, Hugh's failure is not a complete nonresolution. Rather, in line with Anderson claiming Bidwell as the book's protagonist, the town and countryside seem to have reached an iteration of modernity incorporating both rural and urban.

Although Hugh finds a balance between Upland Southerner and migrant Yankee, as well as between ruralized inspiration and urbanized manufacturing, he also becomes a by-product of the system for which he served as both catalyst and most visible success. For a time, Hugh achieves his desire to become "a man among men," but the indefinability of those men follows him and permeates *Poor White.* Near the end of the novel, as Hugh walks around Bidwell thinking about Clara and about the Iowa inventor, his blindness suggests that he cannot continually negotiate the competing and shifting expectations of Bidwell's rural modernity, and he ends up withdrawing from Bidwell's economy. Thus, while Anderson presents an optimistic reading of the possibilities for rural spaces and communities, he also explores the by-products of modern life, including the labor shift between farm and factory, the demise of characters with residual identity definitions such as harness maker Joe Wainsworth, and the individual and communal challenges posed by shifting expectations on masculinity. For Hugh specifically, negotiating the difficulties of constant identity revision—what makes a "shadowy figure" of Hugh, the Iowa man, and even Bidwell itself—functions as both his greatest success and, at the end, the reason for his withdrawal.

Critics generally have not described this final scene as a moment of balanced rural modernity—rather, they pose the factory and its sounds as the scene's dominant element or tend toward an unspecified hopeful future based on Hugh and Clara's relationship. For Brom Weber and David D. Anderson, the whistles are "mocking" (Anderson, "Myth" 276; Weber, *Sherwood* 32), and Anderson argues that they "mark a mechanical superiority" ("Myth" 276). Glen Love focuses on how "the sounds of nature and life are drowned in the shriek of factory whistles" ("Winesburg" 41), which Mark Whalan calls the novel's "inevitable dystopic conclusion" (62). More positively, Stephen Enniss claims that, "with their new knowledge of themselves and with their new relationship with each other, they seem ready to leave behind them that past of confusion, misunderstanding, and loneliness" (97).

My reading of *Poor White* opens a furrow between these. Generally, I agree with Walter Rideout's claim that Anderson leaves Hugh and Clara "head[ing] toward the uncertain future" (*Writer* 1:386)—my sense of the novel's ending is that Anderson has constructed a future in which the machines may prove superior, or Hugh and Clara's relationship may flourish, or some combination of those. That indeterminacy is due to the way Anderson's countryside balances old-fashioned and modern, rural and urban, industrial and agrarian, and past and future. Yet he cannot do the same for the novel's characters, so Hugh and Clara cope with their predicament by returning to the house. They accept their place on the farm and leave behind Hugh's participation in urban industrialism, with the result that any hope rests with their unborn child. Still, even that affective, heteronormative retreat should be read as Anderson's attempt to create a workable alternative arising from their attempts at balance and in response to the challenges they face at the close of the novel.

When those characters retreat, we are left with what Anderson earlier in the novel described as a region and people "rush[ing] pell-mell into a new age" (128). In this description of the socially and economically modernizing Midwest, Anderson's attempt to imagine the modern countryside rests not on the "rush" but rather on "pell-mell," that it signals "a vast disorder" (256) upending cultural hierarchies and allowing poor white characters like Hugh the potential to "find a place where he would be able to mingle freely with men and women" (34). In *Poor White,* that mingling produces a moment that is both energizing and problematic—a modernizing economy and society had started many Midwestern places on a path in which their rural identities became confused and disorderly, merging with and incorporating urbanized values, use of space, and rapid changes in masculine and feminine gender roles. While Anderson sees the creative and social possibilities of the "new age," he retains value in rural products and identities. And while those competing values demonstrate the challenge of sustaining usable rural masculinities in this shifting modern space, they allow Anderson to imagine modern rurality outside the teleologies of urban industrialization to create rural identities and spaces in which so-called old-fashioned elements can thrive alongside and within the modern industrial economy.

CHAPTER TWO

# "THE RUSTIC DREAM"

## *Gender Norms, Rural Time, and the Modern Countryside*

> This was the first time he'd ever wanted to leave the farm, its peace for the first time jarred on his nerves, he wanted motion—motion—something to express his own unrest.
>
> —Dawn Powell, *The Story of a Country Boy,* 1935

In the popular imagination, the American countryside looks something like *The Sunlit Road* calendar of 1935 (fig. 4). On the cover of this biweekly pocket calendar, the sun shines abundantly as a tidy road descends into a valley, disappears into a forest, and presumably climbs into the small town at the back of the frame. The houses display a variety of rooflines, but that difference is mitigated by the comforting visual similarity of white walls and red roofs. It is a bucolic image, marked by expanses of green grass and trees. Aside from the furrows in the lower left corner, this rural scene includes no evidence of agriculture or modern industry. In short, there's very little to disrupt *The Sunlit Road*'s pastoral countryside. The calendar is even bound with a ribbon, tied into a bow that curves off the page much like the road that meanders through it.

That simple binding might also stand in for the simple story this calendar tells about the country. Even on this little throwaway calendar, however, it's not so simple. *The Sunlit Road*'s version of rurality is simultaneously nostalgic and progressive, frozen forever in time but structured within normative temporalities that leave the countryside behind. As you might stroll down the road on its cover, *The Sunlit Road* progresses through twenty-six biweekly pages that delineate past, present, and future, a standard understanding of time also expressed in the calendar's text. Each page includes a short homily expressing the need for character and hard work and, subsequently, the rewards for that behavior. For instance, a homily from late January describes "people in ordinary circumstances [who] are million-

Fig. 4. Cover of *The Sunlit Road* calendar, Dodge Publishing Co., 1935. Actual size is 3 3/4 × 4 7/8 inches.

aires of cheerfulness," and one from late March exhorts the reader to "Be yourself—simple, honest, and unpretending—and you will enjoy through life the respect and love of friends, and the homage of millions of human beings." These join with the cover image to render a wholesome, comforting countryside and a nation that values simple, honest rural people. But while these sentiments are presented as timeless, the calendar itself is not. *The Sunlit Road* is essentially a disposable object—its small size and thin pages place it squarely within modern cultures of consumption and production. As a result, it projects a recognizable, old-fashioned countryside, but the calendar's flimsy material presence undermines both its realism and its nostalgia.

This chapter examines two texts produced the same year as this edition of *The Sunlit Road:* Dawn Powell's novel *The Story of a Country Boy* and poet Lorine Niedecker's one-of-a-kind artist's book, *Next Year or I Fly My Rounds, Tempestuous.* Comparable to the way that *The Sunlit Road*'s ephemeral materiality undermines its pastoral nostalgia, Powell and Niedecker use rural objects to destabilize common idealized stories of the countryside. Their biographies also mirror each other, suggesting one reason why each writes about rural spaces and people, especially those who move between country and city. Both authors were born in the rural Midwest at the turn of the century. Powell lived in Mount Gilead, a small town in central Ohio, from her birth in 1896 until her mother died when she was seven years old, then shuttled among her stepmother and other relatives in nearby small towns until she left for college. Wisconsin-born Niedecker's early years were comparatively stationary. She lived with her parents on Blackhawk Island or nearby Fort Atkinson until she graduated high school. In the early 1930s, both lived in Greenwich Village and associated with Manhattan artistic communities, though their biographies show no evidence that they met.[1] Niedecker's stay in New York was fairly brief—her only extended time in Manhattan was when she lived with poet Louis Zukofsky for a few months in 1933 and again for a "prolonged visit" in 1935 (Peters 49). Powell's life and writing are more bound up with New York, as she lived there from the late 1910s until her death in 1965.

Certain features of these two writers' lives and bodies of work cause critics to categorize them in recognizable ways—Powell is "the American Writer" (Vidal 52) with "Midwestern common sense" (Weiner 23), and Niedecker composed "the speech of the American people, whittled clean" (Cox 29), all while working "in an unplumbed cabin she built on a peninsula beside the Rock River in Wisconsin" (Alcosser 28).[2] To these familiar types, *The Story of a Country Boy* and *Next Year* add the self-made man, the country boy in the city, the housewife, the office girl, the socialist malcontent, the dimwit, the sophisticate, the enthusiast, and more. Powell and Niedecker do not simply employ those labels. They challenge them through modern forms of rural temporality that complicate the gendered experiences of their characters. Conflicts within rural time demonstrate how rural masculinity is expected to conform to old-fashioned, supposedly traditional norms. Yet those same conflicts, often revealed in Powell's and Niedecker's engagement with rural material culture, also show how common idealized visions of rural masculinity come under pressure from the multitude of modern narratives, products, and social movements at play in the Midwestern countryside.

In *The Story of a Country Boy,* Powell superimposes characters' personal memories with scenes that might well be on the cover of *The Sunlit Road,* and the juxtaposition reveals both as fantasies. Early in the novel, Madeleine Greaves—family friend and future lover of protagonist Chris Bennett—revises her relationship to their rural Ohio hometown: "After hearing Chris's interpretation of their hometown she found herself gradually adjusting her memories to fit into his; her recollection of endless walks through still brown woods, pinecones crackling underfoot once identified only with her loneliness and longing for travel, now were revised to show her radiantly happy in calendar pastoral scenes" (19). As a "country boy . . . made good" (271), Chris feels he must come from a rural space conforming to specific, old-fashioned cultural images, such as Madeleine's pastoral calendar, and his nostalgic memory of their hometown becomes the novel's ruling experience. It forms his worldview and demands that other characters conform to it. Chris thereby maintains the animating falsehood that he is the titular "country boy" rather than the industrial manager he has become. Powell critiques those delusions and couches rural temporality in Chris's failures, causing it to function as neither nostalgic salve nor triumphal future. Rather, with its periodic narrative fragmentation, *The Story of a Country Boy* treats rural time as insistently modern, oriented to the present and dependent upon historical, material, and affective contingencies. Over the course of the novel, conflicts between pastoral and industrial narratives cause Chris to lose control of his masculine identity.

Normative gender roles similarly break down in *Next Year or I Fly My Rounds, Tempestuous* as Niedecker demonstrates rural temporality's resistance to tidy narrative patterns. Niedecker's engagement with rural materiality is more concrete than Powell's, as Niedecker composed this short book of poetry by writing on slips of translucent paper and pasting her poems over the homilies of *The Sunlit Road.* Because of its style of construction, *Next Year* enacts a literal material challenge to pastoralized visions of modern rural spaces and their supporting narratives. Materially and poetically, Niedecker demands that the calendar's progressive temporality coexist with a kind of ruralized circularity predicated on seasonal return. She disrupts both, however, when she concurrently draws attention to and papers over the variety of forms and references—pastoral and modernist, regional and national, masculine and feminine—that constitute *Next Year*'s version of rural modernity. The book was created in late 1934 as a Christmas gift to poet Louis Zukofsky, and it remained unpublished until 1997, when it appeared as scanned pages in *Sulfur* literary magazine. In some ways, its creation as a gift to the New York–based Zukofsky reinscribes stereotypical narratives of gender and rurality, which is reflected in Rachel Blau DuPlessis's claim that Niedecker seeks "littleness, a miniature scale almost unthinkable, especially for a female writer who can be culturally coded as minor no matter what genre she chooses" ("Anonymous" 97).[3] Despite this littleness, the poetry and the book itself challenge the notion of gender stereotyping; Ruth Jennison locates such resistance in *Next Year*'s critique of both everyday and seasonal routine while, more broadly, Elizabeth Robinson sees Niedecker's work "as a stretching and alteration of narrative form" (117). Building on these readings, I argue that Niedecker's poems and the book's material construction negotiate and comment on modern rural spaces. In so doing, each absorbs the other's meanings and references, producing a more flexible rural temporality.

Despite their differences—the unexpected formal modernism of Powell's novel, *Next Year*'s absorptive vocabulary—both texts exemplify the insistently modern rural temporalities that structure Midwestern literature. These structures extend from the anachronism of Sherwood Anderson's fully mechanized cabbage-planting machine (discussed in chapter 1) to the acceleration of masculine failure in William Cunningham's and Wright Morris's Great Plains farm novels (the focus of chapter 3). Other Midwestern novels that attend to the material and temporal attributes of modern ruralities include Ruth Suckow's *Country People* (1924), Ernest Hemingway's *In Our Time* (1925), and O. E. Rølvaag's *Giants in the Earth* (1927). Similar attention to contradictory rural temporalities also appears across a wider geographic range in novels such as Jean Toomer's *Cane* (1923) and William Faulkner's *As I Lay Dying* (1930), as well as poetry by Robert Frost, Sterling Brown, William Carlos Williams, and Aunt Molly Jackson. Furthermore,

Susan Glaspell's *Trifles* (1916), Eugene O'Neill's *Beyond the Horizon* (1920), and Thornton Wilder's *Our Town* (1938) are just a few of the plays that consider temporal disruptions in modern rurality. Within these works, as for *The Story of a Country Boy*'s Chris Bennett, "the time's never been just right, that's all" (140).

In this chapter, I argue that Midwestern writers create specific forms of rural temporality that remain resolute in their modernities despite what Powell calls the "rustic dream" (1) of nostalgic pastoralism. Chris Bennett's rural nostalgia and his desire for industrial success appear contradictory, but I will show how each demonstrates his desire for uncomplicated temporality. Powell critiques such simplistic desires through Chris's nominal resistance to industrialism, which hinges on the way his consumerism imposes gender stereotypes on both Chris and his wife, Joy. Lorine Niedecker addresses similar limits of gender normativity by highlighting *Next Year*'s temporal simultaneity, as its material construction unsettles both circular and progressive time. Taken together, Niedecker's allusions to twentieth-century rural life mirror passages in *The Story of a Country Boy* that disrupt an otherwise conventional narrative with flashes of rural objects. Through juxtaposition and multiplicity, Niedecker and Powell reject simplistic notions of the heartland in favor of representing complex gender experiences in the modern countryside.

## "I SHALL PASS THROUGH THIS WORLD BUT ONCE"

*The Story of a Country Boy* depicts Chris Bennett's decline from a position of power in an Ohio manufacturing company. By the end of the novel, Chris has lost his job, run out of money, and returned to his boyhood home. Despite mimicking his management colleagues' profligate spending, heavy drinking, and infidelity, Chris believes that he remains the downhome "country boy" of the title. In this self-image and his memories of home, Chris attempts to fix the countryside within a recognizable nostalgic framework that denies the social and industrial developments of the first third of the twentieth century. Other than Chris's worldview, however, Powell mostly does not indulge rural nostalgia, partly because the novel takes place during the first years of the Great Depression. Powell charts the onset of national economic decline through several reminders of the rural material culture of the 1930s, including gadgetry, road construction, and uneven returns on field crops. While these disrupt Chris's view of himself and his origins, he continues to disregard his own and his company's struggles, not least because his nostalgia for the farm fuels the hope that he will retire triumphantly to the family homestead in Bennetsville. Since leaving as a young man to take a factory job, Chris and his wife Joy have celebrated the farm, "waiting for kind fortune to let them return" (133). Until his shame-faced return, then, he refuses to accept his position in the Great Depression narrative, often falling back on the comforting sentiments expressed in pastoral calendars like *The Sunlit Road.*

Despite the many ways that Powell undermines Chris's pastoral image of the country, he maintains it throughout the novel. Chris's memories, along with his interest in "kind fortune," fit nicely with Madeleine's revised memory of "calendar pastoral scenes," especially in that they mimic the homilies of *The Sunlit Road.* While Powell did not consult this calendar in particular, the series sold well throughout the early twentieth century.[4] According to contemporary trade publications, this series of calendars makes "a distinctive and appropriate holiday gift" ("New Goods") and were popular enough that "folk write from all over the country" to obtain their "yearly visitor" ("Stationery and Novelties" 447). Chris Bennett's self-image as an exemplar of old-fashioned rural folk suggests why Powell writes Chris's sentiments to match the homilies' rose-colored tone. For instance, Chris's willingness to wait patiently for his return to the farm mirrors a page from March 1935 in which *The Sunlit Road* charts a direct, linear temporality. Indeed, Chris might well be charmed by the calendar's exhortation to kindness because, it reminds readers, "I shall pass through this world but once" (fig. 5).

Drawing on assumptions of normative temporal progression, the calendar encourages its audience to capitalize on the opportunity for kindness and good deeds.[5] Not only, then, does *The Sunlit Road* depict time in terms of past, present, and future; it also asserts time's teleology, with readers passing through the present one time on their way to a happy future. The calendar's final page reinforces its nostalgia and echoes Chris's hopeful, progressive temporality: "And so let us be cheerful, without regret for the past with contentment in the present, and with strong hope for the future." Both homilies present a tidily proportioned perspective on rural temporal-

Fig. 5. March 10–23, 1935, page from *The Sunlit Road.*

ity. Past, present, and future stay in their places, as *The Sunlit Road* primarily uses the passage of time to exhort readers to hopefulness and good cheer. When paired with the pastoral cover image (fig. 4), this tone of uncritical acceptance suggests that, even as time goes by, the country remains frozen in picturesque preindustrialism.

Chris Bennett imagines his own life as a corollary to the easily understood version of both rurality and time that might be featured in "calendar pastoral scenes" (Powell 19). After receiving a letter from the farm, the narrator notes Chris's and Joy's feeling that "there is fortune merely in the certainty that somewhere lies happiness" (18). Chris's image of the countryside mirrors *The Sunlit Road*'s brand of pastoralism, expressed here and in the calendar's homilies as a recognizable life grounded in a cheerful vision of farm communities. Both texts are part of "the long-standing association of the [Midwest] with pastoral values and imagery" (Barillas 11) and, of course, such sentiments seem fitting for a disposable, commercially produced calendar. When transplanted into Powell's novel, however, they draw attention to Chris's folly for believing that they are accurate, real, and forever. Rather than acknowledging the changes of a modernizing countryside, Chris and Joy "would sit beaming over their picture of the farm," imagining their future to contain such bygone labor practices as "Chris out stacking wheat and Joy in the kitchen beating up biscuits" (18). Chris does not understand the modern Ohio countryside in part because his thoughts about it conflate—and simplify—past, present, and future.

Echoing Chris's affinity for uncomplicated temporality, contemporary reviews of *The Story of a Country Boy* chart its recognizable narrative progression. For example, blurbs call attention to the normative masculinity of Chris's economic rise: the *New York Times* calls the novel "a portrait of a self-made man" ("Latest" BR23), while, according to the *Chicago Daily Tribune,* it "tells of a man who rose from nothing to a position of great power in the American industrial world" ("Among" 12). In fuller reviews, the novel had a mixed reception, ranging from one verdict that it "is a formless novel which lacks even the appearance of elemental life" (Stone 223) to an opposing claim that the book contains "so much truth so delightfully managed" (Stong 4). Another reviewer splits the difference, describing it as "one of those American novels which is without special distinction but which adds an honest bit to the mosaic of contemporary American life that our fiction is creating" ("Urban" BR9). Each review concerns itself with the way Powell represents American social life. They suggest that the novel tells an array of stories that attempt to uncover something "honest," truthful, or "elemental." Describing Powell's contribution to and creation of a national "mosaic" adds a spatial element to the blurbs' interest in temporal progression. Considering the novel as a "mosaic" emphasizes the simultaneity of multiple narratives, which resonates with my argument in chapter 1 that Sherwood Anderson's *Poor White* combines multiple rural and urban elements within its representation of rural spaces. This chapter explores a similar multiplicity, but with respect to rural temporality. Powell and Niedecker, along with other Midwestern writers, manage the conflicting demands of multiple narrative logics by showing their interdependence in the modern countryside.

Powell represents multiple temporalities from the very earliest moments of Chris's story, demonstrating a concurrence also found in histories of the early twentieth-century United States. Powell writes that, as a young man, Chris moves from country to city to work in a foundry. He stumbles into the job because his friend El "had to finish painting the barn, whereas Chris had an easy week ahead" (15). Chris's easy week turns into a life ruled by the time clock, supporting a modern system of manufacturing whose objective, according to Mary Ann Doane, "was to eliminate unproductive time from the system" (6). When Chris becomes a factory general manager in the growing city of Aviland, he embodies a common early twentieth-century narrative about the products of the countryside—in *The Transformation of Rural Life,* Jane Adams argues that "the growth of urban factories created a strong and ever expanding market for agricultural products" (82). Furthermore, Chris's story exemplifies a broader transition from "local sun time" (Cronon 79) to regional time zones, which allowed raw materials—animal, vegetable, or mineral—to move more readily from country to city. In this case, Chris himself is the agricultural product who is assimilated into an American ideal of urban industrialism that strives toward market-driven productivity. This industrial ideal implies that individuals should contribute to urban development by moving to the city, increasing a smaller community's industrial capacity, or more broadly participating in the manufacturing economy. Chris Bennett does all three when he moves to town for a factory job, helps factory and town grow, and becomes a model suburban consumer.

According to historian Wolfgang Schivelbusch, this narrative is fostered by the rise of railroad transportation, which causes rural products to become commodities judged primarily by their value in the urban market. In turn, Schivelbusch claims, rural temporality became more complicated: "The regions, joined to each other and to the metropolis by the railways, and the goods that are torn out of their local relation by modern transportation, shared the fate of losing their inherited place, their traditional spatial-temporal presence" (41). Powell demonstrates this dislocation by representing the range of Chris's affective relationships with the countryside. As a young man, Chris was active on the farm, poised to take it over from his father. While moving to Aviland interrupts that plan, Chris continues to identify as a country boy. The beginning of the novel shows Chris at his most optimistic, as he makes himself out to be the Midwestern exemplar of a commonly told story of American masculinity: the "country boy outsmarting the educated stuffed shirts" (3). He hopes to return to the farm as a success story, but the novel doesn't allow it. Instead, after a period of poor job performance culminating in an attack by striking factory workers, Chris loses his job and is forced to leave Aviland. Chris's humiliation at the end of the novel aligns with his anxiety in the presence of urban colleagues: "Chris, in the lounge of the Aviland Country Club, used to glance uneasily at the other guests to see if they noticed straw in his hair or some other definite betrayal of his unfitness for civilized interiors" (2). In these instances, Chris simplifies both his story and that of rural people more generally—removed from, in Schivelbusch's words, his "traditional spatial-temporal presence" (41), Chris becomes one stereotype or another. Powell never allows these simplifications to stand. Just as Chris's optimism and anxiety coexist in the novel's opening pages, his rural self-image coexists with the reality of his white-collar labor.

While contrasts within Chris's experiences and feelings cause him to feel restless, divergent temporalities exist peacefully in settings such as Madeleine's gift shop. Madeleine herself fits into the novel's urbanization narrative, as "she had been glad to leave [the small town] for the city" (19). Her shop in the Parma Hotel lobby, however, is described as "a unique refuge from the commercialism of the city, a chic little heaven filled with reminders of stately homes and pleasant ways of living" (155). Because the shop incorporates rural retreat into the urban industrial space, it disrupts both urban and rural temporalities. For example, the shop stands outside urban commercial time but is also removed from nostalgically conceived rural time because of its urban location. Because of this tension, Madeleine's shop feels both old-fashioned and modern. In it, multiple temporalities coexist, as the "chic" space of urban commercial futurity depends upon "reminders" that draw from nostalgia for rural living and ask customers to remove themselves from the city.

In addition to Madeleine's shop, Powell demands that many of the novel's other spaces absorb conflicting narrative temporalities.[6] This is particularly true of Aviland, a growing industrial city that is also provincialized in relation to larger cities. In other instances, though, Aviland and New York City function similarly as the nonfarm: "In Aviland [Chris] thought of the farm as perfect serenity, in New York it had been a refuge from the devils that pursued his spirit" (130). Although Chris thinks of the farm similarly when in Aviland and New York, he does not generally equate the two cities. Throughout the novel, Chris repeatedly rejects city life, saving his strongest feelings for New York City: he has a "futile rage . . . against New York City, itself, a slow, bubbling anger that began each time he got on the trains going eastward" (105). His rejections of Aviland are weaker, partly because "in the broad, suburban streets he was free, he could breathe, he could take great swinging strides" (44). Despite Chris's apparent comfort, throughout the novel he treats Aviland as a "temporary" residence (3) that keeps him away from the farm.

Chris thinks of the farm as the nostalgic foil to the modernizing city, but Powell disrupts these otherwise recognizable representations by suggesting that Aviland and Bennetsville bear notable similarities. Much like the description above of Chris's morning walk through Aviland, he experiences the farm as a place where "a man could relax, his soul could expand, his words needed no guard" (2). In both Aviland and Bennetsville, Chris embodies a kind of normalized rural masculinity. He inhabits them in ways that place him out of time, experiencing both as spaces of freedom and soul expansion that allow him to forget other problems. On one hand, Powell presents a recognizable spectrum of space-time relationships: nostalgically envisioned farm community, industrializing small town, modern metropolis. Read otherwise, the novel rejects that temporal spectrum by drawing key similarities between divergent settings (sometimes despite Chris's own protestations). Building on Elizabeth Freeman's argument that "nonsequential forms of time" allow us to understand temporality outside of standardized historical narratives (xi), this chapter finds that Powell, Niedecker, and other Midwestern authors construct the modern countryside as a temporally and historically absorptive space. In *The Story of a Country Boy,* what seems like a recognizable story within a familiar historical trajectory begins to disrupt itself, a strategy the novel parallels generically and historically. Beyond advancing the novel's plot, then, those disruptions challenge these spaces' accepted meanings and alter their relationships to the teleologies of urban industrialization.

## MIDDLING NATURALISM

*The Story of a Country Boy* depicts US industrialization from the perspective of a self-proclaimed rural character, and the novel derives much of its tension from Chris's responses to both rural and urban spaces. Because the agricultural and industrial depression of the 1930s intensified relationships between country and city, "depression-era literature was rife with tropes of positioning, of location, of place, or rather, of displacement, derailment, missing locations, and missed connections. Spatial order . . . while sharply visible, still tangibly in effect, could no longer be counted on to signify as [it] once had" (Rabinowitz, "Between" 33). The personal, spatial, and economic displacements of Midwestern urban development can be seen in the long-standing prominence of naturalism in the region's fiction. For example, from naturalism's late nineteenth-century beginnings to the social protest fiction of the 1930s, two-thirds of Donald Pizer's exemplary American literary naturalists have significant Midwestern ties.[7] Furthermore, Pizer argues that the best-known naturalist characters "fall from midway—midway both in mind and status—rather than from a height" (7). Chris Bennett is just such a middling character, without refinement or intellect, indicating how this novel shares a geography, a mode, and a set of common concerns with 1930s social protest fiction.

According to historians Andrew Cayton and Peter Onuf, Midwestern regional identity developed alongside "the triumph of commercial capitalism" (44–45). But while industrial growth allowed Midwesterners to define the region as progressive and successful, it also "created new forms of dependency that jeopardized the crucial link between production and citizenship at the foundation of the Republican, bourgeois ideology" (Cayton and Onuf 118). These newfound dependencies marginalized independent producers—articulated elsewhere as the self-made man—while still offering the expectation of economic advancement.[8] Commercial capitalism therefore implies a narrative teleology based in capitalist "triumph," but only for individual participants in the corporate economy. These same structures, however, create the conditions for personal tragedy due to corporate failure, causing members of the white Midwestern middle class to feel less certain that they control their own destinies. In Chris's rise and subsequent expulsion from the factory, *The Story of a Country Boy* exemplifies both potential narratives. Even before Chris loses his place at the factory, he distrusts the urban-industrial success narrative, which Powell compounds by portraying the factory bosses' unethical and immoral behavior. Furthermore, she presents rural proletarian influences as part of Chris's upbringing, exemplified by Chris's father's claim that "this country is going to the dogs, ruined by these damned Morgans and Astors and all these young swells in tailcoats and fancy educations to cover up their feeble minds—what chance has the working man got against them and their millions . . . ?" (6).

Despite the novel's political perspective, Barbara Foley's *Radical Representations* does not mention Powell even when quoting her friends, novelist John Dos Passos and playwright John Howard Lawson, or when discussing other Midwestern writers of social protest fiction such as Tillie Olsen, Meridel Le Sueur, and Josephine Herbst.[9] While Powell is by no means a central figure in this field, Foley's reading of social protest fiction offers a way to classify *The Story of a Country Boy* among other proletarian novels of the period, even with a decidedly middle-class and middlebrow protagonist. According to Foley, by the mid-1930s, proletarian critics "offered no 'formulas' about conversion plots, triumphant workers, or heroic party members: so long as writers addressed some aspect of working-class experience and indicated its relation to the class struggle, they should follow the bidding of their own imaginations" (117). While this novel follows a manager rather than a worker, it fits among other proletarian novels in the way it explores the Great Depression's socioeconomic challenges. Specifically, the novel articulates concerns about the effects of American capitalism on people with proletarian origins who have since risen to positions of power in capitalist structures. Although he was born a poor farm boy, by the start of the novel Chris has become "The Public Figure. . . . The perfect Halfback—the American ideal" (109). The period of the novel, then, explores his personal and economic failures as Powell revises a familiar rags-to-riches narrative within the context of American economic decline.

Chris has invested in the progressive temporality of urban industrialization, and Powell intensifies his downfall by completing it with a worker's strike. While Chris has been comparatively wealthy throughout the novel, the Great Depression has subjected him to similar strictures as the workers. Chris's belief that he remains a "country boy" amplifies the conflict and leads to misunderstandings on all sides. Chris rejects the standardized version of capitalist temporality and its implications for his loyalties and moral character: "He had stood out against his success, by God, kept his head, a simple, honest man to the last, just one of the boys, and they stoned him for it, despised him for it, despised him for not selling his soul, too, the same as they would have done in his shoes" (193). The factory workers don't believe him—they throw rocks at Chris's car and remind him that "he's tied up [with] the Steel bosses, then he comes around trying to tell us he's our friend. You can't be both, Bennett!" (191). Reflexively, they reject Chris's self-perception as "the barefoot boy beneath his disguise" (6). In this particular conflict, both parties seek to escape recognizable teleologies by refusing to accept the normalized progressions of Chris's economic rise. The workers reject Chris's proposed relationship to them because of his social alignments and profligate spending. Chris, on the other hand, denies that he is aligned with the other managers. He relies on a ruralized version of his identity despite his position and spending habits, and the persistence of that self-image disrupts the smooth progression of the industrial success narrative.

Reflecting its mid-1930s publication date, the novel unsurprisingly includes several attempts to ease the felt struggle of the Great Depression. As discussed earlier, Chris attempts to escape the expectations placed on him because of his class position. The novel's more common (and less crisis-oriented) forms of escapism center on the Bennett family's various leisure activities: Joy's devotion to bridge, their son-in-law's saxophone playing, and Chris's turns at the country club, racetrack, and a colleague's bachelor pad.[10] Many of these are upper-class pursuits, appropriate for a family with the means to purchase a country estate, which Chris does late in the novel: "On hot Sundays there was nothing to do but sit on the great screened veranda drinking gin fizzes. At night they drove along the shore or visited the Gorsleys who always had a houseful of distinguished out-of-town guests, or they played cards" (268). Chris finds many of these activities discomfiting, partly because they are aspirational. Early in the novel, he is concerned that country club members would notice "his unfitness for civilized interiors" (2). Chris is also uneasy with working-class leisure activities, seen when he rejects a working girl's invitation to go dancing, declaring, "Hell, I don't dance!" (73). The combination points to

Chris's middling taste and his aversion to any but the most normalized class labels. Thus, Chris appears to be most comfortable when he can adopt whatever position he wants, such as the local cigar store's socially inclusive backroom chess club, where he might see "a Chinese laundryman or a bootlegger or a professor from Miss Millard's School in the Heights" (48).

The novel's most regular escape is Chris's vision of himself. Although he has risen to the position of factory general manager, he still identifies as a "country boy . . . made good" (271), a guiding illusion that provides stability for his character and the confidence to follow a normatively defined success narrative. According to Mary Neth, strong affective ties to rurality were common among country-born people who left to work in the city. Powell establishes this type of stabilizing emotional connection at the very beginning of the novel: "For him always reality was not the rose bedroom but the rustic dream and he was perpetually amazed that others could not see the farm shining in his eyes like a guilty secret. Every year the nostalgia grew. Through his veil of longing he saw his present world and believed that others must see him through the same fog" (1). Here, recalling Chris's unjustified indignance at the workers' attack, Powell indicates one of the novel's key tensions: the narrator will treat Chris's rural identity as a "rustic dream," while Chris believes in its essential reality. Still, Chris appears to be ashamed of that identity, perhaps because he assumes that his "veil of longing" is as visible to others as it is to him.

Given that Powell denies Chris the comfort of a future golden age, she marks his story with nostalgic longing for his past. In *The Future of Nostalgia,* Svetlana Boym links emotional and temporal experience: "Modern nostalgia is a mourning for the impossibility of mythic return, for the loss of an enchanted world with clear borders and values; it could be a secular expression of a spiritual longing, a nostalgia for an absolute, a home that is both physical and spiritual" (8). Borrowing Boym's language, Chris longs for a nostalgically remembered farm in part because of its absolute purity of space and values. Chris envisions the farm at Bennetsville as a real-life representation of a pastoral ideal. Because in his mind the farm matches that invented ideal, it offers an escape from the changing economic structures and confusing moral codes of his job at the factory. Chris's "veil of longing," then, serves as a "rebellion against the modern idea of time" (Boym xv) and allows him an affective retreat from his manufacturing present.

This tendency to metaphorical escape appears to be doomed from the start, and because of it Chris cannot sustain a normative masculine role. In other words, when he fails as a businessperson and can no longer provide for his family, it is because he maintains a nostalgic rural identity. That said, the novel does not treat Chris's feelings for his rural past as entirely nostalgic, nor his homecoming as mythic and impossible—at the end of the novel, Chris and his family return to the farm of his birth, which exemplifies Depression-era migration patterns. According to historians David Danbom and Jane Adams, migration shifted in the early 1930s, and rural populations grew. Through this realistic aspect of Chris's "rustic dream," Powell challenges conventional wisdom on the inexorable march of urban industrialization and offers the potential for what Boym calls "unrealized possibilities, unpredictable turns and crossroads" (xvi).

In that vein, Chris's behavior in the following passage suggests how his "rustic dream" also depends upon his future success and is inflected with elements of commercial modernity:

> Bennetsville was home: their house in Aviland would never be completely fitted out because the forty or fifty years they might spend there were only a temporary absence from their rightful place. The attic of that huge house in Aviland Heights was cluttered with the latest farm gadgets: new fruit seeders and automatic jar sealers for Joy's future canning, milk testers, grain shuckers, every new contraption for every phase of farm life Chris would purchase because he expected every year to return to his rightful home. He would have sent this collection to Dad for immediate use, but old Christopher Bennett declared he had no use for these modern handicaps to labor. (3)

In this passage, Chris becomes the very figure of modern life, purchasing all "the latest farm gadgets" to ensure a comfortable return to the farm. But he never uses them, which associates this behavior with Joan Rubin's argument that the replication and purchase of luxury goods allowed middlebrow culture "to regard gentility itself as a commodity" (3). To revise Rubin slightly, it appears that Chris's gadget purchases allow him to regard rurality itself as a commodity—because he buys these tools, Chris can remain a country boy. Correspondingly, Bill Brown claims that some historicist fiction implies that "possessing a thing comes to feel like possessing history itself" (118), which speaks not only to this appliance-oriented commodification of the country but also to Chris's feeling that his nostalgia is an accurate representation of the past.

While Chris imagines farm labor with a nostalgic glow, he does so through regular (and, perhaps, compulsive) participation in the modern industrial economy. The farm therefore becomes a passive space, of consumption rather than production. It is also a frivolous space, in that Chris buys all "the latest" gadgets without ever using them. He stores them immediately in his attic, where they are likely to remain for "forty or fifty years," by which time they will be obsolete. According to Peter McClelland, a "tradition of inventing" (5) began in the early nineteenth century and contributed to rapid innovations in agricultural technology, which R. Douglas Hurt documents well into the twentieth century. In this passage, as throughout the novel, Chris's vision insulates him from the farm's position in the commercial landscape of the 1920s and 1930s, during which "U.S. farmers suffered bruising market conditions even as they became more deeply integrated into the nation's industrial economy" (Hamilton 44). Agricultural production became integrated with the industrial economy partly through the proliferation of small implements. In this book, though, Chris's gadgets are held separate from the farm. Although Chris is devoted to these gadgets—or at least to purchasing and cluttering up his attic with them—his father resists them as "modern handicaps to labor" (3). His father's work ethic enables Chris's nostalgia, which then becomes entwined with Chris's vision of the future, in which he will also labor on the farm, but presumably using modern, mechanically assisted methods. Their obsolescence never occurs to him, however, reinforcing Chris's "rustic dream" through a preindustrial idyll in which implements had a long utility.

These gadgets combine the temporalities of commercial modernity and preindustrial farm life, which disrupts Chris's nostalgic vision of the farm as well as his middle-class lifestyle. Still, by limiting Joy to domestic food preservation, they leave his middle-class masculinity intact. Thus, while Chris intends to live farm life on his own, more modern terms, this scene's version of modern life does not extend to modernizing gender roles. Chris's demand for narrative independence, coupled with Joy's confinement to the kitchen, indicates Powell's implicit critique of his actions as well as his "rustic dream." For instance, even when faced with utter economic collapse because his and the Balding Company's failings push him out of the factory economy, Chris vows that he will not be compelled to change. He feels that "he could go back [to the farm] someday, probably, but he damn well was not going to be pushed back" (293). Chris insists that he makes his own decisions, which suggests his devotion to notions of patriarchal authority and self-made masculinity. By juxtaposing masculine nostalgia, consumptive practices, and devotion to capitalist narratives of personal advancement, Powell shows how multiple temporal experiences join to confound the trajectory of each available narrative. In short, no matter how badly Chris wants to be a self-made man (or industry titan, or gentleman farmer), the book won't let him.

Thus, while this novel's broad outlines conform to a standard narrative of urban industrialization, Powell also challenges that story, even in a scene underscoring the characters' consumption of modern industrial products. Some of those challenges are material, like those posed by Chris's gadget hoarding, and gesture toward Midwestern socioeconomic characteristics or to the period's rural history. Others relate to the novel's structure, which one reviewer criticizes because the protagonist "behaves so unconventionally that the book and the man, after rather noisy progress, end in frustration" (M.D.P. 596). Using a variety of representational, referential, and even literal disruptions, *The Story of a Country Boy* and, as I argue in the next section, Lorine Niedecker's *Next Year or I Fly My Rounds, Tempestuous* challenge older, more conventional forms of narrative, gender, and space. While these texts engage urban industrialism as a central topic of American modernity, they cultivate rural temporalities that disturb urbanization's inherent teleology. By representing Midwestern spaces and stories that do not rely exclusively on recognizable narrative progressions, Powell and Niedecker offer a countryside in which multiple temporalities, narratives, and identities can coexist.

## TEMPESTUOUS MATERIALITY

*The Story of a Country Boy* and *Next Year or I Fly My Rounds, Tempestuous* each present circular aspects of rural time that evoke the annual repetitions of seasonal work. In Powell's novel, not only does Chris physically return to

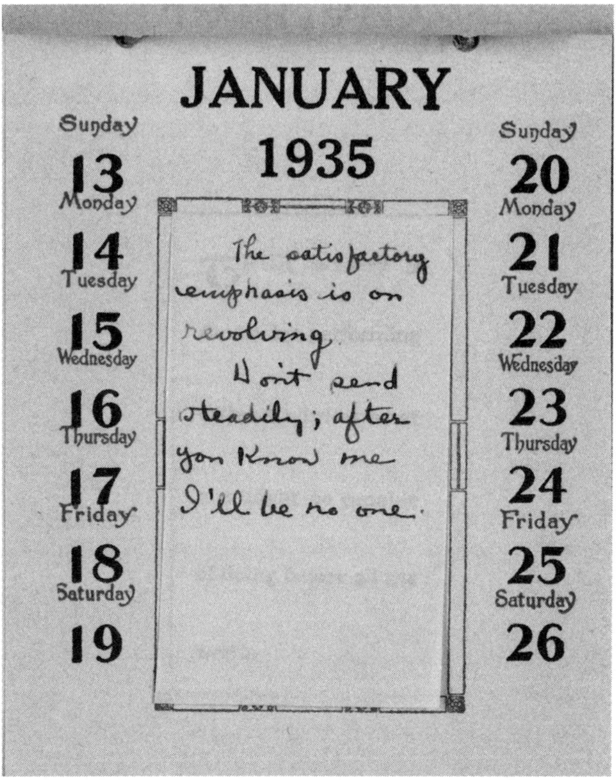


**The satisfactory / emphasis is on / revolving. / Don't send / steadily; after / you know me / I'll be no one.**

Fig. 6. January 13–26, 1935, page from *Next Year or I Fly My Rounds, Tempestuous.* By Lorine Niedecker, 1934. Courtesy of Harry Ransom Center, University of Texas at Austin.

the farm, but he also attempts to do so mentally through his pastoral image of Bennetsville. Material life in this novel, however, denies easy temporal definition. For instance, Chris's gadgets signify both material and economic progress as well as nostalgia for the farm and old-fashioned gender roles, showing how Powell uses ruralized materials to challenge the circular returns of nostalgic temporality. This strategy also appears in *Next Year,* which Niedecker created by pasting her poems over *The Sunlit Road*'s homilies.[11] Similar to Madeleine's gift shop balancing public and private in *The Story of a Country Boy, Next Year* absorbs divergent references: regional and national, nostalgic and avant-garde, masculine and feminine, public and private, mass-produced and individually crafted. This multiplicity allows *Next Year* to disrupt both urban and rural temporalities—even as it evokes common experiences of rural people and spaces, Niedecker's poetry and the book's material construction challenge the expected narratives of rural gender, history, and literature. As a result, despite their different representational strategies, pairing *Next Year* and *The Story of a Country Boy* calls attention to certain ways in which Midwestern literature both absorbs and undermines the prevailing temporalities of rural life.

Critics usually label Niedecker a rural poet, calling her work a "stern refusal of the city" (Peterson 247). Accordingly, the circularity of *Next Year*'s second poem (fig. 6) provides a somewhat standard reading of rural time. This poem's first sentence adopts a tone common to the original homilies—advice given as common sense, suggesting a way for the reader to exist happily within a given situation: "The satisfactory / emphasis is on / revolving" (*Collected Works* 42). Signaled by the single-word line, the poem's emphasis lies on "revolving," which implies a ruralized satisfaction based on temporal circularity. Thus, while the poem adopts *The Sunlit Road*'s hopeful tone, it does so by emphasizing the repetitions of rural time rather than the progressive temporality of "calendar pastoral scenes" (Powell 19).

The poem's second sentence, however, does not lend itself to a smoothly functioning form of rural seasonality. Its first clause, "Don't send / steadily," might be read as recognizing the natural uncertainties in rural life. Critics frequently attribute this issue to Niedecker's biography, as "she lived in an environment in which the natural world always seemed about to overwhelm the human one" (Armantrout 103). But that same clause proposes a fragmentary, halting version of rural time, in both its vocabulary and its unsteady phrasing. For example, the poem's repetition of *o* and *e* sounds demonstrates Niedecker's use of an inconsistent scheme of internal and line-ending rhymes to suggest the likelihood of repetition despite the unpredictability of exact placement. The final clause extends the poem's halting circularity by defamiliarizing the speaker and carving out a space for personal refusals.

This poem's instabilities exemplify Rachel Blau DuPlessis's argument that Niedecker, in her earlier poetry, maintains formal divisions as a way to resist common gender narratives: “Keeping intact edges, precisions, elements of a modernist and objectivist aesthetic seem here to take on a gender function for Niedecker. She will not be absorbed into the same joshing easygoing narratives of gender allure that blur distinctions” (“Anonymous” 105). In *Next Year,* Niedecker uses modernist aesthetics to avoid simplistic narratives based on normative gender roles, but I counter DuPlessis’s claim that she does so by keeping the edges intact. Instead, in this book, she removes those intact edges and intentionally blurs gender distinctions. In the poem quoted above, from the January 13–26 page, the final clause—“I’ll be no one”—effaces the speaker’s gender, declines to provide identifying personal or narratological details, and undermines the reader’s progressive accumulation of knowledge. The poem’s broad referentiality thus destabilizes any single interpretation and offers a rural temporality based on the absorption of gender, historical, and epistemological possibilities.

In effect, the poem’s structure depends upon common understandings of circular rural temporality as well as on how elements of that space disrupt the assumed smoothness of the rural experience. This structure occurs in *The Story of a Country Boy* with Chris’s gadgets and a night-driving scene that I will examine later, as well as in the farmworkers’ terror at an inventor’s appearance in Sherwood Anderson’s *Poor White,* which I discuss in chapter 1. Like these novels, *Next Year* resists the promulgation of rural nostalgia, starting with its opening poem:

> Wade all life
> backward to its
> source which
> runs too far
> ahead. (41)

The poem’s first clause suggests a historically based approach to experience, a reaching back that might be nostalgic, primitivist, or heteronormative. But, as Ruth Jennison notes, “Here, the rural, that place popularly conceived of as ‘behind’ in time, is also, uncannily, ahead” (“Waking” 133). In this poem, the rural space projects nostalgically (or, in an alternate reading, heteronormatively) but quickly subverts itself. The poem’s water imagery partially explains this subversion, as "wading" to the "source" asserts a fluid rurality resisting easy definition. *Next Year*'s first two poems, then, develop a nonnostalgic position that nevertheless accepts the power of nostalgic understandings of rurality. For these poems, the problem of rural nostalgia is that, in the popular imagination, rural spaces become fixed, old-fashioned, incapable of modernity. This also occurs in *The Story of a Country Boy* when Chris Bennett treats his nostalgic view of the farm, himself, and his role as essential and unchanging.

Niedecker, Powell, and other Midwestern authors challenge that static image, using the conflicts between these old-fashioned images and stories to demonstrate the anxieties and fragmentation of modern rural life. Somewhat nonintuitively, then, *Next Year* subverts rural nostalgia partly by referring to ruralized, ahistorical "folk- / time" (57). Lines such as "rock me out" (57) exemplify what folklorist William Nicolaisen describes as the "gentle time" of folk narratives (318). However, the line-break interruption signals that "folk-time" is evocative but fractional, undermining the twinned gentleness of "folk-time" and the homilies' folk wisdom. Niedecker further disrupts simplistic notions of the countryside through poems like the one found on the December 15–28 page (fig. 7), which reflects surrealist influences on her early poetry.[12]

The seeming nonsense of all three sentences serves as a reminder that the poem isn't especially interested in realistic storytelling. Furthermore, beyond surrealism, Niedecker makes a range of cultural allusions in this poem. Religion, for instance, informs the object-transforming use of "transubstantiation." Associated with "downward mouth," however, transubstantiation also seems to say, "Turn that frown upside down." The phrase became popular in the early 1930s, appearing in the 1931 Joe Young song of that name as well as the 1934 poem "Smile!" by homespun Indiana poet Barton Rees Pogue. "Turn That Frown Upside Down" is also the title of a Leo Robin and Ralph Rainger song in the 1933 film *The Way to Love.* In early January 1934, soon after Niedecker returned from her first visit to meet Zukofsky, this movie was featured at the Fort Theatre in Niedecker's hometown, Fort Atkinson.[13] There is no evidence that Niedecker saw *The Way to Love,* but Peters refers to Niedecker seeing movies in Fort Atkinson and exchanging letters with Zukofsky about their favorite films (29, 58, 122). Whether "transubstantiation" is a play on pop culture, a mark of

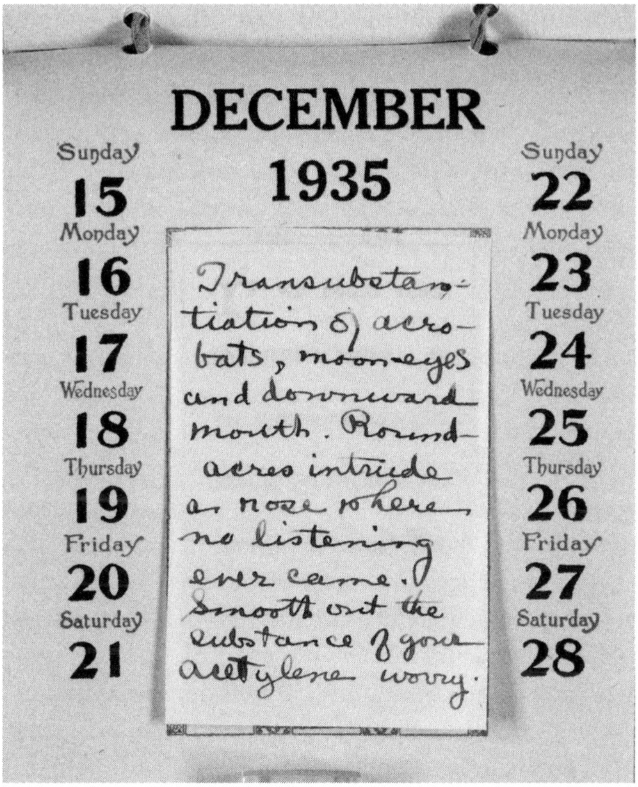


**Transubstan- / tiation of acro- / bats, moon-eyes / and downward / mouth. Round- / acres intrude / a nose where / no listening / ever came. / Smooth out the / substance of your / acetylene worry.**

Fig. 7. December 15–28, 1935, page from *Next Year or I Fly My Rounds, Tempestuous.* By Lorine Niedecker, 1934. Courtesy of Harry Ransom Center, University of Texas at Austin.

surrealism, a religious reference, or a playful nudge to Zukofsky, this poem shows how, though *Next Year* may traffic in ambiguity, it doesn't simply represent an impersonalized—or nostalgic—rural folk.

In addition to *Next Year*'s personal and cultural references, Niedecker also embeds this poem with several regionally specific elements. For example, beyond its potentially romantic connotation, “moon-eyes” holds two ruralized meanings: it is a species of freshwater fish found in the Great Lakes region and an equine ocular disease. Perhaps the most historically marked term in the poem is “acetylene,” a highly explosive chemical compound that was used widely throughout the early twentieth century for welding and illumination (Myers 7). Augustine Davis, one of the inventors of acetylene lighting and welding equipment, had Midwestern roots: he was born in Iowa, lived in Wisconsin and South Dakota, invented his apparatus in Chicago, and sold lighting equipment at the Davis Acetylene company in Elkhart, Indiana (“Augustine” 13). Davis died in 1933, and his obituary appeared in the Wisconsin papers. In Chicago newspapers, acetylene was mentioned several dozen times during the ten years prior to *Next Year*'s composition, most often in negative and neutral references to explosions and welding. But it also figures optimistically: one article notes Wisconsin research contributions and also nationalizes acetylene by arguing that its production “aids U.S. independence” (Evans 13). Another envisions a time “when a democracy makes the acetylene torch its torch of liberty and declares its independence of the past” (Clifford G1), which merges the Statue of Liberty's torch with acetylene's masculine connotations as a national economic force. In the Midwest, acetylene figured into a range of early twentieth-century discourses. Juxtaposing these with the poem's personal and art-historical meanings suggests how Niedecker's reference to acetylene (and, perhaps, *Next Year* as a whole) can only uneasily be gendered, regionalized, or even historicized—even as it demands each of them.

By virtue of its prominence in national regional economic discourses, acetylene locates the poem in time. Poetically, it also draws together its first and last lines, as the relationship between transubstantiation and acetylene reveals one way that *Next Year* remains bound up in capitalist temporalities. For example, while discussing the Du Pont corporation's attempts to increase profits, Evans describes the transubstantiation of acetylene into synthetic rubber: “The Du Pont synthesis has for its primary material, acetylene, which requires for its production only coal and limestone. Salt and water, the chemists say, are the only other raw materials, and all the ingredients are available in unlimited quantities” (13). Within the chemical process are at least two transubstantiations: the creation of acetylene from coal, limestone, salt, and water and then the creation of rubber from acetylene. A third transubstantiation, from synthetic rubber into corporate profit, exemplifies the productivity demanded by industrial capitalism. Furthermore, by way of national exaltations of scientific and economic production, it also evokes transubstantiation's religious connotations. Another article's title links Du Pont's synthesis with the perceived magic of religious transubstantiation: "Wand of Science Transforms the Ogre Coal" (Beck D8). Both articles represent the process of transforming water into rubber as a magical scientific abstraction—water to wine for the modern day. Still, they remain focused on acetylene's materiality and economic effects, mirroring Niedecker's interest in the concrete "substance" of the more abstract "acetylene worry" (67).

As with her use of acetylene to join religion, economics, patriotism, and homespun wisdom, Niedecker composes rural temporality by resituating local materials. According to Elizabeth Willis, Niedecker's "vocabulary was composed of endlessly recycled local elements" (xvii). Willis observes that Niedecker's recycling ranges from actual objects to regional language patterns. Regarding *Next Year,* such poetic repurposing both reflects acetylene's chemical transformations and gestures toward a materially specific kind of rural temporal circularity. Niedecker alters that circularity, however, in the very acts of reuse and revision, which help her demonstrate the limits of stereotypical rural time. Lee Upton contends that Niedecker "is a naturalist of her cyclical experience, yet it is her task as a writer to see the particular dissolve" (29). Extending Upton's claim, I argue that *Next Year*'s temporality is based on neither pastoralized seasonal repetition nor industrial transformation of raw materials. Rather, Niedecker creates an elastic temporality open to a variety of possibilities, a representational strategy that parallels the way historical events both create and undermine the narrative of *The Story of a Country Boy*—such as when the Great Depression disrupts Chris Bennett's success narrative but provides the impetus for his return to the farm.

Niedecker clarifies the disruptive effect of local materials and history through *Next Year*'s material constructedness, specifically the way her poetry obscures the original homilies of the biweekly pocket calendar, *The Sunlit Road. Next Year* was given as a gift and thus may have had some kind of affective resilience, but the book is also an ephemeral physical object: small, printed on thin paper, bound by an easily removed ribbon. *Next Year*'s construction upon such flimsy materials suggests its relationship to Jani

Scandura's work on depressive modernity, especially her interest in "the mechanisms through which refuse is managed, manipulated, and defined" (21). Scandura's terminology highlights the planned obsolescence of *The Sunlit Road.* Intended to be used only once, a page need only last the two weeks designated on its borders. Niedecker repurposes each page of the calendar, managing its reception and manipulating its meaning by using her poetry to obscure the original homilies. She thus redefines both the calendar and the homilies' commonsensical wisdom through her homily-esque poetry and her adoption of the calendar's form.

Indeed, while the calendar's form obviously structures *Next Year*'s temporality, its material construction challenges progressive time, recalling Upton's claim that Niedecker's project hinges on her ability to see "dissolve." In part, this is because, according to Jenny Penberthy, many of the homilies are partially visible underneath the thin paper of *Next Year*'s poems. Their coexistence provides a constant reminder of the past and, further, each page's two-week timeframe presents a historicized yet imprecise temporality in which past, present, and future are together on the page. Elizabeth Robinson points out that Niedecker can "assume that the reader knows . . . a year . . . is an orderly movement of days through weeks into months *and* that the completion of the year results in the commencement of another unit of time that is ostensibly identical" (118; emphasis in original). *Next Year* therefore alters both progressive and circular temporalities by juxtaposing the calendar's understood progressions with material reminders not only of the past (calendar dates just gone by) but also of past uses (homilies barely visible beneath pasted poems).

Because Niedecker composes *Next Year* on top of *The Sunlit Road,* she alludes to the calendar's readership, which since the 1910s had treated it as "a yearly visitor, whose welcome is never outworn" ("Stationery and Novelties" 447). Coupled with the calendar's annual return, the homilies' partial visibility underneath the poems presents a version of rural time that isn't predicated on simple narrative progressions. For example, this homily is found underneath the "transubstantiation" poem:

> If we could read
> the secret history of
> our enemies, we should

find in each man's life
sorrow and suffering
enough to disarm all
hostility. (*TSR*)

The poem and homily share a similar structure: an opening action that is inaccessible (reading a secret history) or incoherent (transubstantiation of acrobats) followed by a personal connection (finding sorrow, the nonlistening acquaintance) and an exhortation to calmness (disarm, smooth out). Juxtaposing the concept of an enemy's "secret history" in relation to a nonlistening "round-acre," then, gives credence both to a potentially personal meaning in the poem as well as to the idea that Niedecker is updating the original homily with a referential modernist vocabulary. Taking the two together suggests how Niedecker uses the homilies: as a limiting form, providing recognizable—if insufficient—narrative structure to the experience of modernity. *Next Year* disrupts those narratives, altering them to the purpose and needs of Niedecker and her intended audience.

Repurposing the calendar also hints at the layers within *Next Year*'s gender construction. On one hand, Niedecker performs heteronormative femininity by creating *Next Year* as a private gift for Zukofsky. On the other, Jane Augustine claims that Niedecker rejects feminine gender roles, instead trying to locate herself "in the gender-free category of poet" by using "the borrowed words of male writers" (139). *Next Year*'s clearest borrowing is the appropriation of the gift calendar, adding thin slips of paper to create an art object from a commercial one. She manipulates the ephemeral object and, in an instance of Scandura's depressive modernity, both redefines the calendar and manages her gender position. As with Niedecker's references to material histories that can be only partially labeled local, regional, or national, she challenges the latent heteronormativity of the homilies' emphasis on devotion and contentment. And while her tiny slips of paper miniaturize national economic forces like acetylene, she manages expectations of feminized privacy by refusing to let the poetry become entirely domestic and making it in the form of an "ironic palimpsest" (Alcosser 30).

Niedecker, then, locates gender partly in *Next Year*'s refusals, which suggests the book's ambivalent gendering rather than the creation of a "gender-free category" (Augustine 139). Despite the personal relationship implied in the gift to Zukofsky, neither the speaker nor the listener is gendered, and the poems do not propose any particular feminine or masculine ideal—except perhaps that a "dull man" (57) should try to be better dressed. As a result, over a homily listing "the things to be / desired for man in a / healthy state" (*TSR*), Niedecker writes that "in all free states / the selves un- / mix" (62). She "un-mixes" normative gender categories within a "free state," revising both the homily's normativity of the "healthy state" and the implication that it is primarily important for men. Niedecker's redefinition of the calendar's gender normativity demonstrates that even a failed attempt to attain a "gender-free category" proposes a revision of masculine gender roles just as it does for feminine.

The failure of normative gender roles structures the temporality of *Next Year* much as it does for *The Story of a Country Boy.* For Powell, those failures designate a divide between Chris Bennett's expectations and his experience. For Niedecker, they join *Next Year*'s material reminder of multiple temporalities as she literally papers over *The Sunlit Road*'s normative sentiment. Virginia Jackson contends that a poem's materiality calls into question standard reading practices. With regard to Emily Dickinson's manuscripts, Jackson argues that "the persistent sense that something is left—those handsewn leaves, those pieces of envelopes pinned at odd angles—keeps recalling modern readers to an archaic moment of handwritten composition and personal encounter, a private moment yet unpublicized, a moment before or outside literature that also becomes essential to modern lyric reading" (10). To remember that Dickinson wrote poems on a used envelope or that Niedecker pasted hers over a single-use calendar is also to recognize that the poems exist within a specific historical moment. Contextualizing these poems implies a relationship between two stereotypically gendered materials in *Next Year:* its feminized private construction and the masculinized materials of the economic public sphere. Their ambivalent coexistence shows how *Next Year* calls attention to gender even while effacing it, and the absorption of that ambivalence—effected by a papering over—parallels its treatment of temporality. Niedecker offers a rural temporality that depends upon neither calendrical progression nor seasonal circularity. Instead, it defamiliarizes both by highlighting a network of meanings and temporal references that indicate the poem's historical specificity without demanding narrative progression or representational realism.

## MATERIAL DISRUPTION AND THE "RUSTIC DREAM"

While *Next Year*'s actual physical construction alludes to the temporal effects of rural materiality, in *The Story of a Country Boy,* the people and objects in the countryside highlight inherent conflicts by affixing simple rural or urban labels. For example, because Chris Bennett spends a large portion of the book claiming to be a farmer when by most measures he would be considered a businessman, it appears that *The Story of a Country Boy* represents modern rurality as antimaterial and ahistorical. But when the Bennett family returns to the farm, Powell upends the novel's rural nostalgia. Mirroring *Next Year*'s unsettling of rurality, *The Story of a Country Boy* fends off pastoralism by representing the farm as an unfamiliar space. Chris's wife Joy remarks, "'It just seems so—so lonesome here. Everything is so different. It's as if it was a strange land. . . . If only I had a little Benedictine . . . or something.' She dabbed at her eyes. 'And you'll miss people—Madeleine—everybody—you'll be thinking about them, Chris'" (310; ellipses in original). Joy and Chris expect that returning to the farm will comfort them, but Joy finds it strange. She expresses their experience in halting, fractured prose, which might be read as feminized sobbing. It is also, however, represented as modernist stream of consciousness, through which Powell establishes the countryside as an essentially modern, present-oriented space. She thus rejects the nostalgic vision of her characters and plunges them into a countryside that includes all of the disappointments they brought with them but none of the temporary balms—alcohol, gaming, infidelity—that they used to escape those problems.

Given the disappointment that Chris and Joy experience upon their arrival and during the "jolting," "incredibly slow" train that "meandered downstate like a lazy mule" (304), perhaps it is to be expected that Chris's return will not conform to his nostalgic expectations, his "rustic dream" from the novel's first page. But then it does: "On the front stoop Chris and Dad sat looking at the stars, drinking applejack, talking. A quarter-moon with its proud Roman profile hung like a medallion on a velvet ribbon in the soft black sky. Far off toward the distant village stretched the dark waiting fields and between their spoken words crept the country night framing each phrase in its gentle silence" (309). Evoking an earlier classical reference, to Greek pastoral poet Theocritus, the moon displays a "proud Roman profile."

Beyond that, the night is gentle, the fields are prominent, and this conversation takes place under the stars at the family farm. Chris and his father engage in a pastoralist, masculine communalism that feels like they were on the cover of *The Sunlit Road* or, as the narrator notes earlier in the novel, as if "Bennetsville never grew" (126).

Their conversation continues, and it seems that Bennetsville may actually belong to the past. Chris's father says, "There'll be a lot of things you've forgot, Chris, my lad. . . . A lot of things about this patch of land you'll have to learn all over" (309). In this passage, Powell underscores the interplay between memory and repetition. Even though the farm is the same as always, Chris will have to learn how to farm all over again—Chris's absence has not changed it, but only him. Chris's inability to step back into the "rustic dream" subverts his nostalgia, while being forced to labor and relearn defies his intent to return as a success. Powell thus asserts "this patch of land" as a present space, not one that conforms to a nostalgic past or a triumphal future. The emphasis on learning also underscores Chris's experience of the farm, which suggests that the novel is concerned with neither realistic representation nor pastoral fantasy. Instead, it presents Chris's old-fashioned, pastoral dream as part of the affective experience of a contradictory, modern character within an equally modern rural space.

Throughout most of this novel, Powell uses fairly conventional representational strategies. In some scenes, however, she abandons all pretense of realism and depicts rurality in a fragmentary modernist style. Just before one such passage, Chris comes upon a crisis at the factory, then flees the scene and leaves town, drunk. On his way out of Aviland, he sees Vida Spencer, the office worker with whom he earlier had an affair. He asks her to join him "on a little trip [to] see grass and sunshine and none of this goddamn factory smoke" (195). Here, Chris expresses his intention to escape to a romanticized rural space containing none of the industrial elements that sully the city for him. Chris's claim that he has "served [his] time in the foundry" (191) indicates that the desire for escape is somehow due to the nature of his industrial experience. Since he has "been working ever since [he] was born down in Center County" (191), the labor doesn't seem to be the main problem. Rather, the place and type of factory labor do not appear to fit the ideals of his rural origins. Furthermore, Chris's comments about the strike and subsequent decision to flee gesture at the novel's problems of temporality. Chris saying that he "served time" in the foundry submits a progressive temporality in which his time generates increasing rewards and responsibilities. But the rural origins of his labor, as well his return to a land of "grass and sunshine," show that the rural space challenges industrial temporality even as it appears to provide the raw materials for growth.

Initially, the countryside conforms to Chris's vision of an idyllic rural escape. After they escape town, Chris and Vida drive for hours, drinking all the while: "On and on through the hushed country night they flew, gloriously, magically free, heads swimming beautifully so that all about them the world stood revealed in its essential topsy-turviness. For miles they shot along a white fence, this white fence belted the world, when it stopped they would pop off into breathless space" (196). Free to explore a magical rural world with a hushed quality that allows them to fill it with their voices and actions, Chris and Vida have it both ways. In this world, they are free to move and comforted by the white fence but are not plunged into danger when the fence disappears. Because Chris is dissatisfied at home and fears losing his position at the factory, this combination of freedom and protection is doubly enticing: he is protected from the dangers of the factory but free to explore sexual behavior outside his marriage or, on the other hand, free to escape the factory but protected from any consequences of his affair. In both cases, Chris's magical freedom within a "belted" world draws attention to the scene's arrested temporality. He is held safely between two options that could be catastrophic within the novel's plot. Here, though, Powell stops the narrative's forward progress, which can be seen not only in the passage's imagery but also its sentence structures. In the first, the simple statement "they flew" is scaffolded by four adverb phrases and a subordinate clause, none of which clarify the sentence's meaning. The second sentence is composed of three independent clauses joined only by commas. The absence of conjunctions means that the relationships between clauses are unclear, suggesting that this is a series of hazy, unprocessed observations.

Chris's breathlessness indicates that Powell will not let the feeling last. In *Next Year,* Niedecker exhorts her audience, "don't send steadily" (42), and this passage similarly highlights unsettling rural experiences. Its first sentence, for instance, emphasizes rural "topsy-turviness," and later Chris "dizzily" watches the moon and stars (197). The confusion only increases when modern life enters the passage:

> An airport lighthouse girdled with ruby lights decorated a lonely meadow, gasoline pumps under spotlights grew so close together they seemed to bark at the car's heels, a rabbit scuttled into bushes and back across the road perpetually, ahead of them a truck with a horse's head thrust sadly out of an aperture changed to a Good Humor wagon, back to the horse, and both were lost in a great illuminated sign across the sky WRAP YOUR ARMS AROUND A BATHING BEAUTY! Then darkness and an endless forest, where trees swished their leaves in a whisper like rushing water, DANGER! (197)

There is copious detail here, but—like the rest of the longer passage—almost no discernible narrative. For example, the glowing airport tower in a field is a provocative image, as are the gasoline pumps that have come alive and chase the car, so too the horse's head that transubstantiates into an ice cream truck. The passage moves between the wilderness of the "endless forest" and the modernity of the airport, gas pumps, and advertisements. The only sense we get of a story is that the car's speed changes a great deal, as Chris passes the truck and then is passed by it. Instead, the details pile upon each other, run-on sentences confusing the scene. That confusion is a key part of Powell's approach. Rather than letting the rural idyll develop, this passage portrays an old vision of rurality, the horse, at the same moment as a modern one, the truck. Through this relationship, Powell addresses the implications of modernization and nostalgia on rural temporality. She dismisses neither, instead placing them in a network of ways that Chris, as a modern, mobile character, might understand and participate in rurality.

Chris's experience flying through the night shows how early twentieth-century enthusiasm for night driving creates an episodic rural temporality. By narrating this scene from Chris's perspective inside the space of his headlights, Powell limits his range of vision. According to Sandy Isenstadt, "Speed simultaneously foreshortened objects and condensed observational time: objects appeared vaguely at first, perhaps as just a flash from a polished surface, bloomed gradually into nocturnal form, then sharpened for an instant and, just as swiftly, were gone, giving way to another baffling flash from the darkness ahead" (218). This passage represents those successive moments of sharpened visibility as a dramatized but not narratively focused version of rural modernity. Similar to the biweekly pages of *Next Year,* what time exists in this passage becomes episodic, a series of fleeting moments in which the roadside materials are "recognized at only the last instant, if at all" (Isenstadt 215). Even though Chris is speeding along the road, he remains in the same space behind the wheel, which causes stationary objects to appear active. As a result, bridges and old men "sprang up," "torches flared," "sudden white crosses loomed," and "an automated traffic man materialized" (Powell 197). Each of these, in their turn, startles Chris and interrupts his attempt to find a rural ideal. These material disruptions are notable within the novel because, according to Isenstadt, one of the chief pleasures of night driving was that headlights "effectively screened out irrelevant information" (218). For Chris, what counts as irrelevant should have been anything deviating from a recognizable, nostalgic rurality. But the components of that space disallow his attempt at temporal return. Flashing nostalgic images alongside evidence of modernization, his episodic vision thus forces multiple successive returns to the present moment.

Thus the rural space invites Chris to fill it with his actions, and it begins magically but then compresses details and time in such a way that it upends his vision of the "rustic dream." As they speed through the countryside, Chris's dream becomes nightmarish: "Cornfields were gaunt armies of shocked corn reviewed by General Moon, their ranks filled in by reserves of tombstones in adjoining fields; graveyards, cornfields, graveyards, cornfields—these fields killed these men who tilled this corn which killed these men who tilled this corn—" (198). By anthropomorphizing the corn and moon, Powell makes this sentence read like a children's story, especially given its chanting repetitiveness at the end. The rhyming chant, however, asserts a nightmarish circularity to the rural experience. Even though its repetitions allude to a common conception of rural temporality, the chant's ghastliness negates Chris's attempt at nostalgic return. Powell thereby dismisses Chris's childish understanding of rurality and returns him to the moment of his experience. Chris's attempt at escape provides only momentary comfort, and even his companion cannot provide the desired experience. Vida's presence and her scant dialogue—limited to exclamations and the question "Where shall we stop tonight?" (198)—serve primarily as a reminder that he is trying to experience a nostalgic pastoralism with a woman who isn't his wife. In other words, Chris performs normative masculinity even as he undermines it. Alongside the material interruptions of modernity, such incongruities demonstrate how the novel's present unsettles its protagonist, showing how something like a field of corn shocks Chris into an agrarian nightmare.

But these frightening appearances do not indicate that the countryside is inherently dangerous. After all, the nightmare develops after Chris sees a traffic signal. For a modern man used to driving in towns and cities, that signal should be a mundane reminder of urban industrialism. In this passage, though, it causes a nightmare, partly because it is a reminder of a modern rurality that doesn't conform to Chris's nostalgic dreams. Indeed, his fright at the traffic signal registers anxieties that, in the early twentieth century, rural roads were no longer "bound up with the commonplace rhythms of agrarian life" (Barron 21). In this way, like *Next Year,* Powell's novel attends to rural history despite avoiding a coherent representation of it. Even as the novel allows Chris his momentary magical dizziness, the rural space also returns him to the present moment, to the combinations of workhorses and trucks, forests and billboards. Accordingly, Powell follows Chris's fright at the "automated traffic man" with "the smell of September woods, of clover fields, of dying bonfires mingled with gasoline" (196–197). This sensation of rurality evokes a range of temporalities, starting with the seasonal smell of an autumn forest. Clover fields imply that this is an unsullied space for pastoral land use; they not only allude to the plants' growth but also the field labor of baling hay as well as the horses and cattle who will eat it. The final image of dying bonfires, however, diminishes this pastoralism—the bonfire, a symbol of community, is weakening, and its association with the smell of gasoline both provides evidence of modernization and suggests accelerated decay.

By presenting modernity and decay in equal measures, Powell demands that the rural be relegated neither to a nostalgic past nor a future golden age: while the clover fields fit into a "calendar pastoral scene," those gasoline-fueled dying embers do not. In this novel, therefore, reminders of modernity—such as the economic struggles of the Great Depression,

Chris's use of a bachelor pad, or the smell of gasoline in the woods—create confusion for Chris, and the rural Midwest refuses to function as a palliative. Similarly, William Cunningham's and Wright Morris's farm novels, which I discuss in chapter 3, portray how Great Plains farm life accelerates masculine failure. They share an attention to obsolescence with *The Story of a Country Boy* and *Next Year,* as each presents a version of modern rurality that is old-fashioned yet modern—it absorbs past and present, industrial and pastoral, masculine and feminine, sometimes even magic and science. For Niedecker, the result of such absorption is a ruralized poetic modernity that uses its materiality to underscore its temporal simultaneities. Her poetry forces the elements of recognizable temporalities to coexist in moments and on texts when it seems they ought not. Both texts, then, placing themselves in the space of the 1930s rural Midwest, negotiate the demands of regional and national narratives by creating or referencing a material network of temporal associations. The coexistence of multiple material temporalities means that neither *Next Year* nor *The Story of a Country Boy* can simply accept the normative trajectory of the self-made man, the progressive teleologies of urban industrialism, or the nostalgic returns of pastoralism. Powell and Niedecker choose to neither embrace those recognizable narratives nor elide the confusing aspects of rural modernity. Niedecker therefore rejects normative gender roles, and Powell refuses to allow Chris to remain a "country boy . . . made good." As a result, the Midwestern space of these texts participates in the confusion, asserting itself in the present tense.

CHAPTER THREE

# "WHERE PEOPLE AND THINGS WEAR OUT"

## *Masculine Fatigue and the Great Plains Farm Novel*

We are bound to the farm by a thousand ties. We belong there as long as the chickens hold out.

—William Cunningham, "Okla. Farmers Plan No Pink Tea for Their Holiday," 1932

I have always liked to work.

—Wright Morris, "The Writing of Organic Fiction," 1977

From the 1936 documentary *The Plow That Broke the Plains* to the 1936 Dorothea Lange photograph known as *Migrant Mother* to John Steinbeck's 1939 novel *The Grapes of Wrath,* many enduring images of the Great Depression are associated with the Great Plains. The Dust Bowl provides a ready narrative: drought conspires with irresponsible farming practices to cause economic and environmental decline, which in turn yields widespread poverty and mass migrancy. According to Michael Denning, "the representation of mass migration became one of the fundamental forms" of Great Depression art, with rural crisis serving as the powerful opening to migration stories beginning in the Dust Bowl, Appalachia, and the Deep South (264). In other words, many Great Depression artworks tell stories of men and women who, confronted with forces beyond their control, sought a better life. They also suggest that there's a way out, that Americans (or at least rural white plains dwellers) can find solace in California, better farming practices, or the love of family.

Dust Bowl migration stories begin with land that has become worn out, fatigued, infertile. As the story goes, when farmland no longer produces, farmers can't farm. So the Joads head west, joining a stream of fictional and real-life "Okies" from the Great Plains to the West Coast. According to agricultural historian David Danbom, however, "Most of the victims of the

Dust Bowl stayed in the region" (227). R. Douglas Hurt adds that many of the so-called Okies were not from the Dust Bowl but rather sharecropping regions to the east. Hurt infers that, because the wheat farmers in the Dust Bowl were more likely to own their land, they had more reason to stay on it. It's not, then, that farmers couldn't farm. Rather, in the face of persistent dust and drought, they found that they couldn't farm in the same way. To help farmers weather the downturn, the federal government enacted a slew of New Deal programs that, according to Michael Johnston Grant, focused on diversifying farm operations, shifting crop rotations, and reducing the amount of tractor farming. The Farm Credit Administration, Resettlement Administration, and Farm Security Administration (FSA), among others, not only supported rural communities generally but, more specifically, were developed to help farmers adjust certain practices.

New Deal rehabilitation programs flourished throughout the Great Plains, and they were documented by FSA photographers. Of course, the most famous images of the Dust Bowl are pictures of environmental devastation. James Swensen suggests that Steinbeck's writing about the Dust Bowl was influenced by images like Arthur Rothstein's *Fleeing a Dust Storm,* which depicts a farmer and two boys running toward a shed amid swirling dust. Taken in April 1936 in Cimarron County, Oklahoma, many of Rothstein's photographs depict abandoned and damaged farmhouses or gardens and farm implements buried by sand. Less well known are several images of the response to the drought, such as the homes of rehabilitation clients or the photos of men repairing fences and making other structural improvements. In *Fighting the Drought and Dust with Irrigation* (fig. 8), Rothstein documents a common rehabilitation activity: a man digging an irrigation ditch. Behind the man in the foreground is a bare, plowed field and, in the distance, a farmhouse, barns, and a windmill. It is a picturesque sight—without the context provided by the caption, this image shows an industrious farmer working the land to provide for his family. Shooting from a low angle, Rothstein depicts the farmer as an avatar of heroic masculinity. Within its context, however, this man's work appears futile. The land is worn out, and it seems impossible that the hand-dug irrigation ditch will rehabilitate the expanse of dust between him and his barns. Still, the dirt he's digging is darker than the soil around it, indicating that there's moisture to be found. In that respect, at least, Rothstein offers a positive image

Fig. 8. Arthur Rothstein, *Fighting the Drought and Dust with Irrigation. Cimarron County, Oklahoma,* April 1936. Courtesy of Farm Security Administration—Office of War Information Photograph Collection, Prints & Photographs Division, Library of Congress, LC-USF34-004109-E.

of a man attempting to preserve his way of life through his willingness to make both behavioral and material changes.

This chapter examines two Depression-era Great Plains farm novels that address a similar effort to cope with forces largely outside the control of their male characters. William Cunningham's 1935 novel *The Green Corn Rebellion* and Wright Morris's 1948 photo-text novel *The Home Place* highlight the responses of individuals and communities to a national economy that exploits rural land and people. In so doing, they reconsider the value of negotiating those challenges—in terms not only of their losses but also their ability to live through them. The farmers of *The Green Corn Rebellion* attempt to dismantle capitalist hierarchies precisely so that they can improve life on their Nebraska farms. Both the content and the publication date of Cunningham's novel represent periods of social unrest in the countryside, which reflects Roy W. Meyer's claim in *The Middle Western Farm Novel in the Twentieth Century* that "farm fiction has tended to proliferate in periods of agrarian discontent" (182). Written during the Great Depression, *The Green Corn Rebellion* dramatizes a short-lived 1917 uprising in Oklahoma in which socialist farmers intended to march on Washington, eating green corn along the way. Protagonist Jim Tetley and his father-in-law Mack McGee organize with the state socialist party to protest working, lending, and social conditions in Oklahoma. Their discontent also filters into the characters' home lives, and Jim impregnates his sister-in-law, Happy. Mack sustains multiple losses—Happy's suicide, learning that Jim was the father, and the failure of the rebellion—which cause his health to decline, and the book ends with Mack's death and Jim's conscription. In *The Green Corn Rebellion,* economic, moral, and social failures accumulate and, amid crisis, the rebellion breaks down.

*The Home Place* represents a similar sense of rural disappointment, but—following wartime privations and the Great Depression before that—it shows the long-term effects of American economic decline. Clyde Muncy has left his home in New York City, and he considers returning to his childhood home in Nebraska. Over the course of a one-day visit to Clyde's aunt Clara and uncle Harry, Clyde and his wife Peg realize that Lone Tree, Nebraska, is not the refuge they hoped it would be. The Muncys feel like they should fit into this community, but they can't overcome cultural differences that have arisen because Clyde chose to leave Nebraska and make a living as a writer. Morris's documentary-style photography gestures toward this mismatch. On every facing page, the black-and-white images are not captioned and often have an oblique relationship to the story. Unlike Arthur Rothstein's photograph of the heroic farmer, Morris shoots from a frontal angle and usually limits the images to a single object or building. As a result, the photographs provide an undercurrent of uncertainty, mirroring the broader economic condition as well as Clyde and Peg's specific circumstances. This novel accepts masculine failure as a precondition of the modern countryside—Clyde has lost his footing (or perhaps his bearings) in New York, while Uncle Harry and the farm are both wearing out.

*The Home Place* and *The Green Corn Rebellion* thus cultivate a modern rural masculinity that acknowledges—even dwells in—failure. Like Sherwood Anderson's *Poor White* and Dawn Powell's *The Story of a Country Boy,* which I examine in the first two chapters, they construct what Jani Scandura calls "a depressive modernity, a modernity that does not follow the forward thrust of mania, speed, and progress, but of depression, idling, and refuse" (4). Cunningham and Morris avoid being overly nostalgic in part by highlighting, in Scandura's words, the "refuse" of modernity. In many Midwestern modernist novels, that refuse often turns out to be the men who have otherwise benefited from socio-industrial modernity. In Great Plains literature specifically, the removal of these men from hierarchies of power is complicated by frontier mythology. Richard Slotkin argues that the frontier functioned as a "safety valve" (138), not least because of the myth that its "natural environment is so rich in resources as to render competition harmless, class conflict absurd, and monopoly almost impossible" (139). For Morris, the Nebraska plains promise an escape for Clyde Muncy and family, who wish to leave New York; in this way, the novel shows how the combination of masculine failures and frontier mythology generates the migrant narratives that were a hallmark of Depression-era proletarian fiction. Cunningham, on the other hand, suggests that when the safety valve no longer exists, men will try to escape the structures that made it necessary. The difference between escaping and being cast out as "refuse" is that, while they may be a consequence of modern life and economics, in the case of the latter, these men do not benefit from their mobility.

Clyde Muncy, Jim Tetley, and Mack McGee hope for a better life, but the struggle to improve their lives not only highlights existing structural inequities. It also wears them out. These novels describe the modern countryside in terms of age—what makes farm men modern also makes them seem old-fashioned. Cunningham and Morris thus demonstrate how regionalism disrupts narrative teleologies. In so doing, they develop a rural masculinity that registers its modernity through the very images and stories that make it feel dated. As a result, Midwestern farm novels resist the prevailing masculine and spatial narratives of the mid-twentieth-century United States.

While these resistances can take the form of rejecting specific narrative temporalities, these novels more often adopt multiple, apparently incompatible ones. The result is often stasis (or slowing) and an emphasis on coping (or endurance), which makes both their masculinities and their modernism feel old-fashioned—making do rather than "making it new."

## GREAT PLAINS MASCULINITY

Of the two main archetypes of Great Plains masculinity—the cowboy and the pioneer—the men in Cunningham's and Morris's novels adhere more closely to the latter. They build on a long tradition of pioneer literature, including Willa Cather's *O Pioneers!* (1913) and O. E. Rølvaag's *Giants in the Earth* (1927), which explore the challenges of homesteading, particularly for European immigrants. These books echo historian Frederick Jackson Turner's assessment of the frontier, which he describes in terms of "the struggle of the pioneer farmers to subdue the arid lands of the Great Plains" (247). Turner originally delivered his remarks at the 1893 Columbian Exposition in Chicago, claiming that by 1890 the US population had dispersed beyond any coherent frontier line. Whether plains novels are set before or after this date, however, they portray this attempt to "subdue" in terms similar to another famous frontier figure, Teddy Roosevelt, who famously embraced the kind of cowboy imagery that was further popularized in Owen Wister's *The Virginian* (1902) and countless turn-of-the-century dime westerns. According to Gail Bederman, "As TR saw it, nature was brutal and primitive—a proving ground of manly prowess" (174). For both cowboys and pioneers, the frontier was a "proving ground" because land and adventure were seen as available for the taking. Annette Kolodny shows that this was possible because "men's fantasies had already attained the status of cultural myth" (12). Of course, those fantasies often didn't work out, but "the fact that a fantasy is frustrated by intractable realities does not mean that it loses either force or vitality" (Kolodny 11).

Depression-era farm novels refute fantasies of a pure, liberating prairie. While the plains remained a place to prove manliness, farmers faced different challenges than their cowboy or pioneer forebears.[1] For instance, in Horace Kramer's *Marginal Land* (1939) and J. Hyatt Downing's *The Harvest Is Late* (1944), banking difficulties and drought complicate the establishment of productive farms on the plains. The plains are not a fantasy land if farming requires expensive machinery, as in *The Grapes of Wrath,* or farmers depend on banks for operating loans, as in *The Green Corn Rebellion,* or they are employed by large corporate farms, as in Paul Corey's *Acres of Antaeus* (1946). Such stories are partly due to the rise of industrial-scale agriculture, which Deborah Fitzgerald documents throughout the 1920s. As a result, the worn-out land of the plains causes even further dependence on banking and lending structures, and Great Plains novels document the resulting material and social anxieties. Minimal crop return, mortgage problems, and social shame are common features in farm novels of this period, including Dorothy Thomas's *The Home Place* (1934), David Cornel De Jong's *Light Sons and Dark* (1935), Marjorie Bayley's *In Friends We Trust* (1938), and Charles Edward Hayes's *The Four Winds* (1942).

In Morris's *The Home Place,* housing anxieties are taken for granted, as they are the reason Clyde Muncy and his wife Peg leave New York City and return to Nebraska. Within the narrative, Morris foregrounds the social consequences of this possible move, as Clyde and Peg encounter resistance from Clyde's family because they don't immediately fit in. These seem to be minor differences, such as that their son—raised in New York—has never seen a croquet ball. But Clyde's aunt Clara, who raised him for part of his early life, seems to feel the difference is more fundamental. Every time Clyde attempts to explain the differences between his family and the current residents of Lone Tree, Clara responds but does not invite further conversation. For example, when he argues that if she "had some idea of how we've been living for the last ten years, we wouldn't strike you as being so strange," she replies, "Well, you're that" (37). When he says, "You've no idea what it's like to live in a big city, Clara—to try and raise a pair of kids in a place like New York," she replies, "I don't know as I'd want to know" (37). Since he left the farm, Clyde has become strange, yet Clara chooses to remain ignorant of the circumstances that cause him to be different from Uncle Harry and the men she knows in Lone Tree.

Clara's stance on Clyde's absence also relates to common perspectives on the family farm. In "Three Visions of Masculine Success on American Farms," Peggy Barlett argues that "for those who hold an agrarian perspective, farming is valued as a family commitment, an integration of work, family, community, and land. Sustaining the family's livelihood is a complex enterprise, but one that is located in a particular place, with relatives and friends nearby" (55). Clara privileges proximity among these agrarian values—for farming to be a success, family members must remain nearby not only to help with fieldwork but also to sustain the local community. Clyde's choice to move away means that he cannot fulfill those requirements. He is related to Harry and Clara and his cousins Ivy and Viola, but his work has taken him away from Lone Tree, both as a patch of land and as a community.

While Clara declines to ask follow-up questions and appears generally disinterested in Clyde's life, her diction belies some uncertainty. She says, after all, "*I don't know* as I'd want to know" (37; emphasis added). Clara hesitates, but she is not simply being polite. Rather, she rebuffs Clyde for his unconventionality, particularly those characteristics that have developed during his long absence from Nebraska. Despite Clara's skepticism, Clyde asserts his fidelity to agrarian values. Specifically, when he claims his place in the family, Clyde reminds Clara of a commitment beyond geography:

> "I'm a Muncy," I said, "as much as Uncle Harry. If he'd been wearing my shoes for the last thirty years he would strike you as silly as I do."
>
> "I doubt that," she said. She tipped her head forward to think about it, and stared at the floor. "Take a good deal more than thirty years." (37)

Clyde argues that he and Uncle Harry differ primarily because of their experiences, a circumstantial difference that has more to do with modern economic mobility than any kind of inborn psychological defect on his part. Morris presents Clara as more open to this claim than his earlier line of argument. In this exchange, her immediate doubt is of a piece with earlier comments on his strangeness. But then she physically reacts, looking down while thinking about Clyde's claim. Earlier in the conversation, when Clara tells Clyde she doesn't want to know about city life, Morris represents only Clara's verbal response. Clyde's thoughts then revert to his wife's claim that Harry and Clara "*don't give a dam*" about them (37; emphasis in original), which reflects his and Peg's self-absorption and also suggests a sense of finality to Clara's thoughts on the matter. In this moment, however, she doesn't reject him entirely. Instead, she considers the possibility and limits her reply to the length of his absence. Though she insists that there is still a difference between Clyde and Harry, Clara seems to be aware that definitions of successful farming have changed and at least some of those changes are beyond Clyde's or Harry's control.

Clyde argues that his attachment to family is not damaged by the time he has spent away from Nebraska, and he goes on to explain how he wants the same for his kids: "Something happened out here, in four or five summers, that thirty years of hell and high water, and twenty years of the city, has not changed in me. That's what I want for my kids. They're Muncys— . . . that's what they deserve" (37). For Clyde, the agrarian value of commitment to family cannot be broken after it has formed. Clara feels differently, and Clyde must make the case that his name and his experience on the farm mean that he belongs there. At this point in the novel, Clyde and Peg intend to move permanently to Lone Tree. They want to provide for his family the kind of life that Clyde had spending summers in Nebraska. But the structure of modern life makes this exceedingly difficult. While Clyde has become a locally celebrated author—featured as a "Creative Native" in the *Omaha World-Herald* (50)—his success doesn't insulate him from economic precarity, and it doesn't make it easier to reintegrate. Rather, the fact that he has spent the last twenty years in the city makes Clara turn away from him. Clyde is silly and strange, his wife won't follow Clara's kitchen rules, and his kids aren't like others she knows—it's only faint praise when she tells him, "They're nice enough youngsters" (37). Generally, Clara seems disappointed both that Clyde has left and that he cannot easily return. Clyde and Clara are equally frustrated by this situation, and *The Home Place* presents these frustrations and disappointments as constitutive of modern life in the Great Plains—the same historical developments that allowed Clyde to move away and become a successful writer are the same ones that caused him to lose that immediate connection with the farm, and they also cause him to return in distress. Despite these layers of failure, Clyde remains hopeful that he and his family can escape the effects of the Depression in Lone Tree.

To Clyde, the plains farm is a place that promises to alleviate some of the burdens of modern life, even though it is implicated in the system that caused those problems in the first place. Similarly, in *The Green Corn Rebellion,* Mack and Jim believe that joining with other Oklahoma farmers will allow them to resist the exploitation they feel from banking and political leaders. In the planning stages of the rebellion, especially, men are shown to gain strength from each other. When Jim and Mack go to a meeting of the Working Class Union (WCU), organizers tell them they are going to march on Washington to put power back in the people's hands, and the men respond with enthusiasm: "After the meeting the men stood around and talked. They were rarin' to go. The sooner the better" (123). Presented with the promise of a new, more equitable political and economic system, the men are excited to move forward. In *Masculine Style: The American West and Literary Modernism,* Daniel Worden shows how *The Grapes of Wrath* demonstrates the need for collective action: "As both Casy's recognition by the police and the farmer's threats demonstrate, masculinity can symbolically resist state and corporate power but flounders when an individual acts alone" (134–135). The way that the men of *The Green Corn Rebellion* seek the company of other men suggests a latent awareness of the power of organizing; Mack, Jim, and their comrades have been exploited long enough that they know they will not succeed on their own. When the men unify to undertake this conflict, they feel as if they are taking control of their situation. The outcome for these men is the same as what Worden finds in *The Grapes of Wrath:* the rebellion does not deliver the socialist utopia they were hoping for.

One obstacle for the rebels in *The Green Corn Rebellion* is that the opposition is primarily local, which reveals a conflict between town and country. Cunningham presents the town men as exploitative: the banker won't loan to socialists, the sheriff unjustifiably beats African American farmer Bill Johnson, and the high school boys prey on both teachers and country girls. Even so, they are able to appeal to institutional authority in a way that the rebels cannot. According to Ted Tetley, Jim's brother and the writer for the local paper, the men who broke up the rebellion were a "little band of patriotic citizens" who overcame "the traitorous band [who] did not have the courage to fight, although they had every advantage. They ran like turkeys" (193). Ted continues, "The Boy Scouts could have defeated this bunch, who fight just like they farm" (193). In this article, Ted challenges the rebels' masculinity by impugning their physical strength, moral conviction, and workplace competence. While Ted's labels for the rebels are rhetorically effective, they are demonstrably false. For instance, Ted questions the farmers' physical ability, but a local high school boy who is a member of their "little band" of patriots has shown that he cannot work as hard as the farmers. As for Ted himself, the only reason he has a newspaper job is that physically he isn't able to do farm labor.[2] According to Jim, the reason that the rebels scattered was that they began to doubt the revolution would be successful and, while the men from town "deserved to be killed maybe. . . . But how are you going to blaze away and kill a man you have known all your life, your own brother, just because he is fool enough to believe the lies the capitalists have told them?" (190). Similar to *The Home Place,* there are clear divisions in this community, but they are occasionally overcome by familiarity and established relationships. These novels thus use plains farmers' impulses to collectivity (socialist farmers joining together) and community (deciding not to fire on your neighbors) to complicate simplistic national narratives about masculinity.

Despite the connections that Jim and the other farmers feel toward other residents of the county, not everyone can participate equally. Whether capitalist or socialist, for instance, women are excluded from the rebellion, known throughout the novel only as wives or lovers. Furthermore, Cunningham also shows that not all men are afforded the same opportunities. Bill Johnson, "Negro farmer and veteran of the Spanish-American war" (150), is forced to eat a live mouse by Glen Rehlin, a farmer known to abuse African American employees. Rehlin forces Johnson to eat the mouse and then lies to the sheriff about Johnson stealing wheat. Rehlin and the sheriff beat Johnson, running off his horses and damaging a wagon wheel that they then make him pay for. Rehlin may be the most overt villain in this scene, but none of the other employees—all white men—come to Johnson's defense. When Rehlin makes clear that eating the mouse is a command, "the other fellows stood around waiting, some of them grinning. Bill felt himself getting trembly again" (153). The other men allow it to happen, at least some of them approvingly. In *Black Masculinity and the Frontier Myth in American Literature,* Michael Johnson explains that the ability to participate equally in groups of men is central to frontier masculinity. This scene, then, is a clear example of the ways "black men are excluded from 'men's relations with other men,' from full participation in the homosocial bonds between white men that constitute the power structure of the dominant culture" (M. Johnson 246).

During the march, Jim notices that the rebels do not openly mistreat

Johnson. Jim attributes this apparent solidarity to the exploitation that white and black farmers have in common, and in this way the novel parallels the actual rebellion. David Chang argues that the long-term exploitation of black, Native American, and poor white farmers led them to take up common cause: "The WCU's single-minded attention to class and the Green Corn rebels' focus on resisting the draft were thus interracial (but not antiracist) because of a class consciousness born of specific circumstances" (187). Because Jim and other farmers have stopped imagining that they are "white landowners-in-waiting" (Chang 187), they are more accepting of Johnson's equal participation in the march. According to Jim, "Up here on the hill Negroes were treated just like whites. It was always like that among Socialist farmers because Socialists knew that all working men white or black, were in the same boat" (178). Though their equality seems evident to Jim, Johnson is more hesitant. When Jim asks him to train the rebels as they wait to begin marching, Johnson questions whether their movement has enough farmers to succeed and expresses concern that other rebels will not tolerate a black man being elevated to a position above them. Johnson is not entirely excluded from bonding with the other rebels—indeed, he gains their respect because of his military experience—but there are still clear limits to his equal participation in the novel's version of the rebellion. By the end, Johnson's position becomes even more tenuous. Most of the rebels run away, and Johnson is captured by the sheriff. Later, he is especially singled out by the newspaper as "the most noteworthy" of the "shabby and worthless lot" (195).

Johnson's plight clarifies how these novels construct masculinity—while he participates in a movement promising greater equality and an improved economic situation, other, related conditions undermine his success. Both *The Home Place* and *The Green Corn Rebellion* exemplify what Barbara Foley describes as the "perspective" criterion of proletarian literature, which 1930s critics defined as novels that approached their topics with an anticapitalist, Marxist ideology. Like many other texts written from a proletarian perspective, these novels suggest how people could join together—either as a family or with other people of their socioeconomic class—to achieve a sense of "social totality" (Foley 126). In this chapter, that means not only the Muncy family's struggles with belonging but also Cunningham's representation of various groups' attempts to determine the character of their community. Morris's and Cunningham's layering of hopefulness and disappointment construct plains masculinity upon the expectation of failure. In *Labor & Desire: Women's Revolutionary Fiction in Depression America,* Paula Rabinowitz argues that this failure is built into the structure of revolutionary fiction: "One pull of the *roman à thèse* is toward closure, toward a single meaning or message; but as fiction, this project is undermined within the text" (*Labor* 76). Compared to *The Home Place, The Green Corn Rebellion* is more clearly a didactic novel, but both complicate their construction of Great Plains masculinity by underscoring characters' attempts to negotiate, challenge, or simply live through the economic and social difficulties of the Depression era.

## REVOLUTIONARY FAILURE, COLLECTIVE DISAPPOINTMENT

Roy W. Meyer does not include *The Green Corn Rebellion* in his survey of Midwestern farm novels, even though, like others in his chapter on social criticism, it fits nicely into both sides of this formulation: "Farm fiction was not always intended as the stimulus to reform; sometimes it was the imaginative re-creation of a reform movement already past" (104). Certainly, its critical reception shows how Cunningham's novel meets Meyer's main criterion for farm fiction—that it accurately "reflects the realities of farm life" (7). Similar to the critical commentary on Sherwood Anderson, Dawn Powell, and Lorine Niedecker, which I address in this book's first two chapters, Cunningham's contemporaries address his representation of authentic American life. According to Alvah Bessie, for instance, *The Green Corn Rebellion* avoids "stylized caricature" of its socialist farmers in favor of an "authentic American idiom" (10), and Helen Neville argues that *The Green Corn Rebellion* "falls easily into the best class of proletarian fiction" (417).[3] David Tilden finds that Cunningham has "genuine insight into the minds, groping but determined, and the hearts . . . of American workers," but he still notes the novel's "mistakes and crudenesses" (F8). Tilden's ambivalence reflects Nathan Asch's irritation with what he sees as the novel's emphasis of romance over revolt: "I don't know why I get so indignant about this book, except maybe because I get angry when I see anything wasted" (311).

Reviewers' disagreements extend beyond the book's aesthetic quality to its treatment of fact. For example, Harold Strauss claims that Cunningham's handling of Jim and Happy's romance is marred by his faulty representation of the rebellion: "A successful proletarian revolution never occurs without a background of abortive rebellions, without a tradition. And some novelists are determined to create this tradition for America, even if they must do it out of thin air, even if they must pretend that farmers rising to defend their private ownership of productive property were class-conscious proletarians" (BR6). As I will discuss later in this section, histories of the rebellion challenge Strauss's account by narrating the 1917 rebellion as a complicated convergence of Oklahoma farmers' social, political, and economic concerns. Labor historians articulate a complex narrative surrounding the causes and aftermath of the rebellion, and the confluence of reviewers' denials and critiques demonstrates the expectation of failure appended to fiction of the Midwestern countryside.

Accordingly, Midwestern novelists often depict conflicts between capital and labor that seem predisposed to end poorly for farmers and other country people. Some novels do this more simply than others; Dawn Powell's *The Story of a Country Boy,* which I examine in chapter 2, takes several common stories of social unrest—socialist soapboxes, economic loss, crushed strikes—and locates them in a country town. In *The Green Corn Rebellion,* rural radicalism fails specifically because of the structures of rural economy and culture. When the revolt begins, it immediately fizzles because of limited organization and a lack of group cohesion. Without the prospect of reinforcements from the statewide socialist party, the assembled farmers disperse to look after their farms and families. These farmers are left with disappointment in themselves, the movement, and their position within capitalist hierarchies.

Even before the farmers begin their march, however, Cunningham suggests that the rebellion will fail. Jim's doubts register while he plows his fields and waits for union leaders to organize: "Working by himself in the field Jim thought it all over and became skeptical. It was just one of the things that couldn't happen, and he would go on year after year plodding behind a plow. Nothing ever did happen to him and nothing ever could" (129). Jim has been going to WCU meetings and is frustrated by delays in the rebellion. He had hoped that at this point he would be marching triumphantly toward Washington. Instead, he is tending his land, alone, the same thing he has done "year after year": trudging behind a team of horses, turning the same soil all over again. This passage alludes to the many repetitions of Jim's life: it shows the annual need to plow his fields and refers to the other plodding he does in them—planting, tending, harvest, maintenance and repair, and so on. These are the acts of a responsible farmer, but none of them promise the glory of revolution.

Jim's burgeoning disappointment develops in dialogue with the hopefulness he feels as part of the organizing effort. Despite his initial skepticism, Jim becomes more optimistic as the rebellion gets closer. On the day before it begins, Jim works on his farm and thinks about what's to come: "It was hard to imagine what would happen in the next few months. If the farmers all over the country were just like the farmers in his neighborhood, there wouldn't be American soldiers going to France to be killed, and America would be the first country in the world to have a Socialist government" (158). Jim is plowing just like he was during his earlier moment of skepticism, but now the plans have progressed such that his expectations have become more specific. In this passage, though Jim notes that imagination doesn't come easily to him, he replicates the plans presented by socialist speakers who have traveled around rousing support for the rebellion: they will repeal military conscription, avoid the war, and install a more equitable government. In the paragraphs that follow, Jim imagines hiring socialist school teachers and ousting the local banker—peacefully, "unless he got smarty and tried to resist" (159).

When Jim tries to picture the rebellion in "Oklahoma City and other big places" (159), his imagination stalls. Jim sympathizes with his fellow farmers but cannot extend the same feeling to poor city dwellers: "When you thought about the cities you wondered how anything could happen that would change things. So damned many people, and you felt like most of them never even heard of socialism. Patriotic, and ready to go to war and fight for the capitalists. How could you ever knock anything into their heads?" (159). This passage demonstrates Jim's limited knowledge of socialism and early twentieth-century American political action. In the Midwest, for instance, Lizabeth Cohen documents the importance of Chicago, which developed as a center of the labor movement in no small part because of "its location at the crossroads of transportation and communication" (12).[4] Unaware of organizing activity in cities across the country, Jim conceives of socialist revolt as a rural affair, enacted by farmers with knowledge and some sense. He hopes that all American farmers are "just like the farmers in his neighborhood" (158) and that his local group will be joined in a confluence of other marches to overthrow the government and enact a socialist vision for American society.

In this novel, revolution is imagined hopefully, as a corrective. Jim remains ambivalent, however, as the rebellion sometimes fades into, as he says, "one of the things that couldn't happen" (129). Similarly, Mack is of two minds: "Well, by God . . . there'll be a time when it will be so a feller won't have to work fourteen hours a day, and will have money to do *with*. I used to think I'd never see it, but maybe I will, and maybe I won't" (103; emphasis in original). Like Jim, Mack constantly toils on his farm, at least until he attends a series of WCU meetings to oppose the Selective Service Act of 1917. According to James Green, "The insurrectionists of 1917 aimed their uprising at the war and military conscription, but their action was linked to a long chain of confrontations between the rural poor and the propertied townspeople of the cotton country" (366). Furthermore, Nigel Sellars argues that farmers saw themselves as the victims of "nonproductive" bankers and industrialists (81). Although the stated goal of the Green Corn Rebellion was to end military conscription, historians agree that the revolt developed over a long history of agricultural industrialists taking advantage of tenants and small farmers.

*The Green Corn Rebellion* taps into this history via Mack's and Jim's feelings that nothing will ever change for them—economically, politically, or in the repetitions of farm life. Not only do farmers in the novel feel victimized by bankers and politicians, then, but they also believe that they have been mistreated for a long time. These feelings mirror the historical rebellion, and they are among the reasons organizers took action. According to John Womack and Roxanne Dunbar-Ortiz, "The leaders were old men [who] . . . actually dreamed of a revolution. And they acted as best they could to make it real. It was their conquerors who baptized their failure a bumpkins' folly" (49). Harold Strauss's review of the novel, which questions the rebels' motivations and denies their understanding of socialist principles, exemplifies this kind of denialism. Womack and Dunbar-Ortiz claim otherwise—that the rebels were thoughtful and politically engaged, and acted accordingly. Alongside plains farmers' long-term exploitation, this account of farmers' motivation suggests the implications of Mack's desire for "money to do *with*": he, Jim, and the other farmers are willing to take the risks of rebellion to gain the rewards that he imagines will also come. In both Cunningham's novel and the actual rebellion, those risks were substantial; beyond the conscription act they were protesting (and which ensnares Jim in the end), the passage of criminal syndicalism laws gave states "the legal authority to suppress radicalism" (Green 346).[5]

In *The Green Corn Rebellion,* the farmers' failure is not simply due to broad organizing challenges or the imposition of repressive legal authority. Specifically, Jim becomes disappointed because the experience of rebellion is just the same as the barnyard, a problem that is ingrained in the structure of the march. The members of the rebellion planned to eat green corn and beef along the way, so they must round up and steal cattle during their march. Their plan, of course, is an awful lot like farm work: "Pushing the cattle through the fields they felt like they were just out at work on a hot morning. The revolution seemed like a dream" (188). This is not Mack's and Jim's dream of the revolution. While revolutionary temporality remains oriented to the future, in this moment it is neither hopeful nor attainable. That future temporality is complicated because the work of revolution is so similar to the repetitions of their lives, which exemplifies Taylor Eggan's description of "the temporality of revolution" as a "simultaneous movement toward change and stasis" (44). Rather than offering Jim an escape from the struggle of life on the plains, the rebellion becomes yet another iteration of this novel's prime experience—unending drudgery.[6]

Jim's combination of disappointment and hopefulness reflects Mack's thoughts on the rebellion: "Us fellers went off half-cocked. . . . We wasn't ready to overthrow the government. You can't get ready overnight or in a month, or even in a year. The American people ain't ready. Them fellers down at Oklahoma City, and this Carson the son-of-a-bitch, they backed down on us. They turned yellow. If we have to be hanged, then I hope every one of them is lynched" (196). Mack is angry that the socialist party organizers failed them, and his concern that farmers "ain't had no trainin' to do anything else" (196) suggests how he accepts some of the blame—Mack had been named a "local commander" (123) and realizes he was unsuited for the job.[7] As Mack continues, he reflects on some of the reasons for the rebellion's failure:

> The Socialist party ain't got enough good leaders. You know how it is with farmin', a feller ought to be born and raised on the farm to know very much about it, and I guess it's like that with revolution: we got to wait till we got thousands of youngsters who don't think or talk about anything but revolution before we can do a damn thing. I won't live to see it. Maybe you will. That kid of yours maybe will help finish the job that we made such a mess of. (196–197)

According to Mack, other than Eugene V. Debs, there aren't enough people with experience to fight against the government and capitalists. He hopes that the socialist fire will burn in Jim's child and other kids across the country so that future Oklahoma farmers will be able to create a better future for themselves. Mack's hopefulness about the revolution has turned into disappointment, but his failures also point the way for future success.

Mack, Jim, and their cohort complain about labor practices and local bankers and subsequently attempt to ameliorate those problems by creating a socialist government. These acts echo Marshall Berman's claim that modernization is thought both to produce problems and then to relieve them. Berman finds that nineteenth-century thinkers such as Baudelaire, Marx, and Nietzsche "denounc[ed] modern life in the name of values that modernity itself has created, hoping—often against hope—that the modernities of tomorrow and the day after tomorrow will heal the wounds that wreck the modern men and women of today" (23). Berman sees their collective voice as deeply ambivalent in the way it accumulates complex and contradictory elements. With this same type of ambivalence, Mack denounces capitalist exploitation of farmers but favors rural socialist organizing, which has been made much easier by railroad, automobile, telephone, and telegraph technologies—all of which are specifically attacked by the rebels.[8]

He hopes that future generations will be able to heal capitalist wounds but still use some of those things that have eased modern rural life. In this passage, Mack focuses not on the material elements of rural modernity but rather on those "thousands of youngsters" who will be raised up in revolution. As a result, he imagines they will be singularly focused on "fightin' the capitalists" (196) and therefore understand what it takes to organize and revolt. He bases this argument on the idea that "a feller ought to be born and raised on the farm to know very much about it" (196). To Mack, this is a comforting prospect, as those raised in revolution will be more successful than he was. But this feeling also reflects certain parochialisms of modern rural life, especially the sense that only those who are fully part of the community could integrate themselves within it. While Mack is hopeful, his reliance on future generations reads as ill-fated, not least because his hope rests on what Berman might suggest is an unlikely premise—that the youth will "heal the wounds" of exploitation in the plains because the squashed rebellion will spawn the organizational strength of a broad political movement.

As when Jim doesn't want to shoot the men from town because they are his neighbors, community relations complicate the rebellion, and they promise to have the same effect in the future. At the end of the novel, all of Jim's hopes have been dashed: the rebellion has failed, he must enlist, he cannot care for his family, and his sister-in-law has died because of him. As a result, he is disappointed and ashamed. When some fellow socialists come to warn Jim that, because he has enlisted, he should never come back to town, Jim worries that his child will hear about his actions.

> "Well, he won't hear nothin' about it so far's I'm concerned," McSlarrow said. "But you know how kids is, and I hope to God she don't stay around here. Maybe if she'd rent the place and move to town it'd be all right, because in town you're quite a hero, and if you git killed in the war your kid'll grow up proud of you."
>
> "Well, if he knew the whole story," Jim said, "he wouldn't feel much proud." (225)

Cunningham emphasizes Jim's shamefulness, which he links to McSlarrow's response. First, McSlarrow pledges not to tell about Jim's affair. Nevertheless, he expects that Jeannie and the boy will hear about it somehow, and he hopes they won't remain in the countryside because they will be treated poorly. Jeannie's move to town and the child's pride in Jim are both based on Jim's death. For him to be a hero, he must be absent. Jim agrees to these terms; at this point, he only hopes that his wife will move to town and live on income from renting the farm, while his child will be shielded from the full story of Jim's past. This child, who is one of those Mack wished would "help finish the job," will have to move away from the rebels because of community infighting. Jim's choices—to rebel, to have an affair, to enlist—mean that his son will be marginalized in both town and country. In this instance, the rebellion does not spawn further socialist action; instead, the responses from the rebels as well as the opposition splinter the existing organization, calling into question their future successes.

In many ways, *The Green Corn Rebellion* demonstrates the desire for, as Florian Freitag finds in other 1930s farm novels, "a collectivization of rural power in order to restore farmers to their rightful ownership of the soil" (225). The rebels hope that banding together will allow them to change exploitative government policies so they can participate free and clear in the local and regional economy. Furthermore, Freitag argues that Great Plains farm novels aim to develop "a community of farmers and a collective consciousness itself" (225) and, as plans for the rebellion come together, Cunningham represents Jim's nascent political consciousness. In *The New Masses,* Karl Pretshold asserts that Cunningham "has shown how revolt, rebellion, the joining together in organization, can enrich and widen lives which seem 'destined to narrowness and meanness'" (24). When Pretshold notes the rebels' apparent "narrowness and meanness," he references Adam Smith's *Wealth of Nations,* positioning these tenant farmers within Smith's "unproductive" servant class (287). According to Pretshold, one of the novel's strengths is that the farmers are not confined to such "narrowness," and he paraphrases Karl Marx and Friedrich Engels to show how collective political action can "enrich and widen" their lives. Pretshold thus locates an impulse in *The Green Corn Rebellion* that Freitag identifies across the plains. But this book also shows the limits of collectivization, in that the rebels' attempts to organize are thwarted partly because of the collectivity that already exists. Rather than becoming energized by the rebellion, Mack, Jim, and the others become fatigued—by their relationships, by their dashed hopes, and by the monotonous similarities between the rebellion and their lives on the farm.

## THE TEMPORALITY OF FATIGUE

In terms of both land and people, fatigue is common in plains literature of the Great Depression. Characters look tired, they act tired, and they're tired of being exploited. They express their fatigue when they are working and when they have quit for the day, when they are on the farm and when they have left. In *The Grapes of Wrath,* even though the Joads have found a spot at a good camp, things don't change much: "Ever'body's so goddamn tired an' wore out an' mis'able" (Steinbeck 238). The two books I examine in this chapter present the experience of wear in multiple ways, from weariness to worn-out tools. Cunningham represents the farmers' revolt as the culmination of years of socioeconomic exploitation, but the main plot of *The Green Corn Rebellion* is the story of an acute crisis, which is fitting for its historical antecedent as well as its composition during the heights of the Great Depression. Published in 1948, Morris's photo-text novel *The Home Place* offers a later perspective, largely excising crisis in favor of the personal and material effects of years of privation.

Because of its attention to organizing for and beginning the march, *The Green Corn Rebellion* purports to show the temporality of crisis. In Cunningham's book, Jim imagines revolutionary time as future oriented, promising rewards of money, time, and equality. But then the revolution fails, and the book's real shock is the similarity between revolutionary and barnyard temporality. After the revolution has failed, Mack is left reeling—he has neither protected his family nor provided for their future, and time starts to break down on him: "Time had been grinding by like it always did when all at once it slipped a cog, caught again, and the grinding went on; but hours had passed, and the sun had whirled half around the world, and there it was high in the sky. Even the dew had dried up" (205). His daughter is dead, the revolution isn't going to happen, and Mack is drunk and waiting to be arrested. Even after these crises, though, time is "grinding by" just the same as before the rebellion. Then it slips, accelerates. Not only is this a break in time, but it feels like something new. Jim noticed something similar, however, on the very first page of the novel. Mack has "little dead spells," and the narrator describes their prevalence: "Everybody has little flickers of death, but with an old person the blank spaces are long and apparent" (3). Mack's postrevolution blackout, then, might be seen—alongside the similarities between revolution and barnyard—as a continuation of rural temporality. And it is. Yet over the course of the novel, as temporalities accumulate and come into conflict, these dead spells have become more pronounced. The rebellion doesn't cause a major change in Mack's "little dead spells," but it does speed them up just a little, making him seem older and causing him to wear out much like the fields in FSA photographs and the Joads themselves in *The Grapes of Wrath.*

This acceleration recalls the experience of the farm in *The Home Place.* When Clyde Muncy returns to his aunt and uncle's Nebraska farm after many years away, he tells his wife Peggy how the farm used to be a fine, productive place. In response, she asks, "What happened?" Clyde replies, "You wear out. . . . Out here is where people and things wear out. You keep winding it up till one day the ticker stops" (19). In this situation, wearing out is a slow process that happens over time, due to repeated use. It is exactly what happens to Mack—and what Jim Tetley fears—in *The Green Corn Rebellion.* In the rural space, failure is inevitable, even accelerated. While this acceleration is related to the countryside modernizing, it highlights the characters' fatigue. The modernity of *The Home Place* is neither acute nor startling. It is a duller version, seen in the economics of poverty, the pressures on young people to leave Lone Tree, and Muncy's forced exit from New York.

Rather than the familiar story of Okies on the move west, this novel represents the lives of those who stayed alongside the "small town expatriates" (Morris 59) who might just come back. Rather than focus on moments of creation or crisis, then, Morris's post-Depression photo-text turns to the narratives that emerge after long-term decline. Given that this novel portrays circulation rather than escape, the concept of wear becomes central, and it features in several contemporary reviews. Charles Poore, for example, notes how Morris "likes to emphasize the gnarled and the worn, the tired and the spent, with the kind of buried romanticism that always goes to make a forthright realist" (13). With his nod toward Clyde Muncy's romantic notion of a farm where he spent a few summers, Poore gestures toward the value that Morris places on coping with wear. Similarly, William Dooley notes the "peculiar charm" that Morris develops by describing "the earthy atmosphere of the place—the much used farm buildings, the house with its sparse but oddly decorative furnishings (not antique, not even quaint), just old and comfortably worn" (BR5).

Morris's representation of objects that are "comfortably worn" indicates how the novel counters discourses of obsolescence. According to Daniel Abramson, manufacturers in the 1920s increasingly offered new models of their products in order to drive consumers to purchase them before they wore out: "Habits of sustained use, of keeping and maintaining an object as long as possible, were superseded by forces of expendability and convenience, novelty, prosperity, and marketing" (32). In some ways, the Great Depression shifted the ways that people participated in consumer culture, which can be seen in New Deal programs that encouraged subsistence farming partly by restricting loans for the purchase of tractors and other machinery.[9] Such policies are often read as nostalgic, an attempt to excavate and return to past practices. Part of the reason they appear retrograde is that planned obsolescence places a continual forward pressure on the market; actions that resist this socioeconomic trend thus also remind one of it. Accordingly, Babette Tischleder and Sarah Wasserman argue that "the past, present, and future all inhere in the obsolete" (9). While *The Home Place* does not represent heightened consumerism, understanding obsolescence's "temporal incongruities" (Tischleder and Wasserman 9) clarifies how the novel still gestures toward these discourses. On some occasions, the relationship is overt, as when Uncle Harry complains about low-quality, ersatz rubber—which he calls "Airsuds" (5). Generally, as with the many instances of threadbare carpets, worn-out shoes, and other objects, Morris's reference to obsolescence is more subtle, seen through the way those worn, old-fashioned objects refer not only to the objects' uses but also to their need to be repaired or replaced.

Morris does not simply represent a series of well-worn household items and farm implements. For characters, *The Home Place* recounts the effects of lives lived under constant strain. This is as true for Clyde and Peggy as it is for Uncle Harry and Aunt Clara. Still, there were differences between rural and urban experience in the 1930s; Deborah Fitzgerald argues that while city folks were surprised at the onset of the Great Depression, farmers had "endured worse" and felt New Deal programs offered some relief (185). Still, according to David Danbom, rural people faced increased economic precarity and, by necessity, "retrenched heroically" (199). The perception that country people such as Uncle Harry and Aunt Clara had "retrenched" and "endured" suggests why the Muncys may have wanted to return to the country. In this novel, when Morris describes the effects of fatigue on people and objects, he shows that living through instability and coping with hardship are valuable traits:

> Out here you wear out, men and women wear out, the sheds and the houses, the machines wear out, and every ten years you put a new seat in the cane-bottomed chair. Every day it wears out, the nap wears off the top of the Axminster. The carpet wears out, but the life of the carpet, the Figure, wears in. The holy thing, that is, comes naturally. Under the carpet, out here, is the floor. After you have lived your own life, worn it out, you will die your own death and it won't matter. It will be all right. It will be ripe, like the old man.
>
> Nothing happens to a man overnight but sometimes what has been happening for years, every day of his life, happens suddenly. You open a door, or maybe you close it, and the thing is done. It happens. That's the important thing. (176)

The constant strain of repeated use makes the characters and the farms break down. Maintenance is clearly part of this world, as some objects—like the cane-bottomed chair—can be repaired, emphasizing how the ruling experience is one of aging and wear. This passage also makes clear that alongside the wearing out of men and women, sheds and houses, there's also a fair amount of wearing in. For instance, the Axminster carpet starts to reveal the way that people have lived in that space. Since the wearing in doesn't stop the wearing out, but actually intensifies it, this passage shows how Morris values fatigue. Indeed, he finds it a "holy thing" that demonstrates a connection to the place and to the action, one that imparts meaning through repetition and wear.

The book's photos verify this kind of valuable fatigue as well as the accumulative, sometimes contradictory temporality described above. One representative photo, a worn-out pair of shoes on a kitchen chair, illustrates the text on the facing page, in which Peggy and Clyde are looking through their neighbor Ed's house and she watches Clyde "stare at the old man's shoes" (143). Throughout the book, only some of the photos illustrate the prose, but tonally they tell a similar story of worn-out people and things that are being valued as objects worthy of attention. Bearing this out, Joseph Wydeven claims that the motive for these photos is "salvage" (40). In the photograph of Ed's shoes, you can see the various kinds of wear in the nap of the carpet, the edges of the chair, and the creases of the shoes. While the shoes bear witness to all their past uses, the photo's composition also implies the future, that they remain ready for use. Except they are sitting on the chair—these shoes are not ready to be put on so much as that they're ready to be moved. There's no one in this photo to use them, however, partly because Ed has just died. In this photograph and the accompanying passage, the shoes gesture toward their future uses, but they also remind Clyde of Ed, of the things he did, and of the fact that he's no longer there. Using Morris's language, the shoes are worn out, but his life has been worn in to them.

Ed's absence thus refers to that last part of the quotation: something has happened suddenly that seems as if it has been happening for years. On the farm, masculine failure accelerates; that's apparent in *Poor White* when Hugh's imaginative abilities decline after he moves into the Butterworth farmhouse, and in *The Story of a Country Boy* Chris Bennett's identity as a "country boy" gets him pushed out of the factory and back to the farm. In *The Green Corn Rebellion,* time speeds up on Mack McGee, and in *The Home Place,* "people and things wear out" despite the care put in to take care of them. The result, formally, is a way in which these Midwestern farm novels create a kind of *old-fashioned modernism* that, as I will discuss in the next section, alters the possibilities and expectations for rural men of the Midwest. In different ways, each book disrupts available temporalities and challenges the representational politics of formal modernism. In this way, they develop a sense of rural masculinity that may feel dated but that nonetheless foregrounds the anxieties of American modernity.

## UNSETTLED MASCULINITIES

The two main male characters in *The Home Place,* Clyde and Uncle Harry, represent different aspects of American masculinity in the mid-twentieth century. Morris shows those differences through their generations, geographies, and jobs: Harry is an old Nebraska farmer, while Clyde is a younger New York writer. Based on these descriptions, it seems that Clyde will be the book's example of modern masculinity and Uncle Harry's role will be more outdated. There's no doubt that Harry fits a number of rural stereotypes—he's a subsistence farmer, resistant to changing his ways, and he's alternately a grumpy and rascally old man. Beyond that, in Clyde's imagination, Harry stands in for the farm, which Clyde had pictured nostalgically before his return. But of course it's not quite so simple. Alan Trachtenberg argues that "for Wright Morris, the pastoral dream-lament has lost its integrity" ("Craft" 42), and the many contradictions in Harry's character suggest how Morris writes against a rose-colored Midwest pastoralism. For instance, beyond his stereotypical characteristics, Harry is resolutely modern in his economic engagement, not only because he endured the Great Depression but also because he is linked to broad economic networks through selling his grain and using modern industrial products such as ersatz rubber.

As for Clyde, he is clearly a modern man, a novelist who has migrated to the city from his country home, achieved some success, and is again considering a cross-country move. Like Harry, Clyde has felt the effects of the Great Depression, but his response is to escape rather than shelter in place, as Uncle Harry has done. When Clyde returns to Lone Tree, he doesn't fit in quite as easily as he hoped he would. Once he and Peggy decide not to rent Ed's house, he asks if Harry and Clara can keep the kids for a few days while they go look elsewhere. Clyde says, "We'll pick up the kids on our way home." When Harry replies, "Where'd that be?" (174), he tacitly accepts that Clyde doesn't quite fit in Lone Tree. Unsettled by post–World War II housing shortages, he is seeking another place where he will feel comfortable living, working, and raising his family. In this, he is similar to many of the other characters I have examined in this book—Hugh McVey wanders until he finds a place that inspires his invention, Chris Bennett hangs onto his rural identity until he gets sent back to the farm, and, as I examine in the next chapter, Sandy Rodgers fits most clearly into spaces that combine the rural and urban aspects of his childhood.

Clyde's slight discomfort in a place where he expected relief echoes Morris's formal approach to this photo-text novel. Unlike *Poor White* and *The Story of a Country Boy, The Home Place* does not have precise passages that are easily labeled modernist. Rather, the book exhibits a dull unsettled-ness in its combination of photos and written text. In each spread, one side has the novel's text and on the facing page is a photograph. The photo is sometimes on the recto, sometimes on the verso, with no discernible pattern. The unsettled-ness in the relationship between photos and text lies in the way that the photographs illustrate the text, but only occasionally or indirectly. Reviewer Charles Poore recognizes the disjunctions in this relationship, commenting that Morris "has put together—fused is perhaps too strong a word—fiction and photography" (13).

Despite some readers' struggles with the oblique relationship between Morris's photographs and prose, *The Home Place* achieved critical acclaim, perhaps because it has clear antecedents in Great Depression documentary texts. Margaret Bourke-White and Erskine Caldwell's 1937 *You Have Seen Their Faces* preceded Morris's first published photo-text, "The Inhabitants," which appeared in *New Directions* in 1940 alongside an excerpt of James Agee and Walker Evans's 1941 *Let Us Now Praise Famous Men.* Morris continued his photo-text project with a book-length version of *The Inhabitants* in 1946 and then, supported by a Guggenheim Fellowship, took most of the photographs for *The Home Place* in 1947. In a *Chicago Tribune* review, August Derleth alludes to the photo-texts' aesthetic of Depression-era hardship, writing that *The Inhabitants* and *The Home Place* are "excellent documentaries, both skilfully blending photografy and prose, both evocative of a way of life in these United States" (G6). Like Derleth, many of the novel's reviewers comment favorably on the combination of photographs and text, which "lends distinction" (Canby 12) to this "brave and beautiful book" (Morgan 237). Some combine praise and lament, finding *The Home Place* a "remarkable experiment in the novel . . . which, unfortunately, the general public stubbornly refused to try to understand" (J. Jackson A5).

While there is clearly a documentary impulse in Morris's photographs, that's not precisely how they function, either on their own or within the novel. As for the photographs themselves, Roy Stryker, the head of photography at the FSA, declined to hire him because he "was puzzled by the lack of people" in Morris's photographs (Wydeven 7). In the context of *The Home Place,* the photos' purpose is only partly illustrative, which causes some hesitation among critics and the public. Morris scholar David Madden suggests that readers "had been confused as to the proper relationship between pictures and text. They expected a journalistic relationship; the author intended a poetic one" (49). In such a poetic relationship, contradictions abound—ambiguities must be interpreted and inconsistencies explained. *The Home Place*'s first three photographs illustrate the inconsistency within Morris's use of images. The first, of Uncle Harry repairing an inner tube (fig. 9), illustrates the action of the novel. The second, of a board lying on the ground, illustrates the setting of the conversation recounted on the facing page but not any of the objects they discuss. The third photo, of a horse-drawn corn planter (fig. 10), does show Uncle Harry's farm but

of *The Home Place* sets the expectation that other photos will perform the same way. The second photo challenges this expectation somewhat. This photo shows a board lying on the ground next to some dried plant matter. There is a broken tool handle on top of the board and a cluster of mint to the side. In some ways, this photo illustrates the narrative. On the facing page, Muncy's son finds a croquet ball half-buried in the yard, and this photo does depict a yard. The text also refers to chickens scratching, and there's a hint of some chicken tracks in the photo. Joseph Wydeven argues that *The Home Place* relies "a great deal on photographic 'verification' and on textual undermining of this verification; both deliberately challenge visual assumptions through probing of the very evidence the books provide" (68). This is another way to look at what Madden called the "poetic" relationship between photos and prose. The photograph appears to verify the idea of the Nebraska farm as well as the novel's story, but it also causes a moment of hesitation, the ambiguity questioning whether photo and text are as unified as they appear to be.

*The Home Place* thus grinds photo and text against each other, but it does so in a fairly light way. Sometimes there's humor in it, such as when the characters are talking about the small town of Lone Tree and the photo is of a single tree. More often, though, the photos depict a farm implement or building or feature a close-up of a structure, product, or tool. The juxtapositions between photo and text aren't shocking, but they don't always match up nicely. Combined with the nearly complete absence of humans (other than photographs on the wall, Uncle Harry is the only person pictured in the book), these oblique relations enable commentary such as that of Walter Prichard Eaton's review: "The photographs are hard and vivid and suggestive, but whether in the combination story-telling they will gain 'character' from the warm human narrative, or whether the narrative will lose warmth from their coldly brutal reality will no doubt depend on the individual reader" (E4). The tone of *The Home Place*—what makes it exemplify a certain strand of old-fashioned modernism—is created by the way Morris takes two types of old-fashioned texts and puts them together to highlight the modernity of both. On one side of the spread, we have a conventionally told story about a man visiting his childhood home. On the other side, Morris places photos of outdated agricultural machinery, old boards, or individual ears of corn that have not been picked by a modern combine harvester.

The tension between photos and text that partially illustrate and partially complicate each other indicates how *The Home Place* develops a more complete picture of each. The book's third photo (fig. 10) shows a horse-drawn corn planter sitting in a dry farmyard and, in the background, parts of a wagon, a barn, and another building. In a time of tractor farming, this photo seems to present a fairly straightforward example of old-fashioned rurality. The prose, however, complicates this expectation. Based on the pattern of the first two photos, it might be expected that the text on the facing page will refer directly to the planter, or perhaps more obliquely to planting season, mechanical repairs, or solo field labor. Instead, the text continues to discuss the croquet ball and the inner tube as Clyde and his son walk down the path to the water pump. This photo does not illustrate the narrative, as none of the objects mentioned in the prose are pictured in the photo. This photograph has a different purpose than the previous two. Rather than verifying the accompanying narrative, the old-fashioned planter and ramshackle barnyard appear more broadly to supply evidence of a declining, outdated rurality.

Focusing on the relationship between text and photo counters this sense of rural decline. Both the story and the photos depict old-fashioned people or outdated materials, and the combination highlights their shared modernity. The writing addresses the complicated social relations between city and country but privileges neither space. Morris portrays Harry as close-minded and Clyde's son as culturally impoverished, but each is limited because of the structures of modern society; if *The Home Place* represents decline, it is happening throughout the United States rather than exclusively in the country or the city. Furthermore, even the corn planter's steel wheels show the modernity of the rural space—first, by alluding to their initial manufacture and, second, by negation (there's no need for an inner tube on this machine), they refer to the manufacture and distribution of synthetic rubber.[11] As individual objects and stories, these do not appear to suggest that Lone Tree, Nebraska, is a particularly modern place. The corn planter is an outdated piece of equipment, and Uncle Harry's resistance to city life and his dissatisfaction with the "Airsuds" rubber (5) tells a common story about a grumpy old man. The pairing, however, reveals not only the complexity and far reach of American wartime economics but also Harry's flexibility in negotiating the challenges of modern America.

Fig. 10. Untitled, 1947 (corn planter), in *The Home Place*. Photograph by Wright Morris. Collection Center for Creative Photography. © 2003 Center for Creative Photography, Arizona Board of Regents.

Clyde forgives Uncle Harry more easily than his cousin Ivy does. As a young, educated farmer, Ivy blames Harry for the state of plains agriculture: "It's men like him . . . who made this goddam dust bowl" (25). Unlike Clyde, Ivy has remained in Nebraska and attended the state agricultural college. His complaint, then, refers to the outdated countryside of these photos and insinuates that he would farm the land differently. It links him to narratives of rehabilitation and productivity that echo New Deal policies and cultural texts like Rothstein's *Fighting the Drought and Dust with Irrigation*. According to Ivy, the rural space is a worn-out failure; Uncle Harry and men like him are the reason that the plains can no longer serve as the nation's breadbasket. In some ways, Morris facilitates this blame. For instance, the book's final image shows Uncle Harry turning back to the barn, away from both Clyde and the audience. But this difference between Ivy and Harry does not result in a predetermined story of modernization in which Harry will get left behind.

Instead, Morris presents the Muncy men using their knowledge to manage life on the land around Lone Tree, and this is what draws them together. Leon Howard writes that in *The Home Place,* "The people who had not gone away had endured hardships that made men" (12). While Ivy is right that irresponsible farming practices contributed to the severity of the Great Depression, *The Home Place* also opposes a reading based in rural decline. It does so partly through Clyde's narrative response: "True enough—but it was men like him who were still around when the dust blew away. As my wife said, there's always something about an old fool" (25). These sentences are presented without quotations marks, suggesting that Clyde does not audibly respond to Ivy. Even in his head, though, Clyde does not dispute Ivy's claim, and he doesn't take issue with the facts of rural or masculine failure. But he does emphasize survivorship through the way Uncle Harry copes with the challenges of modern life. Whether these challenges are burned-up ground, inferior quality materials, or his prodigal nephew with city-raised kids, Uncle Harry responds by plugging on, and Morris implies that both Ivy and Clyde Muncy will have to do the same as they try to, respectively, rehabilitate the worn-out plains or return to Nebraska after the failure of losing a home. This book thus unsettles masculinity by pointing out the differences among Clyde, Ivy, and Harry, but it also draws a key similarity between them, in that each character must persistently negotiate the struggles of modern rural life.

Lone Tree, Nebraska, does not conform to a nostalgic vision of the pastoral countryside. It is not a place where a yeoman farmer tills a productive plain and, on Saturdays, purchases gingham at the general store. Still, this pastoral expectation wends through the book, and Morris's rejection of pastoralism becomes bound up with the actual and expected failures of men. In *The Home Place,* Clyde and Peg Muncy hope that a pastoral life will soothe them. Beyond that, Morris's photos seem to anticipate a reader who likewise expects to see the green, green grass of home. Morris declines, over and over, to fulfill that expectation, and the book becomes a fatiguing experience for the reader, mimicking the worn-out land and old-fashioned farm implements as well as the economic struggles felt by Clyde, Uncle Harry, and other characters throughout the novel. The book's structure bears out this fatigue. Near the end, as the family are discussing relatives and family history, the narrative breaks down: there is less text on each page and the amount of narrative declines in favor of increased dialogue. On a subject—family history—in which the stories should be known and settled, Morris instead shows the challenge of a coherent life on the plains.

Like the losses represented by the Muncy men, and by Mack McGee and Jim Tetley in *The Green Corn Rebellion,* such failures feature in many of the novels I examine in this book. Anderson's *Poor White* pits mechanical modernity against communal labor, and by the end many characters lose their jobs. In Powell's *The Story of a Country Boy,* the protagonist's faulty expectations lead to his dramatic downfall. And Hughes's *Not Without Laughter* finds its protagonist unable to sustain a modern black identity until he leaves his Kansas town. Like many other works of regional modernism—including Willa Cather's *My Ántonia,* Jean Toomer's *Cane,* and Ernest Hemingway's *In Our Time*—these books construct a modern rural masculinity that depends on the inability to achieve a kind of picturesque, old-fashioned pastoralism. This version of modern masculinity doesn't always feel modernist, and it's certainly not a celebration of masculine achievement. If anything, these books share in recognizing economic struggle as a facet of American masculinity. One of their key projects is to think through the affective experience of that struggle. Maybe that's the real modernist move here, to think about the conflicts between seemingly old-fashioned elements—not as something from which to break or transcend, but as a formative part of modernity. In this reading, regional modernism germinates from fissures within realism and naturalism, and modern rural masculinity grows from the fractures caused by our failed expectations of and in the countryside.

# CHAPTER FOUR

# "A DREAMY-EYED BOY"

## *Chicago, Race Records, and Regional Black Masculinity*

> The ideas for my first novel had been in my head for a long time. I wanted to write about a typical Negro family in the Middle West, about people like those I had known in Kansas. But mine was not a typical Negro family.
>
> But I thought maybe I had been a typical Negro boy.
>
> —Langston Hughes, *The Big Sea,* 1940

"Chicago now!" thinks Sandy Rodgers, the protagonist of Langston Hughes's 1930 novel, *Not Without Laughter,* as he rides away from his boyhood home in small-town Kansas. After Sandy's grandmother dies, his mother sends for him to come live with her on the south side of Chicago. As the overnight train crosses Missouri and Illinois, "Stanton, Sandy's Kansas home, was back in the darkness, and the train sped towards the great center where all the small-town boys in the whole Middle West wanted to go" (276). In many ways, Hughes writes Sandy's story as a typical one for black Americans in the early twentieth century. Sandy moves from country to city, participating in the Great Migration that amplified the black populations of northern industrial cities. As Sandy travels toward Chicago, Hughes also highlights one of the great tropes of rural life: its darkness, a lack of illumination that suffers in comparison to the desirable, idealized city.

Even so, Hughes does not simply represent the Midwestern small town as an unenlightened, isolated backwater. It is "back in the darkness" at this moment, but Hughes links Stanton with communities across the country. Sandy's mother has lived in Detroit, Toledo, and Chicago; his aunt has traveled all across the country; and his grandmother's elderly neighbor mentions her "chillen an' grandchillen all in Chicago an' St. Louis an' Wichita, an' nary chick nor child left with me in de house" (35). Hughes makes these connections visible through railroad lines, letters between family members, the travel of jazz and blues musicians, and the distribution patterns of newspapers like the *Crisis* and the *Chicago Defender.* In *Not Without Laughter,* Hughes imagines black life in the twentieth century as a network of people and places that exists outside the plantation-to–New York, south-to-north pipeline that he describes elsewhere as the "conventional" story of the Harlem Renaissance ("Writes" 20).

*Not Without Laughter*'s version of modern black life thus depends upon the accumulation of people, places, and stories. Hughes wrote in his first autobiography, *The Big Sea,* that he wanted to depict "a typical Negro family" (303), and he populates *Not Without Laughter* with familiar character types. Sandy's family alone includes a washerwoman, a domestic servant, two blues performers, a manual laborer, and a middle-class clubwoman. The novel includes a wide range of black experience—the "picturesque" alongside the horrific, the old-fashioned as well as the modern—as it follows Sandy throughout his youth in Stanton. Introducing a 2018 edition of the novel, Angela Flournoy writes, "Sandy is an ideal protagonist for a novel so interested in place and culture—an observant boy with a penchant for finding the extraordinary in the ordinary" (xii), and the novel is structured as an episodic version of boyhood development focusing on ordinary experiences at the schoolhouse, pool hall, barbershop, and the homes of his grandmother Hager and aunt Tempy. This combination of character and setting inspires opposing reactions among Hughes's contemporaries. For instance, a *New York Times* review praises the novel's "excellent contrast in character" ("'Not Without'" 56), and V. F. Calverton gushes, "Here is the Negro in his most picturesque form—the blues-loving Negro, the spiritual-singing Negro, the exuberant, the impassioned, the irresponsible Negro, the Negro of ancient folk-lore and romantic legend" (59). More drily, Mary Ovington comments, "Mr. Hughes' material is old enough" (13).

Much of the scholarship on *Not Without Laughter* addresses its gender politics, clustering around the influence of Sandy's family. His aunt Harriett has gained a great deal of attention because, as Cheryl A. Wall claims, she is one of the first blueswomen represented in literature (39). Kimberly J. Banks argues that Harriett's profession challenges gender norms and that "her objectified condition becomes the mediating point for Sandy's sexual subjectivity" (88). According to Banks, Harriett functions as a model for her nephew because of her public performances as well as the way her identity shifts in response to Hager's dominating influence. Marlon B. Ross also focuses on Sandy's growth in the absence of Jimboy, his wandering father. Contextualizing *Not Without Laughter* with other black male coming-of-age novels of the period, Ross finds that, "depending primarily on women for their gender identity, these boys develop a subtle orientation to the world that strands them between feminine and masculine as conventionally opposed principles of experience and outlook" (330). I share Ross's contention that the novel seeks to balance masculine and feminine influences on Sandy, and I agree with Banks that "the novel is not about fathers teaching sons how to be men" (86). But I build on these readings by expanding the complex of influences acting on Sandy and considering how his gender identity develops in relation to the spaces and communities beyond his family.

Hughes places Sandy both within and outside hegemonic masculine ideals by proposing a range of local and national influences on Sandy's developing identity. In this chapter, I explore the space of the novel, as setting Sandy's coming-of-age in a small Midwestern town outside conventional Harlem Renaissance patterns is one of its supposed innovations. In the words of one reviewer, *Not Without Laughter* "marches into a virgin field and establishes a new frontier for the branch of American letters known as Negro literature" (T. Lewis 9). I argue that Hughes establishes the rural Midwest as fertile ground for black modernity. In Stanton, people, goods, and narratives intersect to form a dynamic regional network. Sandy's development of a regional black masculinity thus requires him not only to balance a variety of masculine and feminine influences but also to accumulate stereotypical and modern characteristics that he cultivates both in his rural hometown and when he travels to Chicago.

Beginning with the novel's final moments, this chapter shows how Hughes constructs a regional masculine identity by combining Harriett's material support with the way that the Chicago streets evoke rural spaces through sound. This geographical blurring echoes Hughes's treatment of the Stanton dancehall as a modernist space where the material and the ephemeral intermingle, where music and social behaviors signify rurality, urbanity, the Midwest, and other regions. Such scenes are somewhat surprising, given the way Hughes populates the novel with stereotypes and folk figures. Ultimately, however, they contribute to modern life in Stanton because Hughes folds folk figures into a network of modern gender expectations, cultural mobility, and physical travel. In so doing, *Not Without Laughter* represents a regional form of black masculinity that engages with local as well as national ideals and is not limited to old-fashioned or modern forms. This reading of Hughes's novel brings together my larger arguments that literary treatments of early twentieth-century Midwestern masculinities seek a middle ground balancing divergent spaces, economic functions, and narrative trajectories. For instance, this chapter builds on chapter 2's focus on rural material modernities, echoes chapter 3's attention to the structural inequities of Midwestern life, and advances chapter 1's interest in the uneasy coexistence of rural and urban elements within the same space. But it also shifts those conversations by addressing the urban space more fully than chapter 1's discussion of *Poor White*'s small town and considering how black masculinities both construct and contribute to regional culture.

## GREAT CENTER, DUSTY STREETS

Sandy's expectations of Chicago are based on popular images of it as the "great center," a city of light amid the "the darkness" of Stanton and the small-town Midwest (276). Sandy imagines Chicago to realize the promise of urban futurity, an image evoking the city's association with the 1893 Columbian Exposition.[1] Predictably, his experience of Chicago falls short of that utopian image: "He hadn't expected the great city to be monotonous and ugly like this and he was vaguely disappointed. No towers, no dreams come true! Where were the thrilling visions of grandeur he had held? Hidden in dusty streets? Hidden in the long, hot alleys through which he could see at a distance the tracks of the elevated trains?" (278–279). While Sandy has been told that Chicago is "a wicked city" (276), he is unprepared for its lack of material beauty. Where he imagines skyscrapers and dreams, he finds dust; where he expects centrality, he finds periphery.

Sandy's expectations for Chicago and his disappointment upon arrival gesture toward the relationship historians find in the early twentieth century between Chicago and comparatively rural communities throughout the Midwest. While Don Kirschner depicts rural migration to the city in terms of stark difference, Jane Adams describes more frequent and fluid transitions. Timothy Spears argues that, because Chicago was growing at this time, there remains "the possibility that, for some migrants, the difference between city and country was slight, and that the movement from one to the other represented a natural, matter-of-fact extension of interests that were first developed in the hinterland" (xvi). Despite such ambiguities, Chicago is often conceived centrally, in terms of its ownership of the surrounding area. For example, even in his excellent study of the connections between Chicago and the rural Midwest, William Cronon portrays the region as "a White City and its thriving countryside" (369). Robert Lewis echoes Cronon's possessive pronoun with his study of "Chicago and its region," which posits the city as the "control center" for the regional economy (7).

Such perceptions of ownership contribute to further ambivalence in images of Chicago and the countryside. According to Cronon, "At the two extremes of the urban axis were the White City and the Dark: the city as pinnacle of civilization versus the city as abyss of moral despair. At opposite poles of the rural axis were similar images: the country as pastoral utopia versus the country as stultifying backwater" (364). These perspectives on the rural and urban Midwest highlight the processes of modernization that were happening in rural spaces in the Midwest and across the nation. Hughes shows these shifts as Stanton's black citizens try to maintain a sense of local community while also providing young men and women the opportunity to travel and improve their socioeconomic standing. In *Not Without Laughter,* such tensions turn into ambivalence. For instance, when Sandy is exposed to the city as a space of possibility, he is also told, "I can only hope Chicago won't ruin you" (276).

Aesthetically and geographically, Sandy's arrival in Chicago recalls the Windy City's development after the 1871 fire that destroyed almost three square miles of the city's downtown area. According to Jon Teaford, commercial activity was largely centralized in downtown Chicago, while residences were located some distance away: "Chicago may have been famed for its tall buildings, yet throughout most of the city the horizontal prevailed over the vertical. . . . In the Illinois metropolis and in other heartland centers mass transit allowed workers to move farther from the core" (77). Between 1900 and 1920, the US Census reports that Chicago's population grew by almost 60 percent, as the city added more than one million residents. Once Sandy arrives, his view—dusty streets and alleys, the el in the distance—illustrates how the uneven development of urban spaces fits into the larger narrative of the increasing size, wealth, and centralization of urbanity in American culture. *Not Without Laughter* seems to exemplify this narrative, as Sandy travels from country to city and experiences its peripheral, impoverished spaces. In this reading, despite Chicago's evident failings, Sandy's move there fulfills its images of centrality and desirability, and his distant view of the city's iconic rail lines reinforces both the city's modernity and the wealth disparities created by its land use patterns.

Despite its affinities with American urbanization narratives, *Not Without Laughter* does not simply report on the increasing importance of the urban space. It also does not detail the inherent contradictions of ruralized subject positions when they are moved to the city, unlike Dawn Powell's *The Story of a Country Boy,* which I discuss in chapter 2. Rather, in the novel's three Chicago-based chapters (of thirty total), Hughes thinks through how Sandy and other rural characters can balance the identities they developed in Stanton with new possibilities found in the city. By imagining an urban space that juxtaposes Sandy's "thrilling visions of grandeur" with the "dusty streets" that also could have been found in Stanton (278), Hughes creates a narrative that runs against the patterns of urbanization. Hughes constructs many of the novel's spaces as simultaneously urban and rural. He avoids incorporating rural people and economics into urban teleologies, instead imagining rural and urban spaces that are equally modern, and in which each includes elements of the other. In this regard, Hughes's approach is similar to Sherwood Anderson's in *Poor White,* which I discuss in chapter 1. Of course, *Poor White* ends with the images and sounds of a modern rural space, while *Not Without Laughter* closes with a scene of city life in which rural and urban elements coexist. By muddying the signs of urban industrialism with those of rural life, neither novel accepts urban futurity as an inescapable endpoint.

Because it resists urban teleologies, *Not Without Laughter* does not focus on the processes of widespread industrialization but on managing its effects. Those effects can be seen in its juxtaposition of the city's outskirts with a marvel of modern engineering and in the urban experiences of the novel's rural characters. For example, after Sandy and Annjee see Harriett sing, Harriett is mortified to learn that Sandy has left school and is working to contribute to the family income: "'Then you'll stay in school!' Harriett affirmed, still looking at Annjee. 'You surely wouldn't want him stuck in an elevator for ever—just to help you, would you, sister?'" (298). Citing high rents, Annjee's meager earnings, and Sandy's dead-end job, Hughes marks the black experience of Chicago with the struggle to survive despite the initial promise of urban life. Through a majority of the three Chicago-focused chapters, the city is closer to Tempy's description of it as a "wicked city" (276) than the hopeful visions of other Stanton residents. But this passage provides a more positive side of the urban experience when Harriett offers to give them the equivalent of Sandy's pay as an elevator operator so he can go to school. Because Harriett makes a good income from musical performance, she can provide some money to Annjee and Sandy and therefore mitigate some of the limitations caused by uneven urban economics.

The struggles that make it difficult for Sandy to get an education also hinder his ability to embody common masculine ideals. In this passage, however, Harriett's support allows him to become a version of the oft-studied "self-made man." George Kent separates these issues, arguing that "this folk sense of making something out of oneself has a lasting impact upon Sandy, but there are also available to him the jazz and blues tradition through his father Jimboy and his Aunt Harriett" (25). Throughout most of *Not Without Laughter,* Sandy's educational achievements happen apart from (or despite) his father's and aunt's influences. Here, though, he explicitly brings the two together. Harriett isn't given to moralizing, but still she charges, "He's gotta be what his grandma Hager wanted him to be—able to help the black race, Annjee!" (298). In this episode at the close of the novel, Hughes does not simply juxtapose Harriett's blues performance with Booker T. Washington–esque self-making; he explicitly joins them. That combination underscores two key issues within the novel: it evidences the material and cultural influences of the blues and suggests that Sandy's masculinity is formed communally, with the guidance of both men and women.

For Hughes, sound offers a method to imagine a balanced modernity for both Sandy and the novel. This approach can be seen in his representation of Harriett's blues performance in Chicago and, as I will discuss in the next section, a traveling jazz band in Stanton. In the novel's closing scene, Hughes focuses on street sounds. As Sandy and Annjee return from dinner after Harriett's concert, they hear a church choir: "Vibrant and steady like a stream of living faith, their song filled the whole night" (299). On Chicago's south side, voice merges with space, "as the deep volume of sound rolled through the open door" and then fills the urban streets (299). Much as Hager's wishes and Harriett's money come from religion and the blues, the choir's song fills the Chicago streets after a blues concert. Regarding this scene, specifically, Steven Tracy notes how "the oral blues tradition supports the gaining of literacy, especially in one like Sandy, who seems able to accept the power and beauty of the blues side by side with an appreciation of the spirituals" (28).

Sandy's development combines these two historically important sound-making traditions in African American communities. Furthermore, this scene highlights the ways they cross regional boundaries and wield significant influence in both rural and urban settings. In the final moments of *Not Without Laughter,* gospel and the blues determine his experience of the Chicago streets. Because the choir's "song filled the whole night" (299), Sandy is reminded of spaces outside his immediate urban surroundings. That filling-in of space does not stop with State Street. It also reaches his rural hometown: to Sandy, the choir's singing feels "like Stanton . . . and the tent in the Hickory Woods" (299). By having Sandy's urban environs echo a rural tent revival, Hughes merges two distinct Midwestern spaces into a single experience. The sound of the choir's song recalls Sandy's past and projects his Harriett-supported future. It also brings rurality into a bustling urban space but avoids privileging either element, which underscores this scene's other mediations. For instance, Sandy hears the choir in the aftermath of a cabaret show, a gambling lesson, and a family argument about the merits of education and labor. Sandy's willingness to absorb each of these elements, and to negotiate their influence on him, proposes a kind of accumulative modernity that Hughes applies to this scene and across the Midwest.

But while *Not Without Laughter* explores Midwestern modernity, Chicago is not exclusively a heartland space. For example, Hughes refers to State Street's reputation as "the greatest Negro street in the world" (284), and he gestures at the city's participation in global systems of cultural and economic circulation when Sandy, Harriett, and Annjee go to a "Chinese café" to get "chop suey instead of going to a regular restaurant" (295).

Hughes accesses both national and international elements using the *Chicago Defender,* a nationally distributed African American newspaper from which Annjee reads reports of "colored troops" fighting in France (286), and Harriett invokes national race issues by expressing a desire for Sandy to "get ahead . . . in this white man's country" (298).[2] In the final scene, Hughes specifically notes Chicago's connections to other US regional spaces when the gospel choir meets "in a little Southern church on a side street" (298). This church's origins (or appearance thereof) in the US South highlight the influence of the Great Migration on Chicago. In some ways, this scene affirms the standard story of Southern blacks moving to northern industrial cities. In others, Hughes writes against that tradition: Sandy comes from the Midwest rather than the South, and the novel's prime urban space is Chicago rather than Harlem, which counters the "foregone conclusion that Harlem should become the center of the new movement" (Bone 54).

Still, while the novel's main narrative moves exclusively within the Midwest, Hughes acknowledges the pervasive influence of Southern regional culture on the experience of Midwestern African Americans. Hager's slavery (82) and the origins of the musicians in a traveling jazz band (105) figure Southern influence historically. Other episodes narrate historical experiences through affective response, such as a neighbor's terror-filled story of Mississippi whites attacking a black neighborhood for "gittin' so prosperous" (85), or Sandy's anger at a drunken white Southerner who commands him, "Boy! I want to see you dance!" (215). In both incidents, an act of Southern racial violence incites an angry response—from Harriett in the former instance and Sandy in the latter. In other scenes, aspects of Southern life evoke an entirely different emotional response. Perhaps because Sandy and Annjee associate the "little Southern church" (298) with their Midwestern home, the "vibrant" choir evokes a feeling of hopefulness: "Them old folks are still singing—even in Chicago!" (299).

Living in "the Black Belt" (279) of Chicago's South Side, Annjee and Sandy experience the city in terms of what historian James Grossman describes as the outsized cultural influence of Southern migrants: "The aromas of southern cooking, especially from the ubiquitous barbecue stands during the summer; the sounds of New Orleans jazz and Mississippi blues; styles of worship; patterns of speech: these were but the most obvious manifestations of the extent to which black southerners reshaped both their cultural heritage and their new environment" (262). According to Grossman, the Chicago experience cannot be exclusively urban because of migrants' influence on everyday sights, sounds, and smells and their continuing association with the nonurban space. Hughes's version of this referentiality relies on Annjee's nostalgia and the memory of Sandy's anger, demonstrating how *Not Without Laughter* accumulates sense experience and gestures to spaces and histories outside of its metropolitan present.

Hughes forms Sandy's modern experience in Chicago not only by highlighting the ephemeral and the momentary but also by emphasizing its simultaneity: both rural and urban, both Midwestern and Southern. The breadth of those influences develops into a version of Chicago in which urban black communities are marked by the ubiquity and intensity of sensory experience. When the narrator describes the choir, then, it is in terms of the strength of their communal voice: "High and fervently they were singing" (298), as they both fill the streets and allude to spaces and experiences outside of the metropolis. That method of exceeding the moment also extends to the novel's rural experiences. Functioning as the converse of the rural choir's effect on the Chicago streets, jazz and blues music move within and signify the modernity of the novel's rural spaces. They also enable Sandy to get his education, a combination highlighting the accumulative modernity that Hughes creates for (and in the forms of) Chicago, Stanton, and his protagonist.

## HINTERLANDS JAZZ AND THE GEOGRAPHY OF MODERNITY

*Not Without Laughter* signals its modernity through jazz music—according to one reviewer, "Once it gains its momentum it moves as swiftly as a jazz rhythm" ("'Not Without'" 56). Hughes represents, associates with, and spatializes certain sounds, and he does so in Chicago as well as in the novel's rural spaces. When a traveling jazz band performs in a Stanton dancehall, Harriett and her boyfriend Mingo sneak out against Hager's wishes. They take Sandy with them because Harriett can't leave him alone and, as Mingo says, "Better the kid than no dance" (94). As when Sandy hears the choir in Chicago, Hughes represents the music in this scene through its spatial effect: "Like a blare from hell the second encore of *Easy Rider* filled every cubic inch of the little hall with hip-rocking notes" (95). While this is a jazz and blues band rather than a church choir, the way that the music both fills its particular space and alludes to other spaces suggests how Hughes uses the sensory experience more broadly. Like so many of the other influences on Sandy, these sounds are both fleeting and formidable, and their placement in rural as well as urban spaces indicates how Hughes counters common narratives of urban modernity. Seen in this light, Sandy does not realize a modern subject position when he moves to Chicago but rather carries it with him from the rural space.

Hughes establishes the rural dancehall's modernity partly by showing the crowd's active response to the music's sounds and rhythms. When Sandy comes back into the hall after a trip to the restroom, "suddenly and without warning the cornet blared at the other end of the hall in an ear-splitting wail: 'Whaw! . . . Whaw! . . . Whaw! . . . Whaw!' and the snare-drum rolled in answer. . . . 'Ever'body shake!' cried Benbow, as a ribbon of laughter swirled round the hall" (99; ellipses in original). Hughes's incorporation of jazz and blues rhythms has been much discussed by scholars of his poetry, so the cornet's wail and the banjo's "plinka, plink, plink" (99) read as a familiar method of representing African American spaces and cultural forms, particularly when paired with Benbow's command, "Ever'body shake!" and the "ribbon of laughter [that] swirled round the hall" (99).[3] This scene takes its particularly modern form as the instruments chime in and the dancers' identities become fluid: "Couples began to sway languidly, melting together like candy in the sun as hips rotated effortlessly to the music" (99). Thus, as the music fills the space and Hughes incorporates the sounds of the instruments, the dancers change, their bodies becoming more communal than individual.

It may be expected that mutability would be essential when country people become more urban. But Hughes demonstrates that rural spaces are themselves sites of modern experience when the jazz band's performance causes the audience's identities to become fluid. According to Shane Vogel, the public intimacy of Harlem cabaret culture developed as a "collaboration between spectators and performers" (22). Hughes explicitly represents this collaboration in his poetry, as poems like "The Weary Blues" and "The Cat and the Saxophone (2 a.m.)" show how audience experience is both separate from and entwined with the musicians performing onstage. Of course, the Stanton dancehall is not precisely the same type of space as the

Harlem cabaret—they differ in layout, in their geographical locations, and in the cabaret's (and Harlem's) more outsized reputation. Hughes's rural dancehall also shares some key elements with Vogel's description of the cabaret, however, including those performer-audience collaborations that "expanded the literary and performative possibilities of blackness and sexuality through the enunciation of alternative modes of thought, feeling, and existence" (Vogel 5).

When Benbow's band creates sounds that allow the dancers to access alternative possibilities and identities, Hughes creates for Stanton a flexible modernity that accumulates many contextually based influences. Josh Kun addresses this issue in terms of the famous story of Hughes writing his early poem "The Negro Speaks of Rivers" while riding a train across the United States to join his father in Mexico: "a train ride that took Hughes not into one nation or another, but into a transnational land of the middle—where cultures and identities have historically existed in a state of contestation, conflict, and hybridity" (153). Kun focuses on Hughes's transnationalism, but his interest in mobility and border crossing also suggests how *Not Without Laughter's* Midwestern regionalism negotiates the conflicted middle ground of US modernity. For Kun, music does not establish "space as a fixed, static, unchanged landscape. The spaces of music may produce maps, but they are maps that move" (21–22). In the dancehall, sound fills the space, mapping and remapping through tempo and instrumentation, as "the piano lazied into a slow drag" or "the drums kept up their hard steady laughter" (99–100) and as dancers alternate between being individuals, couples, and the disembodied "shuf-shuf-shuffle of feet" (106). This kind of remapping may be seen as somewhat at odds with Andrew Berish's argument that music "creates places that are stable and familiar" (23). Indeed, Benbow's band makes the dancehall space profoundly unfamiliar to Sandy through its "ear-splitting" volume, shifting rhythms, and Sandy's fluid perception of the dancers. Slightly shifting Berish's claim, I consider the community of dancers a comforting (if still unstable) experience. In other words, while some parts of Stanton remain, in Berish's words, "stable and familiar," other aspects are more like Kun's "maps that move"—a seeming opposition that allows Hughes to negotiate the accumulative dynamics of rural modernity.

The sounds and dancers remap the dancehall space, and a separate incidence of mapping in this scene occurs through the song titles and variety of blues stylings. When the band switches songs, they play "this time just blues, not the *St. Louis,* nor the *Memphis,* nor the *Yellow Dog*—but just the plain old familiar blues, heart-breaking and extravagant, ma-baby's-gone-from-me blues" (103). Before the band begins to play "just blues," they accumulate geographies through the "Memphis" and "St. Louis" blues. By adopting place names and implying that those sounds somehow define Memphis or St. Louis, Hughes gestures to the practice of place-naming within the "race record" market. Throughout this 1920s explosion of music marketed to African American consumers, record labels advertised and sold records much like those in *Not Without Laughter.*[4] For example, a 1923 Paramount Records advertisement features several songs and groups named after places, including a record by Handy's Memphis Blues Band with the songs "St. Louis Blues" and "Yellow Dog Blues" ("Ida" A10).[5] In a similar 1923 Gennett Records advertisement, two songs are explicitly named after Kansas City, a third evokes the South more generally, and one of the advertised groups is named for a Southern city ("You Can't"; fig. 11).

Thus, even as the novel signals how it will distance itself from known blues geographies, *Not Without Laughter* evokes the actual artists, songs, and places of 1920s race records. Beyond these naming parallels, both advertisements were published in the African American newspaper the *Chicago Defender.* The *Defender* was a key player in the distribution of blues and jazz music, and Hughes explicitly mentions it in Chicago and among several different parts of Stanton's African American community. Within the novel and outside of it, the *Defender*'s widespread availability draws attention to the possible uses and limits of geographically evocative music. Such songs as Benbow's "Memphis" and "St. Louis" blues might be considered nostalgic, part of a country blues tradition, or targeted at shifting African American populations. The narrator's description of musical styles, however, also suggests that *Not Without Laughter* may treat specific geographies as necessarily parochial and perhaps not "familiar" to those outside the boundaries defined in the song.

One reason for skepticism about the geographically placed blues is that the band members remap their origins and affiliations. For example, the band asserts their Midwestern urbanity with the "big bass-drum, on which

Fig. 11. Advertisement for Gennett Records, *Chicago Defender,* 20 October 1923. Courtesy of the *Chicago Defender.*

was painted in large red letters: 'BENBOW'S FAMOUS KANSAS CITY BAND'" (102). The band members' origins complicate that assertion when the narrator describes them as "four men and a leader—Rattle Benbow from Galveston; Benbow's buddy, the drummer, from Houston; his banjoist from Birmingham; his cornetist from Atlanta; and the pianist, long-fingered, sissified, a coal-black lad from New Orleans who had brought with him an exaggerated rag-time which he called jazz" (105). Hughes here introduces an urbanized, "sissified" masculinity to the rural space; it is the first mention of "jazz" in the novel, and this passage gestures to the sounds of the concert space via the blues tradition of introducing the sidemen.[6] Furthermore, those introductions reveal that Benbow and his band come from cities but not the Midwestern one they use as a label. Rather, they come from all over the southern United States, remapping their geographical affiliations in the moment of the concert.

The band's origins seem to indicate that *Not Without Laughter*'s sense of geographical affiliation is limited to urban spaces. By referencing the race record market, however, Benbow's band and jazz performance also evoke rural spaces. Two of the major players in race records, Gennett and Paramount, were based in small towns because they were offshoots of other companies (Starr Piano and Wisconsin Chair, respectively) that depended upon rural materials and shipping lines. Their locations, recording technologies, and Gennett's claim to "the first interracial recording session in jazz history" (Kennedy and McNutt 9) associate racial, mechanical, and social modernity with rural spaces.[7] These connections were not always advertised: Paramount's ad locates that company in rural Port Washington, Wisconsin, but the Gennett ad (fig. 11) doesn't mention its main recording studio in small-town Richmond, Indiana.

The novel shows an awareness of rural affiliation nonetheless, most obviously in the location of the dance but also when it notes the touring practices of African American performers, such as when Harriett gets "some dates booked over the Orpheum circuit" (296).[8] Sandy learns of Harriett's fame from the *Defender,* soon after reading "a few of the items there concerning colored shows" (253). Hughes refers here to a type of column describing the travel of black performing artists throughout the country. A representative column from a 1925 issue of the *Defender* mentions famous performers alongside many lesser-known artists, including dancers, blues singers, comedians, and minstrel shows. The column tracks performers through theaters in major cities and along the road through several small towns (including multiple locations in Kansas) and describes one duo that was "doing the week between Argentine, Kan., and Weston, Mo." ("A Note" 7). Black musical performance draws these spaces together into a networked rural modernity including not only the dancehalls but also recording and advertising practices. For example, the column corrects an earlier report that a Gennett cornetist had signed with Paramount. Starting with Sandy browsing the newspaper, then, *Not Without Laughter*'s version of modern life accumulates African American touring and performance—along with publishing, distribution, and readership—as it generically mirrors its representation of sound as both filling and exceeding the novel's spaces.

Through the *Defender* and the dance, *Not Without Laughter* gestures to the entire field of African American musical production, including such rural companies as Gennett and Paramount. The novel thus exceeds its own pages by accumulating references to the systems and spaces of musical production and performance. Gennett's recording studio, in particular, was a key location within those systems. Built in the Whitewater River Gorge in Richmond, Indiana, the Starr Piano factory and Gennett studio are separated topographically from the town around them. As seen in postcards and photographs from the period, the Gennett studio was hidden below Richmond rather than towering above it. Early photographs of the Starr Piano Factory such as the undated *Starr Piano Factory, View from the North* show the factory and stacks of wood for constructing pianos located in a fairly desolate river gorge. The later *Starr Piano Factory, Aerial View from the South* not only presents the growing factory complex and town around it but also highlights heavy growth on the river banks right next to the factory. Postcards from the era—usually color-enhanced photographs—feature plentiful green space. *River View, South—Starr Piano Factory in Distance, Richmond, Ind.* presents a wild-looking river and banks, while *Starr Piano Co., Richmond, Indiana, 1909* emphasizes the river and *Starr Piano Co., Richmond, Indiana, 1910* isolates the factory within green hills. Almost every time the smokestack is present, whether in postcards or photographs, its ample visible smoke designates the factory's robust activity. Still, these images often suggest the factory was built in the wilderness, amplifying the sense of distance that naturally occurs because of the steep sides of the river gorge.

Rick Kennedy's history of the label emphasizes Gennett's isolation through Richmond's geographic distance from major cities: "With the Richmond studio situated in the hinterlands, its business depended on signing bands passing through town" (30). Kennedy places Richmond in the "hinterlands," echoing *Not Without Laughter* as well as Cronon's and Spears's histories of Chicago. Each of these texts implies that Chicago is—to borrow from Hughes—"the great center" of a vast periphery, set apart from "the darkness [of] the whole Middle West" (276). This language implies an affective distance also present in images of the Starr-Gennett complex. Kennedy's turn to the language of mobility similarly complicates Gennett's

Fig. 12. Photograph of Starr-Gennett complex, circa 1920s. Courtesy of the John K. Mackenzie Collection, Indiana Historical Society, M0428.

seeming isolation. The acts he describes as "passing through town" recall not only the *Chicago Defender*'s travel columns but also, more explicitly, the blues-singing "adventurers and vagabonds" of *Not Without Laughter* who "passed through Stanton on the main line" (248).

The railroad tracks ran right through the Starr-Gennett complex (fig. 12), which complicates its image as a wild, rural place. The photograph reproduced here foregrounds multiple sets of tracks, an icon of mechanical modernity that both dominates the frame and draws the eye outside it. The tracks, the factory buildings, and the truck used for on-site field recording are thereby drawn into a relationship emphasizing the different sounds and mobilities of modern rurality. This photo displays the prominence of modern socioeconomic networks in Richmond, Indiana. Despite the images and narratives that make out Richmond as a wilderness space, the factory and railroad tracks indicate how modern mechanics and economics are embedded centrally within the community. Not only do the Starr Piano Company and Gennett Records use the railroad to ship pianos, phonographs, and blues records to consumers outside of rural Indiana; the railroad also brings performers from all over the country to the Gennett studio. This factory complex in small-town Indiana is, therefore, a key site of interaction among several modes and discourses of American modernity.

Sometimes, as suggested in figure 12, those components of modern rural socioeconomics appear to fit neatly together. At others, they are more ambivalent or disruptive. For instance, at the Gennett studio, "the trains could generate enough commotion to interrupt recording sessions" (Kennedy 28). Furthermore, the unseen river just behind the camera in figure 12 recalls a scene from *Not Without Laughter* in which Sandy and his father Jimboy are fishing on the river when "the train came by behind them, pouring out a great cloud of smoke and cinders and shaking the jetty" (72). After the train passes, "sending back a hollow clatter as it shot past the flour-mills" (72), Sandy and Jimboy are left with the stillness of the "gold of wheat-fields" on the opposite bank (73). Much like its function in Wauseon, which I discuss in the introduction, the railroad creates important cultural and economic links in *Not Without Laughter.* Trains transport people and inspire "the railroad blues" (129), and Sandy dreams of becoming a "railroad engineer" (119). When Hughes juxtaposes a pastoral scene with the railroad's raucous industrial modernity, he shows their fitful coexistence. Similarly, Gennett's "hinterlands" location and its relationship to touring artists suggest an ambivalence in the modern rural space that echoes the photo's interactions between the placed buildings and the tracks' implication of movement.

The sonic ambivalences of modern rurality also inflect the dance in *Not Without Laughter,* particularly when Hughes highlights the dancehall's rural location. As Benbow's band play the "plain old familiar blues" (103), they not only inspire alienation and connection among the dancers but do so in connection with the land under their feet:

> Bodies sweatily close, arms locked, cheek to cheek, breast to breast, couples rocked to the pulse-like beat of the rhythm, yet quite oblivious each person of the other. It was true that men and women were dancing together, but their feet had gone down through the floor into the earth, each dancer's alone—down into the center of things—and their minds had gone off to the heart of loneliness, where they didn't

> even hear the words, the sometimes lying, sometimes laughing words that Benbow, leaning over the piano, was singing against this background of utterly despondent music. (103–104)

As the passage begins, dancers respond to the music, locking their bodies tightly together, each couple joined as one. The passage then turns to their loneliness and, while the rhythms unite two people's sweaty body parts, that same music's despondence creates a space in which they go alone. The music sends each dancer into themselves and outside the space of the dance into the earth. This scene universalizes a feeling of modern alienation in the rural space. Despite the bodily connections and the modern music, which could both be urbanized, Hughes describes the dancers' affective isolation in terms of the earth, a connection to the local space that he writes terrestrially. Thus, in this "little dance-hall in a Kansas town on Friday night" (105), the experience of sound creates an uneasy balance between connection and isolation, which produces the modernity of this rural space.

Whether in the Chicago streets or the Stanton dancehall, sound similarly fills and exceeds its space. In some ways, such as the representation of black bodies, the dancehall's modernity exceeds even that of Chicago. For example, when Sandy and Annjee attend Harriett's concert in Chicago, they find "a typical Black Belt audience, laughing uproariously, stamping its feet to the music, kidding the actors, and joining in the performance, too. Rows of shiny black faces, gay white teeth, bobbing heads" (291). In Stanton, Hughes curtails the fixed stereotypicality of "shiny black faces" as Sandy sleepily watches the dancers: "Dresses and suits of all shades and colors, and a vast confusion of bushy heads on swaying bodies. Faces gleaming like circus balloons—lemon-yellow, coal-black, powder-grey, ebony-black, blue-black faces; chocolate, brown, orange, tan, creamy-gold faces—the room full of floating balloon faces—Sandy's eyes were beginning to blur with sleep" (102). The diverse crowd fills the hall and interacts fluidly. In Stanton, the dancers are bound neither by the structured audience-performer relationship of the Chicago theater nor by expectations of a typified homogeneity.

While that representational difference relates to disparities between the theater and the dancehall, I contend that Hughes's rural space offers the possibility of modern plurality. The "vast confusion" of bodies and behaviors in the dancehall counters the homogeneity implied by a "typical Black Belt audience" and, more broadly, the incorporated centralization demanded by life in Chicago. There are echoes here of Houston Baker positioning the blues at a crossroads that he defines as "polymorphous and multidirectional, scene of arrivals and departures, place betwixt and between" (7). Whether sounds and stories or "arrivals and departures," this novel's accumulations produce ambivalence through diversity. George Hutchinson identifies such multiplicity as a key part of early twentieth-century African American literary culture when he claims that the foundational 1925 anthology *The New Negro* "does not hold out a single gauge of black 'authenticity'; in fact, it implicitly opposes any such gesture. It is not overwhelmingly pastoral in orientation. It does not attack, suppress, or even ignore the cultural hybridity of African America—quite the opposite" (432). *Not Without Laughter* similarly opposes a notion of singular authenticity. But it does so at a more localized level, allowing a pastoral rurality to exist alongside poverty, personal and institutional racism, and the sonic modernity of blues and jazz music. And while the novel presents the difficulty of balancing these accumulations, it also gestures toward the promise of a rural modernity that can absorb them.

Still, the dance—and Stanton more generally—is not without its stereotypical features. These start with the scene's treatment of gender. While the scene relies on actions that disrupt gender norms of the period, such as Harriett sneaking out against her mother's wishes, it also reinscribes common narratives of gender behavior. For instance, when Sandy goes to the restroom, "all the fellows were shouting loudly to one another and making fleshy remarks about the women they had danced with" (98). Furthermore, his sleepy vision of the dancers includes "girls pulling the strings—each boy a balloon by a string. Each face a balloon" (102). These boys and girls display the novel's continued fidelity to normalized versions of early twentieth-century African American behaviors and experiences, even as the characters are inspired by the music's modern intensity and Hughes challenges those stereotypes in other ways. This ambivalence shows the difficulties of performing modern black masculinity; as Hughes compiles the sounds, influences, and experiences of the rural black experience, the anxieties of Midwestern rurality are both offset and amplified.

## STANTON'S STEREOTYPES—FROM "PICTURESQUE" TO "LOW-DOWN"

While Hughes represents *Not Without Laughter*'s rural spaces as modern in some ways, the repetition of stereotypical gender behavior reveals the limits of rural modernity in this novel. So, too, does the extensive use of character types, which may be related to Hughes's desire to make the novel representative of the people he knew growing up in Kansas: "I am interested primarily in life, not local color, so I have chosen as a setting for this first novel of mine not what have become practically conventional life backgrounds for Negro tales, that is Harlem and the South, but rather what I feel is more truly American—the average, small Main Street town" ("Writes" 20). Hughes nationalizes the Midwest and clarifies that he is writing against the grain of the Harlem Renaissance. Furthermore, by opposing "life" to "local color," he describes his intention to write averages, which designates both an impulse to universalism and a sense of conflict about representing local particularities. Hughes often portrays characters' typicality through the work they perform.[9] Thus, Hager is a washerwoman and ex-slave; Jimboy, a bluesman, manual laborer, and soldier; and Annjee, a domestic worker and lodge member. Hughes forms each character using multiple types, and Sandy himself progresses from assisting his mother and grandmother to his own jobs at a barbershop and hotel. Like those of the novel's other characters, then, Sandy's identity evolves among several representative approaches to work and self-definition.

An effect of this emphasis on labor roles is that the novel includes several stereotypes of rural African Americans, a representational strategy often met with approval by white critics. In the *New York Times,* for instance, a reviewer claims that Hughes, "in turning to the country for his setting has exploited material that is even more picturesque. More than that, he has come to closer grips with this material than have his white contemporaries" ("'Not Without'" 56). Hughes's perceived fidelity to the "picturesque" life of the rural Negro relates to his own interest in representing "life" but also suggests the inclusion of Negro stereotypes that were approved by white audiences and critics.[10] Mary Ross's review in the *New York Herald Tribune* calls attention to this phenomenon, noting "a wholly understandable tendency to 'cash in' on the gifts for which the domineering caste expressed admiration" (5). This kind of representation caused problems for Hughes early in his career, when he was castigated for his less flattering depictions of Negro life. In *Not Without Laughter,* according to Sterling Brown's review, Hughes "presents all of this without apology" (63). Building on Brown, I argue that this novel's interactions between the modern and antimodern, as well as between typical and exceptional, drive this book's modernity.[11]

Sandy's father Jimboy shows the complicated balance of representing stereotypical behaviors that don't, in the end, add up to a stereotypical character. Brown describes Jimboy as a "likeable scapegrace, . . . guitar plunker and rambling man" (61). Brown refers to three common African American character types, and Hughes presents each of these aspects of Jimboy's personality. Still, even in a scene of back-porch guitar playing, Hughes does not simply stereotype him: "Jimboy was home. All the neighborhood could hear his rich low baritone voice giving birth to the blues. On Saturday night he and Annjee went to bed early. On Sunday night Aunt Hager said: 'Put that guitar right up, less'n it's hymns you plans on playin'. An' I don't want too much o' them, 'larmin' de white neighbors'" (59). Each of Brown's three types are on evidence in this passage: Hager is wary of Jimboy's guitar playing, and Hughes highlights his rambling by noting that Jimboy is at home this particular Saturday. Furthermore, this scene takes place in Hager's backyard and depends on the religious, racial, and communal pressures of small-town Stanton. Since Hager remarks that black music—even hymns—could be problematic for their white neighbors, Jimboy playing the blues is especially notable. When the narrator notes that "some of the blues lines had, not only double, but triple meanings" (63), it becomes clearer that Jimboy is not simply a "picturesque" stereotype; his every action in this scene challenges what is acceptable for African American men in small-town Kansas.

Jimboy confronts Hager's and Stanton's proprieties simply by playing songs in the backyard and acting as a "likeable scapegrace." His lack of decorum demonstrates an aspect of black masculinity that relates to scholarly arguments that early twentieth-century black manhood relates to but does not mimic normalized white masculinities of the period. Marlon Ross, for example, "frame[s] black manhood as a dialectical process in which black men themselves . . . have constantly upset the Jim Crow regime simply by working through their own and others' efforts to identify, discipline, subject, and re-form their sense of their manliness" (8). According to Ross, black male agency disrupts the social order of Jim Crow America and, as a result, black masculinities claim both relation to and distance from the patterns and expectations on white men. The passage referenced above indicates several expectations for black behavior under Jim Crow, including Hager's complaints about Jimboy playing the blues and the threat of violence underlying the white neighbors' alarm. Jimboy, then, while appearing to be a layabout "guitar plunker," disrupts the order of Jim Crow by playing the blues, which allows him to create a sense of manliness in opposition to the disciplinary demands placed on him by Hager and others. Hughes repeats this process with other characters, such as when Hager ventriloquizes white behavioral preferences but insists upon Sandy's education, or Harriett's unashamed sexuality that nonetheless supports the goals of black uplift. Even Sandy, who has taken a job as a bellhop at the town hotel, working alongside—as Hager says—some "low-down" men and "bad womens" from "the Bottoms" (205), refuses to obey the commands of a drunken white Southerner.

Hager dislikes Jimboy not only because of his backyard guitar playing but also because she fears his influence on Sandy. She calls Jimboy "a lazy coon" (128), and her dislike is well known in the community: "All the colored people in Stanton knew that Hager bore no love for Jimboy Rodgers" (32). Hughes points out the limits to Hager's perspective, however, when Annjee defends him: "Jimboy's all right, but he's just too smart to do this heavy ditch-digging labor, and that's all white folks gives the colored a chance at here in Stanton" (142). Jimboy loses jobs due to his race and his intelligence, not because he is lazy. In this light, Hager's fears may be somewhat misplaced. When Sandy is caught lying about stealing a nickel from the church collection plate, he expects Jimboy to support him, but "his father's usually amiable face was stern this time" (126). Jimboy then scolds Sandy for lying: "I'm not much, maybe. Don't mean to say I am. I won't work a lot, but what I do I do honest" (127). Even while Jimboy admits his work ethic is not equal to Hager's demands, he supports her in teaching Sandy to behave ethically. He also contradicts her teachings in other ways, such as his admission that he's "not much, maybe." This comment seems to preclude greatness achieved through self-discipline and hard work. Jimboy's potential lies in his self-definition according to a different kind of manhood: an honest everyman with neither great achievement nor great fault. Thus, even when their interests align, the novel asserts philosophical differences between Hager and Jimboy, which highlights how Sandy's development functions as the novel's contested middle ground.

While many characters actively shape his work ethic and morality, Hager is his primary care provider and a particularly powerful influence. Her vision for Sandy combines Christian teachings with the dream that he will become a great man like Booker T. Washington:

> "Colored boys, when they gets around twelve an' thirteen, they gets so bad, Sandy," she would say. "I wants you to stay nice an' make something out o' yo'self. If Hager lives, she ain't gonna see you go down. She's gonna make a fine man out o' you fo' de glory o' God an de black race. You gwine to 'mount to something in this world. You hear me?"
>
> Sandy did hear her, and he knew what she meant. She meant a man like Booker T. Washington, or Frederick Douglass, or like Paul Lawrence Dunbar, who did poetry-writing. Or maybe Jack Johnson. But Hager said Jack Johnson was the devil's kind of greatness, not God's. (195)

According to Hager, it's centrally important that Sandy "stay nice" so that he can become a "fine man." In this formulation, boys' changing nature causes them to lose the potential for greatness. Sandy understands Hager to approve of Washington, Douglass, and Dunbar, but including boxer Jack Johnson in Sandy's list of great men complicates the requirement for niceness in achievement. Hager's intention to groom Sandy for service to God causes her to complain about Johnson: "That's what you get from workin' round that old barbershop" (195). When she notes that Johnson married a white woman, she asks, "What he care 'bout de race?" (195). This passage thus suggests that the influence of the men at the barbershop may not stop Sandy from achieving greatness, but he won't gain Hager's approval for it.

Hager resists the barbershop's influence, which indicates that she intends to remain the primary influence in Sandy's life. In the first paragraph above, she is the grammatical subject of half the sentences—and when she says, "She's gonna make a fine man out o' you," she is acting on Sandy, who in this sentence is posed as a passive participant. But Hager also tells him, "I wants you to . . . make something out o' yo'self" (195). This sentence begins with Hager as the subject but then the direct object, "you," is modified by an infinitive phrase expressing Sandy's future action. In this sentence, Sandy participates more actively, which reflects discourses of self-made masculinity, especially when paired with Washington, Douglass, and Dunbar. Of course, the teachings of those men are not strictly individualistic, not least because of their relationship to each other. Using the example of W. E. B. Du Bois, Hazel Carby delineates the way such "race men" influenced each other: "The map of intellectual mentors he draws for us is a map of male production and reproduction that traces in its form, but displaces through its content, biological and sexual reproduction" (25). In some ways, Hager favors a similar communal model of masculine achievement. Her concern about the barbershop's influence, however, implies that she would assert differences between masculine and feminine communalism even though lines of intellectual mentoring were frequently drawn through communities of men.

Despite Hager's concerns about the influence of men, she continues to encourage Sandy to be a "fine man" along the lines of the period's well-known black leaders. Throughout *Not Without Laughter,* Sandy's female relatives encourage his self-discipline, though Harriett and Tempy favor education over a combination of education and manual labor, which is Hager's preference. The novel therefore recapitulates the debate between Booker T. Washington and W. E. B. Du Bois, seen when Harriett gives Sandy school money and in Tempy's scorn, "Du Bois wants our rights. He wants us to be real men and women. He believes in social equality. But Washington—huh!" (242). Like Hager, Tempy and Harriett see Sandy as a potential link to prominent African American men of the period, and he functions as a figure of possibility who can surmount the perceived failures of his father. Their ideological argument splits along generational lines, with two separate visions of how to overcome past and present racial inequalities to secure Sandy's future. Hughes's intervention here is that he does not force Sandy to choose. Instead, Sandy thinks, "I guess they are both great men" (243), which suggests that Sandy's masculine identity development hinges on balancing competing viewpoints—in this case, two race men who might stand in for "old-fashioned" and "modern." He manages the challenges of his present moment by finding the middle ground between philosophies of greatness, disagreements among family members, and even rural and urban spaces.

*Not Without Laughter* thus underscores Sandy's attempt to negotiate the number of influences, spaces, and models that the novel incorporates into his development. For example, beyond his family's debates about the political sphere, Sandy reads widely. He is introduced to Douglass and Dunbar while living with Hager, then Charles W. Chesnutt at Tempy's house. Furthermore, through Tempy and his job at a bookstore, Sandy reads the work of a number of white authors, including Harold Bell Wright, Gene Stratton Porter, Carl Sandburg, Vachel Lindsay, and Edgar Lee Masters. While Douglass might be placed easily into a political tradition with Washington and Du Bois, these other authors represent a literary option that complicates Sandy's ability to choose a specific model for his identity formation. Notably, each of these authors might be labeled regionalists, and the white authors are all Midwestern, which recalls Hughes's plan to portray "a typical Negro family in the Middle West" (*Big Sea* 303–304). Like many of the authors that Sandy reads, Hughes engages a tradition of Midwestern literature representing small towns and rural spaces. In focusing on Sandy's encounters with a range of local color and regional modernist literature rather than his judgment upon it, *Not Without Laughter* demonstrates that even when rural spaces and characters appear to be nostalgic or typical, they illuminate the multiplicities of American modernity.

## REGIONAL BLACK MASCULINITY

Through Sandy's coming-of-age, *Not Without Laughter* incorporates a wide range of character types, literary allusions, and sonic modernities. This method of compilation inflects the novel's modern Midwestern space and takes its clearest form in passages where Sandy is subject to multiple people and influences.[12] Therefore, Sandy's experiences on the streets of Chicago, in the dancehall, or listening to his father sing blues lyrics become the novel's defining moments. Each of those scenes incorporates a range of characteristics—typical and unexpected, rural and urban, masculine and feminine—that Sandy must balance as part of his burgeoning masculine identity. Most often, these are public moments, leading Kimberly J. Banks to claim that the novel "is quite self-consciously invested in the production of masculinity through masculine public spaces" (97). Stanton gender norms become apparent in mixed-gender spaces such as the dancehall, and Hughes also elaborates upon the spatial and cultural aspects of masculine subjectivities through Sandy's experiences at two iconic black masculine public spaces: the barbershop and the pool hall. Sandy learns about Harriett's success while reading the *Defender* among the "adventurers and vagabonds" at Cudge's pool hall (248), and he shines shoes and sweeps the floor every Saturday at Pete Scott's barbershop.

In particular, Sandy's job at the barbershop adds to the complex of influences on him: Hager's focus on work and self-discipline, Jimboy's and Annjee's absences, the New Negro influences of Harriett and Tempy, the blues, and now a homosocial community of men:

> The barber-shop was a new world to Sandy, who had lived thus far tied to Aunt Hager's apron-strings. He was a dreamy-eyed boy who had grown to his present age largely under the dominant influence of women—Annjee, Harriett, his grandmother—because Jimboy had been so seldom home. But the barber-shop then was a man's world, and, on Saturdays, while a dozen or more big laborers awaited their turns, the place was filled with loud man-talk and smoke and laughter. Baseball, Jack Johnson, racehorses, white folks, Teddy Roosevelt, local gossip, Booker Washington, women, labor prospects in Topeka, Kansas City, Omaha, religion, politics, women, God—discussions and arguments all afternoon and far up into the night, while crisp kinks rolled to the floor, cigarette- and cigar-butts were thrown on the hearth of the monkey-stove, and Sandy called out: "Shine, mister?" (188)

Sandy is a marked presence in this community for his age and his female upbringing. In the "man's world" of the barbershop, Sandy is dwarfed by the number and size of the clients and set apart by both youth and bearing. Hughes describes Sandy as "dreamy-eyed" because he has grown up among women, implying a hard-eyed practicality among the men in the barbershop that does not exist in his female relatives. But aside from Hager's grand dreams for Sandy, she is not given to idealism or fancy and does not encourage it in Sandy. Hughes implies that, in addition to their casual misogyny, the barbershop patrons are guided by different definitions of practicality, a difference that also recalls Jimboy's moderated ambitions. In this passage, the barbershop clientele expand Sandy's worldview, not least because they are a group of productive, working male role models whose concepts of respectability and appropriateness diverge from both Hager's and Jimboy's.

Because of those differences, Sandy must learn appropriate behaviors for the context of the barbershop. For example, when clients tease him, Sandy finds "that so-called jokes are often not really jokes at all, but rather unpleasant realities that hurt unless you can think of something equally funny and unpleasant to say in return" (189). To counter the men's unpleasantness, Sandy learns to play the dozens, responding to jokes about his nappy hair with a quick "So's your pa's" (190). He also participates in the lively atmosphere of the barbershop by saying he would shine a chorus girl's shoes for free (193) and by telling the men, "If you don't want a shine, stay out of my chair and do your arguing on the floor!" (192). Despite this apparent confidence, and perhaps affected by the power differential at the barbershop, Sandy remains silent when the men begin discussing his aunt Harriett. After a "young teamster" expresses his preference for dark-skinned women like Harriett, another patron replies, "'I admit Harrietta's all right,' said the old man; 'all right to look at but—sput-t-tsss!' He spat contemptuously at the stove" (191). Even though Sandy has discovered "the protective art of turning back a joke" (189), the way these men sexualize Harriett with a mixture of compliments and insults is more complicated than jokes about his hair. Sandy's silence therefore may not signify approval so much as the way he is learning to respond and adapt to new circumstances.

The men's conversations force Sandy to adapt because their "man-talk" differs from his experience on Hager's porch. While the men at the barbershop engage in similar sustained discussion, the conversations at Hager's are generally local in nature, and the most frequent subjects are family and gossip.[13] The barbershop conversation is more wide ranging, including sports, race, politics, religion, and sex. They also cover a great deal of geographic ground, discussing local, regional, and national concerns. Their conversation does not advance along a clear trajectory, however, and when they discuss "Teddy Roosevelt, local gossip, [and] Booker Washington"

(188), the men sandwich local concerns between two national figures, as Hughes entwines them in a nonhierarchical relationship. Further complicating the relationship between spatial registers is that the conversation's greatest precision comes in its turn to regional concerns over "labor prospects" in Midwestern cities.

This conversation contains a vast middle ground that includes several Midwestern spaces and refers to the differences between country and city, men and women, and "white folks" and blacks. Sandy's awareness of these differences marks the barbershop as a liminal space between contestation and inclusivity. As men in the barbershop discuss their experiences, they stake out identities, creating a perspective that allows for the influence of national interests such as "baseball, Jack Johnson, racehorses" (188) as well as local gossip and discussions of where in the region they might find a job. Coursing through "Omaha, religion, politics, women, God" (188), this conversation demonstrates how these men incorporate local, regional, and national characteristics into unresolved, nondirectional identities. As a result, they create and sustain masculine identities upon contested space, a lesson that Sandy learns in the dancehall, on the streets of Chicago, and by playing the dozens. Much like these men, he incorporates a wide range of influences without slotting himself into conventional Harlem Renaissance narratives.

Thus Sandy's invocation of Stanton as he hears the church choir on the novel's last page suggests the continuing importance of Sandy's background and hometown as well as the dialectical relationship of rural influences to the urban setting. Conversely, Hughes also represents Stanton as an individualized locality responsive to outside forces. When Hughes describes Stanton's sidewalks, alleys, backyards, houses, and stoops, he draws attention to specific local places, then explores confrontations between national forces and local individuals within them. This technique can be seen in the barbershop, dancehall, and the novel's opening cyclone. During its impending arrival, Hager says that it's "Sho' gwine to be a terrible storm" (20) and later exclaims, "It's a cyclone!" (20). This difference illustrates how Hager names the specific local manifestation of what had been, until then, unnamed and threatening but not concretely harmful. The scene's detailed description, noting the kinds of houses owned and the specific damage caused by the cyclone, indicates the storm's local aspect. Hughes's description is not confined to the physical, however, as he also creates a racial component:

rather than simply noting a white death and moving on to Stanton's black community, Hughes makes Hager both sympathetic to and actively desired by the white neighbors. He thereby underscores the importance the novel places on individual locales and experiences. With that, the novel complicates common conceptions about not only race relations but also, more generally, understandings of American life that depend upon increasing centralization.

Hughes clarifies *Not Without Laughter*'s resistance to compulsory urbanization through conflicts that arise regarding Sandy's education and coming-of-age. Throughout the novel, Hughes describes Stanton-based influences coming into contact with those from outside. One such passage is Sandy's daydream as his mother prepares to leave for Detroit:

> When he got big, he would go to Detroit. And maybe New York, too, where his geography said they had the tallest buildings in the world, and trains that ran under the river.... He wondered if there were any colored people in New York.... How ugly African colored folks looked in the geography—with bushy heads and wild eyes! Aunt Hager said her mother was an African, but she wasn't ugly and wild; neither was Aunt Hager; neither was little dark Willie-Mae, and they were all black like Africans. (175; ellipses in original)

Sandy's thoughts drift between cities and travel, modern infrastructure, race, Africa, appearance, family, and heritage. Perhaps the most striking part of this passage is Sandy's ignorance about Harlem. *Not Without Laughter* takes place during the few years before the United States entered World War I, amid massive demographic shifts in New York and other northern cities. At the time of Sandy's prewar youth, Harlem had not yet become, as novelist James Weldon Johnson claimed in 1925, "the great Mecca for . . . the ambitious and the talented of the whole Negro world" (301). Nevertheless, according to the US Census, New York City had the largest African American population of any northern city in 1910, more than double that of Chicago (*Negro Population* 93). Therefore, in highlighting the greater significance of Detroit, Chicago, and Kansas City to Sandy's family and community, Hughes challenges the assumed spaces and narratives of African American modernity.

Proceeding from Sandy's understanding of New York as a fabulous place that excludes people like him, *Not Without Laughter* highlights how Hughes offers an alternate narrative that uses the conflicts and accumulations of the Midwestern space to represent the African American experience more broadly. In this passage, Sandy's ignorance is one step in his learning process, which also includes reading the geography and then questioning it based on his acquaintances and experience. Just prior to this passage, Sandy laments his mother's impending departure and takes responsibility for helping his grandmother in Annjee's absence. Then, when he begins to elaborate his vision for the future, Sandy imagines increased mobility and independence. Although traveling to Detroit and New York were common among African Americans in the early twentieth century, Hughes presents Sandy's future as a modern fantasy because the geography book is shown to be an unreliable source. Sandy realizes the book's inaccuracy when it presents "ugly African colored folks . . . with bushy heads and wild eyes" (175), while contemporary readers likely understood that there were, in fact, "colored people in New York" (175). The geography's unreliability also denotes a limit on Hager, Tempy, and Harriett's emphasis on classroom education as a path through which Sandy may define himself and achieve greatness. For him to make effective use of the geography as a learning tool, he must balance the book's representations with his own experience.

Sandy's daydream suggests he will gain that experience by leaving Stanton and moving to the city. While that narrative trajectory places *Not Without Laughter* within standard Harlem Renaissance coming-of-age traditions, considering this passage as a whole undercuts its conventional qualities. In particular, the way Sandy mediates the textbook's treatment of Africans implies that he could similarly manage his urban fantasy. From the geography, Sandy learns that African people are unkempt, wild, and ugly. But Hager tells him of his great-grandmother, an actual African, and he understands that the published fantasy of the primitive Negro is, at minimum, not entirely true. Sandy's ability to question the book's representations indicate that, once his initial wonder over engineering marvels has passed, he may begin to ask similar questions of urban life. Indeed, his experience in Chicago finds him tempering stories of a city where "buildings were like towers and the lake was like a sea" (284) with the mundane familiarities of messy children and porch conversation. Rather than perpetual idealization and its implied urban endpoint, Sandy's identity balances outside ideals with his particular experience of local and regional influences.

Those influences come from within and outside his family, vary in age and social class, and reflect numerous local and national types. Through these inclusions, *Not Without Laughter* critiques the centralized teleologies of urban industrialization. Whether moderating fantasies or mediating the different kinds of greatness of Washington and Du Bois, Sandy's identity development is predicated on balancing the old-fashioned and the modern. As a result, Hughes allows the specific influences on Sandy's identity to exist concurrently, their conflicts without resolution. I have explored this coexistence in other chapters, including the combination of farm and factory sounds in *Poor White,* the material and temporal simultaneity of a pastoral pocket calendar with Lorine Niedecker's poetry, and the similarities between barnyard and revolutionary temporality in *The Green Corn Rebellion. I*n the conclusion, I will demonstrate its contemporary implications. In *Not Without Laughter,* Hughes incorporates Sandy's racial, gendered, and spatial experiences, amplifying the intersectionality of this "typical Negro boy" in a "typical Negro family in the Middle West" (*Big Sea* 303–304). Hughes thus offers a comprehensive, balanced version of black Midwestern masculinity. He does not attempt to achieve idealistic visions of manhood or follow racialized patterns of masculine identity development. Rather, *Not Without Laughter*'s version of old-fashioned modernism is a more achievable middle ground marked by moderation and experience.

Hughes's representation of that middle ground requires locating the novel outside of the conventional North-South poles of the Harlem Renaissance. Through its Midwestern setting, *Not Without Laughter* includes a broader portion of the black community in the national conversation. In some ways, this novel's Midwestern regionalism charts the Harlem Renaissance in a fashion similar to the transnationalism of texts by Hughes and other prominent black writers of the period.[14] By compiling the influences on Sandy and participating in this remapping project, Hughes attempts to provide a more diverse picture of common experiences and achievable identities. Bernard W. Bell seizes on this attempt when he opposes Hughes's "folk realism" to the "folk romances" of Claude McKay and Zora Neale Hurston, which attempted "to discover a usable past, to define and explore their culture" (113). Hughes, on the other hand, "strive[s] for the truth of a particular environment and the social rituals of common folk" (B. Bell 128). Hughes recognizes the variety and urgency of environmental forces acting on young black men like Sandy. When Sandy must negotiate the jokes of grown men, his grandmother's desire for him to be a race leader, the many valences of jazz and blues performance, and the challenges of rural and urban spaces, Hughes highlights the conflicted, complex nature of his identity development. Hughes's resistance to defining him—as rural or urban, naïve or studied, a laborer or intellectual—creates a black Midwestern masculinity that is both referential and decentered, comprehensible only through its conflicts. Sandy must constantly remap his understanding of himself and the people and spaces in his life. As a result, he is a figure of possibility, incorporating the hopes, trials, and experiences of his family, his community, and the novel itself.

# CONCLUSION

## *Contemporary Manhood and the Entrepreneurial Midwest*

Before leaving Wauseon, I needed some coffee. I bought a large drip, a sandwich, and some beans at local roaster Red Rambler Coffees, then headed straight west on US Highway 20A. After about ten miles on the perfect one-mile grid of northwest Ohio, I turned north, on my way to talk Midwestern literature in East Lansing. Along the way, I passed several family farms, picturesque springtime cornfields planted close to farmhouses and barnyards. As icons of heartland nostalgia, such imagery oversimplifies the narrative of the small farmer.[1] But only if we let it. The gambrel roofs on those barns, for instance, recall the lumber industry of the early twentieth century, as gambrels became widespread only when sawmills began manufacturing their trusses.[2] And the endless cornfields are a scenic illustration of the scope of twenty-first-century commercial agriculture, which I also saw when I passed the tidy board fence and four long, low barns that are the sanitized road-facing presence of a large-scale dairy operation (never mind the manure lagoons behind, or the polluted water of nearby streams).[3] As I've argued throughout this book, a more complex picture of the Midwest emerges when we account for actual histories and move beyond superficial oppositions—whether the country and the city or the family farmer and the urban industrialist. This was true in Bidwell, Stanton, and Lone Tree, and it's true today in Wauseon and other communities throughout the Midwest.

Back to that coffee. Since everyone in Wauseon had recommended Red Rambler, I found the shop up on the northeast side of town, where it's located in a strip mall formerly anchored by a Kmart. I could tell from all the recommendations that Red Rambler fulfills co-owner Jo Michelson's hope to make it "a place where people can come and socialize and have conversation and meet with friends over good beer, good food, and good coffee" (qtd.

in B. Cunningham F1). When Jo and her husband Mel opened Red Rambler in 2003, though, they had never roasted their own coffee. Their friends were skeptical about the business, figuring that Fulton County wouldn't support a specialty coffee shop.[4] Still, the Michelsons pressed on. They had lived in Wauseon for many years, working in sales and administration, and they counted on their network within the community and their knowledge of its needs and interests. As the business grew, they observed their customers' tastes. As Jo told me, "I have found that many coffee snobs are also beer snobs"—so when the shop moved in 2015, they began brewing beer.[5] Combining the coffee shop with a microbrewery has allowed the Michelsons to expand their hours and create a more comfortable atmosphere, and now you can reliably find people chatting at the bar, working on their laptops, or grabbing a cup for the road.

In many ways, the history of this Wauseon coffee shop echoes the themes of *Old-Fashioned Modernism.* The Michelsons may be competing with both national chains and local perceptions, but their initial bet on Wauseon has paid off. Over the years, Red Rambler has grown primarily through word-of-mouth advertising, and they now sell to restaurants and coffee shops throughout northwest Ohio, southern Michigan, and northeast Indiana. As Mel said, "If it's sized right, what works in Ann Arbor, Michigan, works in Wauseon, Ohio, just maybe on a smaller scale" (qtd. in Cathey). Red Rambler doesn't tell a story of the "heartland"—it isn't a success because it's quaint. It's also not a story of "flyover country." Rather, it's an example of two Midwesterners who are attentive to the needs of their community, understand their own limitations, and know how to call on local knowledge and expertise. This coffee shop, then, is part of a longer struggle for Midwestern identity. Despite a national push for centralization, profit, and efficiency, people and communities in the Midwest promote local and regional outcomes—allowing for growth and modernization, but moderating those through experience, tradition, and local needs.

## AIMLESS MASCULINITY

Throughout this book I have provided several examples of "old-fashioned modernism" in which rural modernity is bound up with the performance of masculine gender norms. Jack Greitzer's mural, for example, expresses fear over the decline of agricultural communities in the early twentieth century but also challenges that perspective, as the mural's four men are working to modernize local agricultural systems and improve life for people in Wauseon and throughout Fulton County. *Poor White*'s Hugh McVey likewise enhances local life when he invents a cabbage transplanter and corn harvester. In so doing, he both relieves farmworkers' labor and facilitates Bidwell, Ohio's development into a modern rural town balancing agricultural implement factories with the farms that inspired them. *Not Without Laughter* features two similar combinations, as Sandy Rodgers combines modern experiences with his traditional upbringing, and Chicago incorporates rural cultures into the urban space. These novels also portray the complications and failed promises of such attempts at balance, which other texts pick up in various forms, including Chris and Joy Bennett's home in *The Story of a Country Boy,* where they accumulate new labor-saving gadgets but retain normative gender roles, and Lorine Niedecker's artist's book, *Next Year or I Fly My Rounds, Tempestuous,* which is both dependent on and resistant to industrial consumerism as she pastes poetry over the homilies published on a biweekly pastoral pocket calendar. Similarly, the men of *The Green Corn Rebellion* and *The Home Place* attempt to create better futures for themselves but end up wearing out, fatigued with competing expectations and narratives.

Such unsettled narratives increase the possibility that these characters will stagnate or become aimless. Writing at a time when regional economies and cultures were in flux, Midwestern modernists attempt to imagine alternative possibilities for Midwestern men beyond the subsistence farmer or the company man. Still, they struggle with the reactive nature of "old-fashioned modernism," not least because these authors and their characters are resisting both nostalgic pastoralism and industrial futurity. In the present day, when the Midwestern economy is in the midst of another shift, such anxieties have resurfaced. In contemporary Midwestern literature, white men are forced to adapt and, when they fail, get stuck in untenable jobs and relationships. In some ways, this stagnation narrative is a response to national economic patterns, so books from outside the Midwest, such as Daniel Woodrell's *Winter's Bone* (2006), Philipp Meyer's *American Rust* (2009), and Steve Weddle's *Country Hardball* (2013), also depict rural America as a place where white men's options have diminished.

While unstable rural economies are not exclusively a Midwestern phenomenon, the Midwest does loom large in the national narrative surrounding them—in this case, as the Rust Belt. When the factories close, rural and peri-urban men struggle with the loss of income and status. Midwestern fiction shows the resulting violence and desperation, and Frank Bill's *Crimes in Southern Indiana* (2011) and Donald Ray Pollock's *Knockemstiff* (2008), set in Ohio, develop a country noir aesthetic similar to that seen in Woodrell, Meyer, and Weddle. Others are less engrossed with violence. Michael Martone and Bryan Mark Furuness's *Winesburg, Indiana* (2015) adapts Sherwood Anderson's *Winesburg, Ohio* (1918), updating the original's ennui for the postindustrial age. J. Ryan Stradal's *Kitchens of the Great Midwest* (2015) fits somewhere between, including some country noir violence as it mainly skewers the obsessions and dissatisfactions of farm-to-table foodie culture. *Kitchens of the Great Midwest* circles around Minnesotan Eva Thorvald, "America's bad-girl chef" (265), who organizes destination dining events that spawn breathless *New Yorker* articles. Most of the book's chapters feature one of Thorvald's friends or acquaintances, telling her story indirectly. "Venison," for instance, focuses on her boyfriend's brother, Jordy Snelling, who sells Thorvald some venison he no longer wants.

Like those of many of contemporary regional literature's male characters, Jordy's life has stagnated. He is twenty-five, unemployed, and directionless. He lives with his mother, who is in hospice care for late-stage cancer. Despite their cohabitation, Jordy prefers not to be alone with her because, he wonders, "What if he fucked something up?" (178). In the story, his brother Adam has agreed to come stay with their mother on Saturdays so Jordy can go deer hunting up north with his conspiracy-obsessed father. On the first day of the season, Jordy bags a doe. He plans to make the venison meatballs his mother has requested, but she dies while he's out hunting, and Jordy no longer wants the meat. He also has no plans for it, mirroring his general lack of purpose throughout the story. Twice in the chapter, he drinks to blackout. Once, his friends lock him in the garage because he's getting "chippy" (181). Before he passes out, he punches a hole in the garage, causing several hundred dollars' worth of damage.

Jordy's behavior exemplifies contemporary discourses of toxic masculinity.[6] His anxiety and his anger demonstrate what Vandello et al. call the "precarious nature of manhood," through which they show that "anything that makes salient its precariousness, or calls one's manhood status into question, should be especially anxiety provoking" (1326). In "Venison," Jordy faces multiple kinds of precarity, and he fails nearly every test of his masculinity: he has no job, he is unable to care for his mother, and he unsuccessfully attempts to date the hospice nurse. Jordy proves himself only when he shoots the doe, and that happens in an isolated setting with only family members present. With his friends and in public places, Jordy attempts to prove himself by drinking heavily and fighting. Such behaviors have a long history in American rural life. According to Ted Ownby, since at least the mid-nineteenth century, recreational competition—which includes hunting, fighting, and drunkenness—has been a way for American men to prove themselves to each other.

Despite these aggressive means of proving his worth, Jordy is not typically rageful. He tries to be helpful to his mother and the nurse, and he doesn't insult his uncle in the same way his father does. Still, he is casually misogynistic toward a friend's "hot but annoying girlfriend" (192), and he fails to counter his father's jokey insults. Jordy's role models range widely in terms of their employment, politics, and demeanor, and his frequent befuddled musing suggests that he could turn out to be reliable as easily as resentful, kind as likely as cruel. By the end of "Venison," Jordy has taken several of his mother's leftover OxyContin pills. While he had earlier refused them, the last lines of the story imply that this behavior will continue: "This was going to be another four-pill kind of day. He could just tell already" (209). When Jordy feels physical or emotional pain, he turns to drugs.[7] And it feels understandable: this is a way for him to cope with both his personal failures and his socioeconomic context.

Whether Jordy becomes part of the most recent iteration of the rural decline narrative—the opioid epidemic—it's clear that he is in danger of either remaining aimless or degenerating more dramatically. His interaction with Eva Thorvald provides him another possibility: participating in specialty economies. Were Jordy of a more entrepreneurial mind-set, he might obtain the deer tags of his friends and family, a possibility he considers in a different context earlier in the story. If he did that, he might make a cottage industry out of supplying Thorvald with local products for her high-end cuisine. But he doesn't. He thoughtlessly accepts her offer of a hundred dollars for the venison, which he later regrets because "he always fucked up every kind of negotiation" (209). Still, that possibility exists. His brother Adam already bakes bread for Thorvald, and, partly because her mother also died of cancer, she offers to help Jordy in any way she can. In this instance, Jordy has stumbled into a way to manage some of the difficulties of contemporary Midwestern life. He appears unlikely to take full advantage of it, but Stradal does offer niche entrepreneurship as a possibility for Jordy and the other men in the story. This narrative has roots in "old-fashioned modernism," and not only because of the opportunity to participate in stereotypically masculine activities within the context of a new economy, à la Greitzer's manual laborers in a modernizing rural space. Jordy's story also parallels other texts discussed in this book. For instance, his formless musing mirrors Hugh McVey's dreaminess, his drunken behavior echoes Chris Bennett's ill-conceived road trip, and his material life reveals the failures of modern gender roles much like Lorine Niedecker's poetry.

## NICHE MIDWEST

In *Kitchens of the Great Midwest,* Jordy's aimlessness is related to his limited opportunities. In Bonnie Jo Campbell's 2009 short story "Boar Taint," it's slightly different: men lack direction because they are comfortable in outdated economic structures. "Boar Taint" is the closing story of Campbell's *American Salvage,* a National Book Award finalist that represents the experiences of the working class in postindustrial small-town Michigan. "Boar Taint" tells the story of Ernie and Jill, farmers living in a socioeconomically marginalized community of unelectrified farms and decaying houses. Fittingly, this place appears to be "tainted." But Campbell rethinks rural decline by exploring Jill's and Ernie's responses to the systemic and material challenges facing American small farms. Jill, a graduate-educated agricultural scientist and the story's main protagonist, attempts to earn extra income through a boutique hog-breeding and roasting operation. Her husband, Ernie, on the other hand, is more resistant to change. Even though their neighbor has lost his farm to an agricultural conglomerate, Ernie keeps working "the same corn, oats, and beans he'd been harvesting for the last three decades" (152). In this story, farm entrepreneurship is related to the different ways that men and women experience the countryside. Ernie, for one, continues to farm as he always has, despite evidence that his is a declining way of life. On the other hand, Jill has been doubted by Ernie, her family, and herself, and—creating a version of "old-fashioned modernism"—through her entrepreneurial hog-roast scheme, she adapts their agricultural practice to a changing economy.

While Campbell accesses national imaginaries of the rural Midwest as a space in decline, she also exposes the limits of that narrative, partly by using and then undermining several genre conventions. "Boar Taint" has elements of family psychodrama, the outsider narrative, and hard-luck rural realism. Most prominent among these, however, are the conventions of film's most abject genre of rural decline: hillbilly horror.[8] Early in the story, Jill travels to the isolated Jentzen farm to purchase a boar that she saw advertised on a grocery store pinboard for the too-good-to-be-true price of twenty-five dollars. Jill's arrival at the Jentzen place aligns with film scholar Carol Clover's description of rural horror films such as *Deliverance* (1972) and *The Texas Chain Saw Massacre* (1974), in which "country dwellers are disproportionately represented by adult males . . . [who] do no discernible work and are commonly shown lying about the home farm in the middle of a workday. . . . When we do see country families, something is always terribly wrong with them" (125). Rural horror exploits cultural anxieties by depicting a debased masculinity that is bound up with narratives of rural decline—in these films, there are more men than women, and they don't contribute to society or their families, which have become damaged, presumably beyond repair.

For the first half of the story, "Boar Taint" appears to meet all the requirements for rural horror. Jill walks up the rotting steps as dusk fades to night, and when she "stepped inside the hot, dark kitchen, [and] felt her work boots press grit into the plank floor" (154), genre convention dictates that the sole prematurely aged woman with "swollen ankles and two missing teeth" (156) be surrounded, and potentially held prisoner, by such men. And the scene delivers. Jill sees a "motionless," "shriveled old man" (154) and then three more men and a boy: "The thick bodies, the big table, the chairs that didn't fit under the table, the stove jutting out—it all made the room feel crowded, as though it would be difficult for her to turn and run if she needed to" (155). To borrow Clover's words, the Jentzens are "surly, dirty, . . . and slow" (126). Ernie has told Jill about the family's history of poverty, and these figures intensify Jill's apprehension, suggesting the near-total decline of this rural space. The dilapidated house, its unresponsive residents, and Jill's fear promise her entrapment and murder by debased rednecks. Then she loads the boar and leaves, muddied but not bloodied.

At this point, the story pivots away from the certain violence of hillbilly horror, and Campbell explains the workings of the rural space through its uncertainties. Throughout the story, Jill questions her own judgment and expects similar doubts from Ernie and her family. Once she notices the full extent of the boar's injuries, she wonders what her father would say about this venture: "Would he make clever remarks about failing farms and inbred families at the ends of dirt roads where everybody had six fingers on each hand?" (164). Jill's family disapproves of her decision to farm, and here Jill imagines how that disapproval draws on images of rural backwardness. Her father's expected negativity adds to Jill's self-doubt, which begins with economic and agricultural concerns and is intensified by the physical fear she feels on the Jentzen farm. While Jill is on her way home, the narrator articulates the relationships among what Jill saw, her family's concerns, and her own interests: "Until Jill had seen the Jentzen woman, she hadn't understood what her family feared for her. She'd known that, like all the farmers in this downward spiral, she and Ernie could lose everything, but she'd hoped her ideas for extra income could postpone the end indefinitely. Maybe she was, instead, hurrying the end along" (162). Rather than the certainties of a stereotypically declined rurality—whether that's the worn-down farmer from a Depression-era photograph or the incestual violence of the rural horror movie—Jill is primarily focused on the economics of farming. Her self-doubt causes her to regret an experimental bean crop that has failed and worry that the milking operation may go belly-up. At the end, though, the story offers Jill reason for optimism when the boar revives despite its apparent ill health.

The promise of Jill's pig-roast scheme shows how "Boar Taint" reflects the material realities of late twentieth-century farming culture. While Deborah Fitzgerald documents the industrialization of American agriculture beginning in the early twentieth century, she notes that small farms still exist today, working "not only in commodity production but increasingly in specialty, niche-oriented markets" (189). Beyond Jill's local hog-roast ambitions or Eva Thorvald's destination dining events, the prevalence of agricultural niche markets in the contemporary United States can be seen in such trends as farm-to-table restaurants and artisanal pickle makers, not to mention coffee shops and craft breweries.[9] Specialty economies like these suggest a broader structural upheaval that leads to such cultural anxieties as those expressed in horror tropes. Indeed, anthropologist Kathryn Dudley's description of contemporary rural life reads as if it could be a literary analysis of "Boar Taint": "Although we rarely think of the economic disorder stalking the American countryside as a form of terror, there are profound parallels in the traumatic social isolation that attends the state-sanctioned loss of community" ("Entrepreneurial" 191).

Hillbilly horror fits naturally into these concerns over isolation and economic decline. Its generic conventions, however, tend to overwhelm or eliminate some of the specificity of the farming enterprise. Those erasures suggest why, after leaving the house, as the Jentzen boy leads Jill to the boar, Campbell turns away from horror and addresses Jill's new venture in concrete terms.

> Your uncle tried to castrate a full-grown hog?" Jill should have waited to pay until she'd seen what she was buying, confirmed that this creature was going to do the job she needed done. If her whole pig-roast operation were going to depend on this dull-looking animal, maybe she should say screw it now before wasting any more energy. All along, she and the neighbor had assumed they'd be able to borrow somebody's boar hog for breeding, until they discovered that everybody local was out of the pig business and that they would have to artificially inseminate at thirty bucks a pop. She had been a fool to think that the solution would be as cheap and simple as buying this hog. She could still drive away, she thought, forget that twenty-five dollars and let these people and their pig and their house continue to collapse. She could still pour all her energy into corn and soybeans. (158)

Concern over the boar's intact genitals is an overt reference to masculine castration anxieties, and it also stands in for the uncertainties of farm entrepreneurship (after all, for the scheme to succeed, this boar needs to breed). As Campbell accounts for the difficulties of entrepreneurial diversification, she embeds a history of commodity agriculture in Michigan. To recap, small farmers were forced out of the pork industry because of the rise of agricultural conglomerates, which makes it difficult for entrepreneurs to start new businesses. Jill notes that there's always the possibility of returning to monocultural agriculture, which has been Ernie's practice all along. As she well knows, however, corn and soybean farming is also increasingly centralized, so industrialized monoculture would only delay the farm's decline.

Despite these economic and biological challenges, Campbell presents the hog-roast operation as a feasible option. Jill has identified a viable niche market—roast pork for "any sort of graduation or anniversary party" (163)—which she can fill without disrupting the farm's dairy and grain operations. Shoshanah Inwood and Jeff Sharp argue that this kind of "entrepreneurial stacking" is common among multigenerational farms in Ohio and Michigan, especially after commodity prices fell in the 1980s.[10] Although Ernie is not an entire generation older than Jill, her education and his experience fit the pattern identified by Inwood and Sharp. As seen in the story's final paragraph, this new business will take advantage of both:

> Jill stepped back, away from the men, inhaled the clean, damp air, and released her shoulders. She had built the new hog pen to the neighbor's specifications: posts driven down four feet, woven wire buried underground to prevent digging, sides six feet high, a double thickness of two-by-fours, nailed and then screwed. One corner had a shelter from weather, and another corner had a squeeze pen, where she could trap and medicate animals. She had the medicines and ointments to nurse this weak monster back to strength in time for the gilts to become fertile at about 220 days. With six breeding females, each birthing ten piglets per litter, two litters per year, and with these men to help her, this plan was once again looking very promising. This boar had turned out to be exactly what she needed, a creature even bullets could not stop. (166–167)

In many ways, "Boar Taint" faithfully re-creates an image of the Midwest in decline. The neighbor has lost his farm, the Jentzens seem to exist only as a stereotype, and there are no boars to borrow. Having absorbed that cultural narrative as well as her family's specific concerns, Jill attempts to improve her and Ernie's life by buying this maltreated boar hog, which, from the moment she saw it, seems like a failure. Still, Campbell presents the scene optimistically, as Jill takes comfort in the quantifiable—constructing the pen, identifying the correct medication, developing a production schedule. Perhaps Jill has no choice here; she has become part of a system that compels risk. And she is willing to take the risks that Ernie and her neighbor are not, which is partly because she needs to prove herself as a newcomer and a woman and partly because her skill set allows her to consider the farm in new ways.

Campbell rethinks rural decline through this combination of uncertainty and opportunity, which is linked to her construction of gendered behavior. Even though Jill's self-doubt crops up throughout the story, she is the character with the clearest upward trajectory. Notably, in the above passage, Jill's optimism increases when she steps away from the men. The story doesn't leave them behind, as Ernie revives the hog and the neighbor knows how to build the pen, but they contribute to the venture more in experience than energy. Jill's leadership is necessary because Ernie and the neighbor are both symbols of recent or impending failure; their neighbor has lost his farm, and Ernie does not appear motivated to change his conventional methods. By the late twentieth century, improved technology and farm consolidation resulted in fewer farmers and a shift in perceptions of the countryside: "The depopulation of the rural landscape has created a new, ghostly version of the pastoral ideal" (Dudley, *Debt* 9). Campbell responds to this vision of the Midwest by imagining a way for rural communities to thrive—specifically, through entrepreneurship. Jill identifies a local specialty market and then uses local knowledge to help her fill it, as her hog-roast business modifies conventional agribusiness for modern socioeconomic systems; she quantifies, but without the pressure to centralize. In this version of the Midwest, like the Wauseon or Bidwell versions, even the developments are in support of rural life.

"Boar Taint" thus upends multiple heartland stereotypes, but not before it uses them to set the scene. This story begins with a Michigan farming community that appears desolate because of the rise of corporate agriculture, and Campbell nurtures this ghostly pastoralism through the waning light, the farm's isolation, and the Jentzens' appearance. Using these tropes of rural horror, she incites a paranoid fear in Jill. According to David Bell, hillbilly horror reveals the anxiety underlying rural decline: "Here are societies which seem idyllic, but which are malignant, at a dead end, and viewed in the grip of their own death throes. That condition is the real horror of the rural" (103). In this story, the conventions of hillbilly horror parallel the danger of farm loss. They generate fear because they threaten pastoral images of the Midwestern countryside. In both instances, that threat comes from men and men's behavior. The Jentzens' poor white appearance disrupts American ideals of the yeoman farmer, while Jill's neighbor has lost his farm, and Ernie is headed down the same path. In other words, Campbell's male characters challenge Midwestern masculine stereotypes but replace pastoral imagery with other easily recognizable versions of downtrodden Midwestern men.

However, like Hugh McVey in *Poor White,* Sandy Rodgers in *Not Without Laughter,* Clyde Muncy in *The Home Place,* and many others, this story offers a way for Ernie to negotiate the difficulties of life in the rural Midwest. For Ernie, as with Jordy Snelling in *Kitchens of the Great Midwest,* that means following the lead of the story's central female character. Because Ernie supports Jill's entrepreneurial schemes, rather than resisting out of a notion of patriarchal control, their farm has a chance to survive. That willingness means, in the end, that this story does not argue for the certainty of loss or decline in the Michigan countryside, for either the community or the people in it. When Campbell turns away from hillbilly horror tropes, she indicates that this rural space is not so clearly malignant as the worst of rural stereotypes. But while she writes optimistically of the quantifiable steps Jill takes to fill a community-based niche market, "Boar Taint" also suggests that rural Michigan is not so idyllic as the pastoral would have it. This is a place and people that are caught up in the uncertainties of an economic structure that demands entrepreneurial risk. Campbell thus rejects two inadequate, overdetermined representational strategies and turns instead to a kind of practical materialism—one that, in this case, is driven by women's experience. The sense of practicality in "Boar Taint" is not an old-fashioned belt tightening, a hide-the-money-in-the-mattresses asceticism that might be more comfortable for Ernie. Jill offers a way to participate in developing niche economies while still drawing on conventional agricultural knowledge. This is what old-fashioned modernism looks like in the postindustrial Midwest.

Campbell has constructed rural Michigan as a place where national economic trends may cause individuals and communities to decline. This is not unlike Hugh McVey losing his job in Bidwell, or Clyde Muncy retreating to Lone Tree, or the cabbage farmer being overwhelmed in the Wauseon post office mural, or even the Michelsons' friends worrying that their small town wouldn't support a nice coffee shop. But, like these examples, "Boar Taint" and *Kitchens of the Great Midwest* include possibilities for ameliorating those same problems. We have, then, a story—and a region—that both accepts and rejects the concept of rural decline. Midwestern literature acknowledges the power of conventional narratives of masculinity, economics, and rural life, but it does not capitulate to them. The men in these texts do not always have a clear direction—for Hugh McVey, that comes out as dreaminess. For Jim Tetley, restlessness. For Jordy Snelling, aimlessness. But Midwestern literature is preoccupied with accumulating, balancing, or absorbing different ways of experiencing the countryside, particularly those that harness uncertainties and cultivate some combination of the pastoral and the futuristic, the nostalgic and the dynamic, the old-fashioned and the modern.

# NOTES

## Introduction: Masculinity and Midwestern Modernism

1. Monagon and Liscombe's 1877 *History of Fulton County, Ohio* chronicles the early history of Wauseon, as do Mikesell's 1905 *The County of Fulton: A History of Fulton County, Ohio, from the Earliest Days* and Reighard's 1920 two-volume *A Standard History of Fulton County, Ohio, an Authentic Narrative of the Past,* which both provide a comprehensive history of the town's economy, institutions, and economic trends, as well as a great deal of biographical information of the town's citizens. Two midcentury publications celebrate local and national milestones: *Official Publication of the Wauseon Centennial,* from 1954, and the *Official Souvenir Booklet* for the US bicentennial in 1976. That same year, the Fulton County Historical Society compiled brief histories of Wauseon people, groups, businesses, and landmarks in *Fulton County, Ohio: A Collection of Historical Sketches and Family Histories.* Recently, Krumm updates these histories with the 2014 photo compilation, *Wauseon.*

2. Greitzer's painting was well received in the region, not least because it presents Wauseon as a site of New Deal progressivism. E. B. Turnepseed, the Dearborn, Michigan–based supervising agent of the Detroit, Toledo & Ironton Railroad Company, wrote, "I have seen several of these paintings, but this is the first that portrays the railroad as a vital factor in the development of a community" (Letter to Geer, 29 Nov. 1938). Prominent citizens in Wauseon also wrote letters to the postmaster, George Geer, to praise the mural. Insurance agent and local politician Harry E. Schwall "felt that it was most realistic and appropriate for Wauseon" (Letter to Geer, 23 Aug. 1938), and banker George C. Davies wrote that "the artist has succeeded with great cleverness in combining the past with the new hope" (Letter to Geer, 2 Sept. 1938). Postmaster Geer praised the mural's beauty as an addition to the post office lobby, though he reports that not everyone was pleased with the subject matter: "The editor of one of our county papers has expressed the view that in his judgment a picture of one of our school buildings would have been better than a picture of the D. T. & I. depot with a cabbage patch" (Letter to Rowan, 6 Sept. 1938). Geer passed Schwall's and Davies's letters on to Edward Rowan, superintendent of the Section of Painting and Sculpture in the Treasury Department's Public Buildings Branch, who in turn sent them to Greitzer. Greitzer responded that "it certainly is gratifying and pleasing to know that it is liked by those who must 'live with it'" (Letter to Rowan, 15 Sept. 1938). Though Greitzer expresses his pleasure in this instance, the comment

sounds like faint praise when linked to a letter he wrote during the planning stage: "I felt I had done a rather successful job with the material of a town so colorless that it offered no inspiration" (Letter to Rowan, 13 Mar. 1938).

3. See Krumm for an image of the DT&I depot and a brief account of Henry Ford's involvement in the railroad, which began in 1920 (35). In *Twilight Rails,* Grant mentions the DT&I in relation to Ford's supply line and systematic efficiency (42).

4. In a letter rejecting Greitzer's initial sketch of postal workers, Section of Painting and Sculpture administrator Edward Rowan advised him to "take some theme related to the locale whether it be figures at work in the streets or a landscape and develop that material into a mural design" (Letter to Greitzer, 18 Oct. 1937). In response, Greitzer updated his design to focus on four workmen with the town's water tower and one of its two railway stations in the background (Letter to Rowan, 6 Dec. 1937). A September 1938 article from the *Fulton County Expositor* comments approvingly that the mural "is a composite painting of a group of photographs taken at various points in Wauseon" ("New Post Office"). Wauseon postmaster George Geer sent a clipping of this article to Rowan along with a letter confirming his satisfaction with the painting's quality and placement.

5. According to Melosh, New Deal art relied on "a common vocabulary of manhood and womanhood," which served as "a strategy of containment" against calls for equality (4). Kroiz examines the pedagogical purposes underlying regionalist art and argues that it "reveals an interweaving of rural and urban, traditional and modern" (1). For other sources on public art and the influence of New Deal art programs on American culture, see Musher, Grieve, Park and Markowitz, and Marling.

6. Cabbage and other vegetables were not historically major crops in Fulton County. Reighard attributes Wauseon's early twentieth-century wealth to dairy production and "industrious tillage" of corn, oats, and wheat (136–137). According to the 1940 Census of Agriculture, the value of dairy products sold by Fulton County farmers was approximately seven times that of vegetables, and the difference was nearly as great between grains and vegetables. Regarding the anxiety of farm loss, the total number of cows kept for milking and acres planted in grains increased throughout the 1930s. In each category, however, the number of total farms decreased, which echoes national narratives of increasing centralization throughout all sectors.

7. Greitzer never mentions the farmer's cooperative in his correspondence with Rowan, but a 1937 fire insurance map shows the Fulton County Farm Bureau located along the DT&I tracks about two blocks south of the depot. The building, which formerly housed companies manufacturing windmills and oil burners, stood vacant in 1923. By 1937, the Farm Bureau had moved into the facility and installed several oil tanks and a pump house across the street. The three-block area surrounding the co-op is crisscrossed with railroad spurs and transfer tracks, and it contained several factories, flour and feed mills, and lumber yards, as well as the town's electrical plant. For reference, see the Sanborn and Sanborn-Perris maps from 1893, 1899, 1905, 1910, 1923, and 1937, as well as "New Wauseon Industry," a *Fulton County Tribune* article on the Economy Oil Burner Company.

8. See Henning for the history of agricultural cooperatives in Ohio, including dairy and poultry cooperatives in Fulton County; Barron for the ways that grain elevators and other

types of farm cooperatives helped farmers increase their market power across the rural North; and Rosenberg on how these organizations link the "industrial ideal" of American agriculture to notions of rural manhood.

9. According to Lieberman, representations of electricity in literature reflect the rise of "systems thinking" in American culture. For histories of rural electrification, see D. Brown, Kline, and Jellison.

10. Racial exclusions are also part of Wauseon and Midwestern history; Vega's *Latino Heartland* and Gupta-Carlson's *Muncie, India(na)* explore hostilities underlying the tendency to whitewash Midwestern history and culture. As for Wauseon, Reighard documents the removal of the Potawatomi people from Fulton County. Later, the bicentennial souvenir booklet calls attention to the euphemistic treatment of nonwhite residents by putting "'traditional' Fulton County residents" in quotation marks and claiming that "their lives have become fuller and more meaningful" because of the cultural contributions of Latin American immigrants (Guilford 85).

11. The booster's prominence is especially evident in novels of the period, from Sinclair Lewis's *Babbitt* to lesser-known works such as Sherwood Anderson's *Poor White* and Dawn Powell's *The Story of a Country Boy,* which I discuss in chapters 1 and 2. The small-town Babbittry of Midwestern modernist novels occasionally extends to critical appraisals of the region, such as Odum and Moore's claim that "the great region which we have called the Middle States may be characterized as the most American of them all" (462) and R. Weber's that "for a time, Midwestern literature virtually *was* American literature" (3). Such representations—both literary and critical—relate to twentieth-century American nativism, which can be seen in reviewers' and literary critics' description of the "American" character in the texts I examine in this book (as I discuss in chapter 1, this occurs most sweepingly with Anderson); see Michaels. On the gendering of boosterism in the Midwest, see Abbott and Handy-Marchello.

12. For studies of "the heartland" and "flyover country" as terms applying to the Midwest, see, respectively, Higbie and Harkins.

13. Several Midwestern authors appear in midcentury literary surveys (see Cowley, Kazin, and Hicks, among others), and Midwestern regionalism has been a subfield of American literary studies since at least the 1923 publication of Van Doren's *Contemporary American Novelists, 1900–1920.* More recently, Casey's *A New Heartland* compellingly balances literary and cultural studies, "reconceptualiz[ing] modernity by focusing on rurality and women" (4). Book-length studies of the region's literature and culture pass through Midwestern exceptionalism (Shortridge, R. Weber, and Lauck), comparative studies with other regions (Dorman and Holman), and an interest in the land influenced by ecocritical studies (Pichaske and Barillas). Like Watts, each of these studies addresses "the entanglement of regional and national cultures" (xxv), as do essay collections edited by Cayton and Gray, Mahoney and Katz, Steiner, Lauck, and Kosiba, which display a range of scholarly approaches to Midwestern literary, cultural, and historical studies.

14. Generally, this book follows the US Census Bureau's definition of the Midwest: a geographical area stretching roughly six hundred miles to the east and west of the Mississippi River, from the Ohio River to the Canadian border, which includes the states of North and

South Dakota, Illinois, Indiana, Iowa, Kansas, Michigan, Minnesota, Missouri, Nebraska, Ohio, and Wisconsin. I recognize that this definition can be contested in a number of ways, particularly in terms of the region's expansiveness and its lack of firm, natural borders—which is one reason that chapter 3 includes *The Green Corn Rebellion,* an Oklahoma novel; certainly, my conception of the region is indebted to Benedict Anderson's "imagined community." Several essays in Cayton and Gray's *The Identity of the American Midwest,* which cover a range of historical periods, discuss the challenges of cohesively defining the region's culture and geography.

15. Olson's *Chicago Renaissance: Literature and Art in the Midwest Metropolis* and Rideout's *Sherwood Anderson: A Writer in America,* vol. 1, provide detailed accounts of Anderson's abandonment of his business interests in Elyria.

16. See Lutz, Mahoney and Katz, R. Jackson, Joseph, Foote, Lockwood, and Hsu for further studies of US regionalism that have influenced this book. There is also a notable transnational turn in studies of literature and space, which can be seen in essay collections by Brooker and Thacker and Doyle and Winkiel.

17. Perhaps the great unstated space in this formulation is the suburb, which appears infrequently in the central texts examined in this book. See Jackson's *Crabgrass Frontier* for the history of suburban development in the United States, Jurca's *White Diaspora* on the novel's participation in constructing and altering their cultural meanings, and Wilhite's description of them in "Contested Terrain" as "the endgame and final outpost of US regionalism" (618).

18. Van Doren argues that several major early twentieth-century Midwestern authors, including Sherwood Anderson, Sinclair Lewis, and Ruth Suckow, rejected a sentimental "cult of the village" (146). While Lauck productively calls attention to several authors who did not fit into this formulation, my argument in this book shares more with Lutz, who explains that such a revolt "might more accurately be considered the incorporation of the village" into cosmopolitan modernity (129).

19. In her discussion of masculinity in New Deal art, Melosh quotes Greitzer's thoughts on community service as a heroic ideal, though she does not mention the marginal comments by Edward Rowan, superintendent of the Section of Painting and Sculpture in the Treasury Department's Public Buildings Branch, who wrote, "You may have had this purpose in mind but the result is not convincing" (Letter to Greitzer, 18 Oct. 1937). Rowan's next letter to Greitzer, dated 6 Apr. 1938, makes no mention of this peevishness.

20. For the history of the changing culture of recreation, especially for single people, see Peiss on working-class women and Chudacoff on the subculture of bachelorhood.

21. Masculinity studies scholars often address common figures of American masculinity through the intersection of their national, regional, economic, racial, and sexual characteristics; see Carby, Kimmel, Leverenz, Nelson, Ownby, and Rotundo.

22. For feminist literary scholarship on modernism and modernity, particularly exploring questions of available narratives for women, see Gilbert and Gubar's foundational *Madwoman in the Attic.* For studies of women's relationship to the structures of modernity, including their racial, sexual, and regional implications, see Felski's *The Gender of Modernity*as well as works by Benstock, DuCille, Yaeger, Lindemann, and N. Miller.

23. In the early years of the twentieth century, several circuses raised their tents in Wauseon, often at the Fulton County Fairgrounds. Most local newspaper articles mirror the *Fulton County Tribune*'s assessment of the John Robinson Circus's 1915 performance: "Everybody seemed to be satisfied with the big parade and the performances" ("The Circus" 1). Local newspapers often mention the railroad as part of the process of bringing the circus to town. For instance, in 1917, La Tenna's Big Three Ring Circus came to town on a "special train" ("Circus Day" 5), and when Robinson passed through Wauseon in 1911, it was hauled on the Lake Shore "on eight flat cars, four stock cars and five coaches" ("First" 4). In 1916, when Buffalo Bill and the 101 Ranch Wild West Show performed in Wauseon on their way to Chicago, the *Sandusky Star-Journal* noted that, as he had gotten older, Buffalo Bill had started traveling in "a private Pullman car, having his own chef and servants" ("Buffalo" 8)

24. See Stover for the history of American railroads, including the B&O-C&O merger (282–283) and H. Grant for a more specific focus on Midwestern lines in the first third of the twentieth century.

25. This book follows Ching and Creed's description of "rural" and "urban" as a culturally insistent yet geographically and demographically blurred distinction. Scholarship addressing the history and representations of these extremes includes, among others, Kirschner on rural conceptions of the city, D. Campbell's discussion of the gender dynamics of local color and naturalism, Herring on urban slumming narratives, and Farland, who claims that "for modern American poets, pastoral confronts not the degradation imposed by change and modernity, but a degradation seen as *internal* to agrarian life, presenting a panoply of social problems in need of technical expertise" (911; emphasis in original). These common images suggest that one space or another might pull strongly at specific minoritized groups, which can be seen in Grossman's account of advertisements for high wages designed to lure African Americans to Chicago as well as in Halberstam's concept of queer "metronormativity."

26. Modernist studies' articulation of multiple modernisms has influenced my interest in expanding the archives and available spaces of literary modernism; in particular, see Hegeman's *Patterns for America,* Herring's *Another Country,* and Scandura's *Down in the Dumps.* This book is also in conversation with studies pairing literature with US political and economic practices, such as those by Denning, Foley, and Szalay, as well as Michaels's examination of American cultural nativism. Furthermore, see Moglen, Flatley, and Nieland on the affective experience of modernity, and several texts negotiating the formal and/or cultural elements of specific types of American and transnational modernism: McGurl, J. Brown, Clark, North, Whalan, Doyle and Winkiel, and Rabinowitz's *Black & White & Noir*.

27. To develop his definitions of region and regionalism, Duvall compares writers from New England, the Southwest, the West Coast, the Midwest, and the South in terms of their attention to "specific locale," calling the South "the most self-conscious of all the regions during American modernism" (252). The South is the only region that gets its own section in Duvall's essay, and it not only has a long tradition of dedicated scholarship (see, for instance, Yaeger, Davis, and Weaks-Baxter) but also a prominent place in studies comparing multiple regions (see Holman as well as Herring's *Another Country*). In this book, the South appears in *Poor White*'s cultural nod to the Upland Southerner (see Etcheson) and, in *Not Without Laughter,*

through Chicago's community of black southern migrants and a front-porch discussion of racism in various locales.

28. This is not to say that utopianism doesn't exist in Midwestern literature and culture. Indeed, Sutton describes the prevalence of utopian societies in the nineteenth-century Midwest, and several scholars have explored utopianism in rural and Midwestern literature. I take an approach somewhere between Robert Dorman's argument that regionalism is a "utopian means" to resist urban industrialism (xii) and Maria Farland's claim that modernist poets use pastoralism to confront rural decline yet "remain suspicious" of modern means of improving rural life (911).

## 1. Manufacturing Rural Modernity: The "Vast Energy" of Midwestern Masculinity

1. Although there are conflicting accounts of the first recorded use of natural gas in the Midwest, Bownocker, Kerr, Lynd and Lynd, and Maslowski describe oil and gas production as a major industry in the region, noting both its local importance and its contribution to nationally known companies such as Rockefeller's Standard Oil Company.

2. In *The Incorporation of America,* Trachtenberg describes the "economic incorporation" that took root in the late nineteenth century, and Fitzgerald shows how such centralization results in an "industrial ideal" in twentieth-century American agriculture. Adams, Barron, and Danbom document the many ways technology and modern economics facilitate changes in rural life, which are related to the developing markets of Midwestern cities seen in Teaford and Cronon.

3. Rideout somewhat breathlessly describes *Poor White* as an "unusual book-combination of parable, Biblical prophecy, Whitmanesque poem, and storyteller's tale" (Introduction xx). More commonly, scholars such as Fiedler, Hegeman, Clymer, Farland, Gelfant, and Hogue critique Anderson for infusing sentimentality and nostalgia into his representations of rural and small-town life, and Van Doren describes Anderson and several other Midwestern writers as constituting a "revolt from the village" (154). The volume of nostalgia-related scholarship on Anderson pairs easily with critics who connect him to calcified notions of national and regional identities. Following Butcher's 1920 review, in which she flatly states that *Poor White* is more than the story of a man or a town, "It is America" (9), midcentury critics make claims on Anderson's "authentic" portrayals of small towns (Kazin 209), the Midwest (Hicks 229), and America (Parrington 241).

4. This claim departs from a common refrain in Anderson criticism that argues that Bidwell "succumbs to the forces of history and becomes the city" (Gelfant 64). My argument lies closer to Love's suggestion that Anderson's tone is "reconciliatory" and that his characters attempt "to cope with an inescapable and complex urban present" ("Horses" 236), though I contend that his present is not so inescapably urban.

5. Power highlights regional heterogeneity resulting from these groups' "contact and blending" (vii). On migrant Yankees and Upland Southerners, see also Etcheson, Wilson, and

Gray. Brooks and Hegeman take up similar issues of inter-American cultural conflict between "Puritan" and "Pioneer." The influence of Yankee Puritanism in this novel also relates to Max Weber's description of the entwinement of Protestantism and capitalism, which suggests a reading of Anderson's construction of rural modernity in terms of "forever *renewed* profit" (17; emphasis in original).

6. My discussion of Hugh's actions draws on foundational queer studies scholarship. For instance, Sedgwick's concept of "male homosocial desire" animates Hugh's intent to become "a man among men," and this chapter elaborates on alternate rural spaces and possibilities using Halberstam's study of "queer spaces" within "metronormativity," which she describes as the standard narrative of queer urban migration.

7. Wray's description of the "disturbing liminality" of white trash evokes Cook's claim that the poor white is a figure of "moral, emotional, and intellectual incongruity" (5). Building on this approach, Herring's *Another Country* explores "white trash" as a stylistic category participating in a broader strain of late twentieth-century queer critical antiurbanism, Ferrence describes how redneck identities designate "a refusal to play the game of polite America" (76), and Seguin argues that depictions of poor whites in novels of the 1920s depend upon a narrative emptiness that sets rural poor white characters apart from representations of black folk traditions. Interestingly, among studies of the southern poor white in literature, neither Cook (who has a section on Anderson) nor McIlwaine mentions *Poor White*. This may be due to the novel's setting in the Midwest or because, after Shepard's insult, Anderson largely obscures Hugh's origins as "poor white trash" from the banks of the Mississippi (12).

8. As Seguin associates novelistic representations of rural poor whites and blacks, Harkins's study of the hillbilly in popular media notes how the middle-class viewing public could read poor white hillbillies "as a fascinating and exotic 'other' akin to Native Americans or Blacks" (*Hillbilly* 7). See also H. Smith on primitivism in frontier literature and mythology.

9. Van Willigen and Eastwood note the Bemis transplanter's similarity to those produced by Tiger and New Idea (89), and Hansen dubs it "the best one" on the market (426).

10. Clymer calls attention to the novel's temporal disruptions when he notes that Hugh's "inventive methodology [is] . . . historically obsolete" (502) when compared to the advances made by figures such as Henry Ford.

11. See Fitzgerald on "the emergence of an industrial logic or ideal in agriculture" in the twentieth-century United States (3). Rauchway contextualizes that production shift within a broader US economic history while Adams and Nordin and Scott trace the history of industrial farming, focusing on different locations and aspects of Midwestern agriculture. Of particular note, Neth identifies one way that treating the farm as a business challenged values often associated with family farms: "Some farm men had to put strategies that emphasized capital and production ahead of those that emphasized labor, family, and community" (5).

12. S. Meyer shows how the transition from artisanal to factory labor includes skilled machinists but then in the early twentieth century shifts to unskilled production workers. Because workers felt emasculated in the new economy, they alternated between destructive behaviors such as fighting and drunkenness and more reputable activities such as organizing unions.

13. Bunge and Atlas have addressed Anderson's problematic treatment of women, and Whalan extends that analysis to Anderson's representation of nonwhite characters and homosexuality. Despite such concerns, many scholars and reviewers insist that he somehow captures the essential "human" qualities of his characters. Howe, Chase, Kazin, Enniss, Pichaske, Rosenfeld, and David D. Anderson, among others, comment on this universalizing impulse, allowing them to treat Anderson's writing as a celebration of the individual and/or an all-inclusive critique of modern life. The grotesque—denoting, alternately, a denunciation or humanization of his characters—is also a dominant theme in Anderson criticism, explored by Kazin, Parrington, Schorer, Dunne, and O'Connor. Furthermore, for explorations of primitive elements in Anderson's writing, see Hoffman, Cargill, Love, and Frank, who claims that "the burden of Sherwood Anderson's books [is that] they are a playing of wistful flames over the muck heap" (94).

14. Agee and Evans's *Let Us Now Praise Famous Men* famously walks the line between documentary and fiction, while the Lynds' *Middletown,* a sociological study of a small Midwestern city, shares several narrative and descriptive characteristics with *Poor White.* On sociology and the novel, see Rochberg-Halton's essay on Chicago, Denning on the "cultural front," and Hutchinson's and Marlon Ross's studies of African American reform movements and the Harlem Renaissance. Generic (or modal) confusion is also a feature of Anderson's literary reputation: Pizer and Donald place him in a naturalistic tradition, while Kazin forcefully disagrees, and Whipple finds that despite his naturalist characteristics, Anderson does not arrive at the "hard-and-fast philosophy" expected of naturalism (97).

## 2. "The Rustic Dream": Gender Norms, Rural Time, and the Modern Countryside

1. In her biography of Niedecker, Peters does not mention Powell or her friends. Niedecker and her known acquaintances are likewise absent from Page's biography of Powell.

2. Furthermore, Powell is said to have an "ear for American lingo" (G. Howard) and "stoical Midwestern humor" (Gibbons 146), and Rovit contextualizes her within the Lost Generation, whom he describes as "artists who streamed like lemmings from the American hinterland" (285). Correspondingly, Niedecker has been regionalized not only because she "inhabited a periphery" (Alcosser 28) but also because her poetry was influenced by "the pressure of vast provincial American space" (Tomlinson 7).

3. Gender-based criticism on Niedecker generally follows DuPlessis's claim that "the resistances Niedecker makes in her poetry involve her critical discomfort with gender norms" ("Anonymous" 97). Related to DuPlessis's focus on "littleness" (97), Niedecker's association with the Wisconsin countryside is often used to marginalize her: "In her case, 'local' has been interpreted as 'minor'" (Tarlo 192). She is frequently described as a "mediator between nature and culture" (Augustine 139) or between the "technological" and the "natural" (Peterson 254). Niedecker's marginalization is also seen in her critical subordination to Zukofsky, who frequently is named as her mentor. As a young poet, she sought him out, and they are rumored to

have been lovers, a claim perpetuated by their friend Jerry Reisman but discounted by Scroggins as impossible to confirm.

4. The 1935 edition of *The Sunlit Road* is 3 3/4 × 4 7/8 inches. The calendar was published by the Dodge Publishing Company throughout the early to mid-twentieth century, running from at least 1913 (see Potter and Teich) to 1942 (see "Elevator Calendar Prescribes Philosophers' Weekly Way of Life" in the Columbia University student newspaper). Horder's 1908 *The Sunlit Road: Readings in Verse & Prose for Every Day* appears to be a forerunner, and several of the calendar's homilies were collected in Trine's 1915 *Along the Sunlit Road: Reprinted from the Sunlit Road Calendar.* Dodge advertised in the trade journal *The Bookseller, Newsdealer and Stationer,* which claimed in 1916 that "this series is one of the most popular that has ever been offered" ("Stationery, Novelties" 763).

5. In *Hidden Rhythms,* Zerubavel argues that humans produce normalcy via temporal experience. He develops that argument in *Time Maps* by demonstrating the social element of imposed temporal narratives such as progress, decline, and circularity. Furthermore, each of the texts in this chapter, especially *The Sunlit Road,* draws on temporalities of mass production, which Olsen claims are "orchestrated by things, mainly ephemeral consumer objects mobilized in support of this regulatory ideal of progressive time" (111).

6. This claim, and its contributions to the chapter's larger argument, benefits from the insights of several scholars of feminist and queer time: Halberstam on the problems associated with standardizing a narrative of metronormativity; Herring on rewriting queer relationships to narratives of urban progressivity; Muñoz's use of critical indeterminacy and consideration of utopianism as a "future in the present" (49); Rohy's claim that queer temporal anachronism is contained within the structure of normative time; Felski regarding how studies of temporality reliant upon epochal change paper over fundamentally uneven temporal experiences; Grosz in terms of the relationship between corporeality and time; and Cvetkovich on the effects of materiality and habit on the experience of memory and time.

7. Pizer's exemplars of American literary naturalism include Frank Norris, Theodore Dreiser, John Dos Passos, and James T. Farrell, who all were born or worked in the Midwest, and Kramer finds a strain of Chicago naturalism stretching from Dreiser to the Depression. This trend continues with many of Hapke's representative female social protest writers, including Tillie Olsen, Meridel Le Sueur, Agnes Smedley, and Josephine Herbst.

8. US-based masculinity studies (see Bederman, Cawelti, Chauncey, Kimmel, and Rotundo) devote considerable attention to the figure of the self-made man—including his rise and decline and the effects on American expectations of masculine gender performance. A ruralized version of this concern over masculine dependency can be found in the Great Depression's effect on the US and Midwestern agricultural economies. Danbom discusses the federal government's incursion into agricultural markets, indicating how the US economy incorporated in both the public and private sectors. Nordin and Scott note a comparatively heavy Depression-era debt load for farmers in Midwestern states, and Fitzgerald describes reactions to the "cruel myth" of "much-vaunted independence" for debt-ridden farmers (125). Neth argues that poorer farmers depended economically on their wealthier neighbors in some Midwestern communities, which results in neighborly cooperation but also uneasiness and blame.

9. Page and Rice each note the influence of communist playwright John Howard Lawson on the novel's politics, but they differ on how to describe those politics, a possible reason *The Story of a Country Boy* remains uncited as a proletarian novel.

10. The Bennett family's leisure activities mirror historical trends of the period. K. R. Walker finds that recreation increased in the Midwest in the years following World War I, while Neth argues that it was more easily accessed in towns and urban areas, an example of which is the rise of cheap restaurants and cafeteria culture noted by Chauncey. According to Peiss and Rotundo, recreational activities had been on the rise for several decades among various socioeconomic classes, though each note that men had a broader array of possibilities to choose from—a difference that manifests in *The Story of a Country Boy* with regard to Chris's and Joy's various forms of leisure.

11. Critics use a variety of terms to describe *Next Year*'s form. Alcosser calls it a "single-edition artist book" (30), Burt claims that it is "as much an artist's book as it is a set of poems" (326), and Pinard and Robinson refer to it as a single poem. Penberthy's *Collected Works* typographically calls attention to this confusion, using a different font for *Next Year* than she uses for the titles of other books or poems.

12. Nicholls, Golston, Jennison, and DuPlessis have addressed Niedecker's surrealism, which she makes plain in another poem from *Next Year* that refers to Salvador Dali's 1934 painting *Archeological Reminiscence of Millet's Angelus* (51).

13. Based on a 1961 letter, Penberthy determines that Niedecker's visit to New York happened in late November and early December 1933 (23). According to *The Jefferson County Union* movie listings, *The Way to Love* played at the Fort Theatre's "Bargain Nite" on January 11–12, 1933 ("Fort").

## 3. "Where People and Things Wear Out": Masculine Fatigue and the Great Plains Farm Novel

1. Rural queer studies has further complicated our understanding of frontier masculinity. See Halberstam on Brandon Teena's trans masculinity, R. Henry's discussion of queer sexuality in late-nineteenth and early twentieth-century Colorado, Bateman on homosocial relationships and queer desire in Horatio Alger novels, Rosenberg on the contribution of 4-H to both industrial agriculture and normative sexuality, and C. Johnson on queer sexuality among migrant laborers and in the all-male camps of the Civilian Conservation Corps.

2. Ted has a "disease" which has left him with a "queer" body, and Jim feels their parents only sent him to school because "Ted was crippled and couldn't do work on the farm" (44, 25, 32). Cunningham implies that Ted's vindictiveness is because of his disability, which is consistent with Mitchell and Snyder's findings that physical disability serve as visual shorthand for villains in film and literature.

3. Cunningham's attentiveness to both farm life and the American labor movement started early (according to O'Dell, Cunningham's father was a farmer who supported socialist leader Eugene V. Debs) and continued throughout his life. During his undergrad years at Oklahoma

University, folklorist and radical regionalist B. A. Botkin was Cunningham's English professor and mentor (for more on Botkin, see Wixson and Hirsch). After college, in addition to writing novels and journalism, he taught at Commonwealth College, a prolabor university in Arkansas; worked for the Federal Writers' Project; and, later, became an editor for the Soviet news agency TASS.

4. Teaford documents labor organization and unrest in Midwestern cities from the late nineteenth century up through the Depression era, while Dubofsky notes the cooperation between the Industrial Workers of the World and agricultural unions in the Great Plains. Zieger's history of twentieth-century labor unrest includes rural strikes in the mining and textile industries as well as urban organizing efforts among steel and auto workers, and Perlman and Taft show how activism in western mining camps led to more widespread class war.

5. Criminal syndicalism laws, which were used to suppress radicalism and free speech, were enacted in 22 states starting at the end of the first world war. See Dowell and A. White for the history of these laws and their deployment against the Industrial Workers of the World, one of the unions active in both the fictional and historical Green Corn Rebellion.

6. While Rideout critiques the novel for Jim's unclear motivations, he argues that Jim's and Happy's indiscretions happen because they are "bored by the drudgery" of the farm (*Radical* 216).

7. Within their histories of the rebellion, Burbank and Bissett show how it consolidated opposition to the state socialist party, and Burbank describes the party's attempt to sidestep blame.

8. For the links among individuals and markets created by railroads, automobiles, telephones, and the telegraph, see Cronon, Kline, Adams, Fitzgerald, and Danbom, as well as Stover for the history of railroad building on the prairies. For the implications on political action of telephone and telegraph technology, see MacDougall.

9. New Deal programs such as the Farm Security Administration and Resettlement Administration promoted mixed farming as a way to endure the Great Depression and possibly improve the land. Hurt explains how such loans were designed to facilitate "self-sustaining" farming practices (*Dust* 95), and M. Grant describes how government agents "informed their clients that draft animals, rather than machine power, were best suited for their operations" (115).

10. For Morris's anxiety about the difference between "readers" and "lookers," see his interview with Bunnell, "Photography and Reality."

11. See Harp for the development of synthetic rubber and its increased use during World War II.

### 4. "A Dreamy-Eyed Boy": Chicago, Race Records, and Regional Black Masculinity

1. See Cronon and Spears regarding the effect of the 1893 World's Fair on popular conceptions of Chicago.

2. Grossman maps the *Defender*'s circulation throughout the US South, noting correspondences between the number of copies received and African Americans' percentage of total population (76–77).

3. A great deal of Hughes criticism addresses his use of music as a formal and historical device. In this regard, there has been more work done on his poetry (for example, see Kun and Baker) than on *Not Without Laughter* (more comprehensively, see Rosenblatt and Wall). Hughes draws on similar characteristics of jazz music to those Muyumba hears when listening to Charlie Parker, in which he describes "the music's complicated emotional reality: laughing to keep from crying, crying to the point of laughter, laughing hard enough to draw tears, crying that sounds like laughter, laughter that sounds like weeping" (21).

4. For histories of race records and the development of markets geared to African American consumers, see K. Miller, Kennedy, Kennedy and McNutt, and Calt.

5. According to Brooks and Spottswood, W. C. Handy was among the first published blues artists, recording as early as 1912. His most famous songs, recorded for several labels, including Paramount, Columbia, and Okeh, were the "Memphis," "Yellow Dog," and "St. Louis" blues, directly echoing *Not Without Laughter*. Furthermore, the blues provided Hughes subtle access to folk legend. Brooks and Spottswood describe Handy's song "Aunt Hagar's Children Blues": "The unusual title was a reference to the biblical story of Abraham, Sarah, and Sarah's black handmaiden Hagar, from which blacks sometimes referred to themselves as Hagar's children" (426).

6. From Louis Armstrong to Duke Ellington to W. C. Handy, the number of sidemen who became well-known band leaders suggests an upward mobility (or at least some fluidity) in jazz and blues that may have incited interest in introductions among audience members and possibly among the performers themselves. Pereira counters this reading, however, finding that August Wilson's play *Ma Rainey's Black Bottom* poses sidemen as content with their role, especially as compared to other possibilities for black men of the period. Ennis claims that the jazz press contributed to the phenomenon of introducing sidemen as an educational and evaluative strategy. See Ramsey and Smith and Brooks and Spottswood for numerous band leaders' history as sidemen and Vacher for oral histories of several sidemen, including midcentury musicians as well as those who played with the familiar band leaders of the 1920s.

7. In comparison to jazz recording, blues has a rich rural history. For example, Oliver discusses early field recording and rural "proto-blues"; Brooks and Spottswood archive early jazz and blues artists who came from, toured through, and recorded in rural areas; and McNutt extends this conversation into the mid-twentieth century when he notes the ruralized locations of several "regional music centers" across the country. Turning from the field of jazz and blues recording to specific individual labels results in spotty and confusing partial histories, of which Gennett and Paramount are representative. Along with several lost documents, this confusion stems from widespread use of pseudonymous recordings for reasons both social and commercial, multiple recording locations (Gennett had a studio in New York City as well as the main Starr-Gennett complex in Richmond), and the practice of contracting pressings with other labels (such as the blues records that Paramount contracted with Gennett in 1929). See Kennedy, Kennedy and McNutt, and the John K. MacKenzie Collection at the Indiana Historical Society, which contains several record-keeping documents as well as the manuscripts of MacKenzie's incomplete, unpublished history of Gennett.

8. The Orpheum circuit consisted of a coordinated booking and theater system in large

and small cities across the United States. See Wertheim regarding the development and conflicts among the Orpheum circuit and general vaudeville business practices and Erdman on vaudeville performers' changes to their routines when passing through more rural parts of the country.

9. Hughes's representation of typical black labor in the Jim Crow era is borne out by Litwack's discussion in *Trouble in Mind* of domestic labor and other common jobs held by Southern blacks, as well as by Kimmel's account in *Manhood in America* of struggles over black membership in white unions. See also Ross's *Manning the Race* for a description of literary representations of black labor.

10. For example, Frank bemoans the loss of refinement and increased vulgarity when "the Negro peasant" who "draws from the soil and sky in whose cycles he is seasoned" moves to Harlem (109). Bone later submits that the deployment of "stereotype with counterstereotype" mimics and responds to the racist plantation tradition (22).

11. In his study of Hughes's 1930s short stories, Holcomb suggests that Hughes wished to distance himself from *Not Without Laughter* because it was written, with the approval of Hughes's patron Charlotte Osgood Mason, as "a narrative about the Negro folk striving to enter the middle class" (430). True enough, the family's hopefulness centers on Sandy's education and future economic achievement, but I counter that Hughes critiques uplift ideologies through the complicated relationships among the novel's wide range of middle-class and folk figures, which places my reading closer to Winters's concept of "melancholic hope," defined as "a tension-filled interaction between the past and present" (248).

12. Anthologies such as Alain Locke's *The New Negro* (1925) demonstrate the trend to document the Harlem Renaissance (and African American life more generally) through a wide range of literary, artistic, and scholarly texts. See Hutchinson regarding Locke's methods for choosing what to include in *The New Negro* and Pinkerton for the way it creates a "renaissance orthodoxy" (541). North analyzes Zora Neale Hurston's "The Eatonville Anthology" (1926) alongside Nancy Cunard's *Negro* (1934), which he describes, respectively, as "utterly miscellaneous" and "generically indiscriminate" (186, 189). Regarding *Negro,* Winkiel argues that it attempts to "fill in the present with found scraps of that hidden past" (510), which relates to Garvey's study of African American scrapbook making during the Harlem Renaissance. Jean Toomer's *Cane* (1923) and the lone issue of the magazine *Fire!!* (1926) also reflect this accumulation of genres, though with a more literary focus.

13. A notable exception comes in the chapter "White Folks," with a discussion of racism started by Harriett that leads to Sister Johnson's story of Southern racial violence, which recalls novelist Wallace Thurman's review comment that Stanton "vacillates uncertainly, spiritually and physically, from one side of the Mason Dixon line to the other" (143).

14. Hughes's transnationalism can be seen in several texts, from "The Negro Speaks of Rivers" to the travels he documents in *The Big Sea* and elsewhere. Kun productively studies Hughes's connections to Mexico and Latino musical traditions, while B. Bell mentions Hughes's international travel alongside several Harlem Renaissance works with an international component, by authors such as McKay, Bontemps, and Larsen. For a contemporary claim on the Harlem Renaissance's relation to wider patterns of Afro-transnationalism, see

Du Bois's essay in *The New Negro*. Transnationalism—and the Harlem Renaissance more generally—has also been associated with discourses of primitivism; see Lemke, Bone, and Huggins.

## Conclusion: Contemporary Manhood and the Entrepreneurial Midwest

1. In "Publishing from Flyover Country," Oman shows how recent Midwestern literary magazines subvert common "heartland iconography" through images that make reference to, among others, economic decline and futuristic technology—histories that disrupt the nostalgic image of the well-tended barn and farmyard.

2. A gambrel roof has two slopes on each side, and the bottom slope is a good deal steeper than the top. According to Hauser, a gambrel offers more storage space in the hay loft but requires more skilled labor than gable roofs and other styles of barn architecture (58). Noble and Wilhelm note that gambrel roofs became more popular in the Midwest after Joseph Wing innovated barn roof architecture in the early twentieth century with a self-supporting, braced-rafter design (156–157).

3. Vreba-Hoff Dairy—a Wauseon-based company—was known for polluting waterways around its locations near Hudson, Michigan, and, in 2001, water quality activists organized a "tour de manure" protesting the environmental practices of Vreba-Hoff and several other confined animal feeding operations in the region (Arrigo A12). In 2007, the Michigan attorney general fined Vreba-Hoff and ordered the company to thin its herd at the two Hudson locations (T. Henry, "Mich." B1). In 2010, a finance company took control of Vreba-Hoff's three Michigan locations (Vellequette; Kevin Walker), which by 2013 were sold to Milk Source Dairy, based in Kaukana, Wisconsin ("Foreclosed"). While Milk Source "takes pride in its reputation as an environmentally responsible dairy producer and wants to distance the farms from their Vreba-Hoff days" (T. Henry, "New"), in 2014 a Michigan citizens group drew attention to Milk Source's possible contribution to toxic algae blooms in Lake Erie (Matheny A1).

4. During my visit in May 2018, the other coffee shop in Wauseon was Biggby Coffee, a Michigan-based chain that was founded in East Lansing in 1995. Over the last ten years, Biggby has nearly tripled in size, from 100 stores in 2008 to over 260 in 2018; see "Biggby Hits" and "Biggby Ranks."

5. The Michelsons' head brewers have been home brewers that they knew beforehand, and their beer has been well received in Wauseon and throughout the region; see Cathey, Church, B. Cunningham, and Kubacki. According to Kravatz, the Ohio craft beer industry grew dramatically after changes to licensing fees in 2013.

6. According to Connell, hegemonic masculinity validates patriarchal control through the assertion of authority, and its structures are related to complicit, marginalized, and subordinated masculinities. Bridges and Pascoe argue that when these various iterations of masculinity are combined into hybrid forms, white heterosexual men feel diminished and, accordingly, Faludi's *Stiffed* details the loss of control felt by American men over the course of the twentieth century and Kimmel's *Angry White Men* contextualizes white men's anger with their percep-

tions of socioeconomic futility. One response to such feelings of loss is to valorize patriarchal values, which, as hooks shows in *The Will to Change,* encourages violence in American men. More specifically, sociologists have studied elements of toxic masculinity in many of the communities Jordy is part of and the discourses he would be exposed to. For instance, Pascoe explores the centrality of homophobia and heterosexuality for American high school boys, and Fine et al. demonstrate how white working-class men construct their identities in opposition to women and nonwhite men. Jordy's hunting and drinking relate to Holt and Thompson's argument that men create an active persona through their consumption practices, while caring for his mother both feminizes him and provides certain social benefits, as shown by Ribeiro et al. Finally, Jordy's lack of initiative even as he sells the venison seems to complicate Bird's findings that Midwestern male small business owners need to be their own bosses.

7. The rise of opioid prescriptions for pain treatment in the 2010s has led to widespread increases in addiction rates, particularly in nonurban communities. See Meldrum for historical context on some of the consequences of opioid prescription practices, Wilkerson et al. on rural-urban and demographics, and Ray et al. on the rise of opioid overdoses from 2010 to 2015 in Marion County, Indiana, which includes Indianapolis. For state-level interventions, see Wickramatilake et al. As for the factors affecting policy and government responses, McGinty et al. note a shift to public health solutions in news media framing of stories of opioid addiction between 1998 and 2012, though in a similar timeframe Kennedy-Hendricks et al. find that social stigma toward addicts leads to more punitive policies.

8. Building on Clover's analysis of rural horror, D. Bell develops the term "hillbilly horror" to explain how 1970s rural slasher films represent the clash of urban and rural cultures, and Oman contextualizes 1980s rural horror within the American farm crisis. Blake studies the post-9/11 resurgence of hillbilly horror films, arguing that they critique the state and help contend with national trauma. Hayden, on the other hand, claims that representing rural people as grotesque stereotypes is a metronormative act that allows viewers to distance themselves from actual problems in rural life, and McCollum finds that post-9/11 "heartland horror" movies reject hillbilly horror tropes, instead portraying a society in which the monster is not so easily recognizable.

9. For farm-to-table and other locally oriented or sustainable agricultural systems, see Holthaus as well as Hinrichs and Lyson. Zukin and Hensley each show how local food movements in New York City trade on the authenticity of place. Chapman et al. and Murray and O'Neill explore the relationship of the craft beer movement to discourses of locality, authenticity, and entrepreneurship.

10. Walzer and Blanke claim that small farmers are ideally suited for entrepreneurial activity, while Ferguson and Olofsson caution about the slow returns of entrepreneurial ventures. Ikerd argues that niche markets can help reduce farmers' dependence on industrial agricultural systems. Relatedly, McIlvaine-Newsad et al. claim that entrepreneurial farmers improve local quality of life, and, more broadly, Korsgaard et al. study how rural entrepreneurship can revalorize place.

# WORKS CITED


Abbott, Carl. *Boosters and Businessmen: Popular Economic Thought and Urban Growth in the Antebellum Middle West.* Greenwood, 1981.

Abramson, Daniel M. *Obsolescence: An Architectural History.* U of Chicago P, 2016.

Adams, Jane. *The Transformation of Rural Life: Southern Illinois, 1890–1990.* U of North Carolina P, 1994.

Agee, James, and Walker Evans. *Let Us Now Praise Famous Men.* Houghton Mifflin, 1941.

Alcosser, Sandra. "Avant-Gardist in the Forest." *Antioch Review,* vol. 62, no. 1, 2004, pp. 28–36.

"Among New Books." Review of *The Story of a Country Boy,* by Dawn Powell. *Chicago Daily Tribune,* 24 Mar. 1934, p. 12.

Anderson, Benedict. *Imagined Communities: Reflections on the Origin and Spread of Nationalism.* Verso, 1983.

Anderson, David D. "Anderson and Myth." 1976. *Critical Essays on Sherwood Anderson,* edited by David D. Anderson, G. K. Hall, 1981, pp. 267–283.

——. Introduction. *Home Town,* by Sherwood Anderson, Appel, 1975, pp. i–x.

Anderson, Sherwood. Introduction. *Poor White,* Modern Library, 1926, pp. v–viii.

——. *Poor White.* 1920. New Directions, 1993.

Ardrey, Robert L. *American Agricultural Implements: A Review of Invention and Development in the Agricultural Implement Industry of the United States.* Self-published, 1894.

Armantrout, Rae. "Darkinfest." *Radical Vernacular: Lorine Niedecker and the Poetics of Place,* edited by Elizabeth Willis, U of Iowa P, 2008, pp. 103–112.

Arrigo, Barbara. "Upstream, Downstream Tour Will Open Eyes, and Noses, to Mega-Dairy Farm Threat." *Detroit Free Press,* 2 June 2001, p. A12.

Asch, Nathan. "Novels No End." Review of *The Green Corn Rebellion,* by William Cunningham. *The New Republic,* 23 Oct. 1935, pp. 310–311.

Atlas, Marilyn Judith. "Sherwood Anderson and the Women of Winesburg." *Critical Essays on Sherwood Anderson,* edited by David D. Anderson, G. K. Hall, 1981, pp. 250–266.

Augustine, Jane. "'What's Wrong with Marriage?': Lorine Niedecker's Struggle with Gender Roles." *Lorine Niedecker: Woman and Poet,* edited by Jenny Penberthy, National Poetry Foundation, 1996, pp. 139–156.

"Augustine Davis, Inventor, Is Dead." *New York Times,* 20 Jan. 1933, p. 13.

Bailey, Liberty Hyde. *Cyclopedia of American Agriculture.* Vol. 2, *Crops,* Macmillan, 1917.

Baker, Houston A. *Blues, Ideology, and Afro-American Literature: A Vernacular Theory.* U of Chicago P, 1984.

Banks, Kimberly J. "Gender Performance and Sexual Subjectivity in *Not without Laughter:* Sandy's Emergent Masculinity." *Montage of a Dream: The Art and Life of Langston Hughes,* edited by John Edgar Tidwell and Cheryl R. Ragar, U of Missouri P, 2007, pp. 86–105.

Barillas, William David. *The Midwestern Pastoral: Place and Landscape in Literature of the American Heartland.* Ohio UP, 2006.

Barlett, Peggy F. "Three Visions of Masculine Success on American Farms." *Country Boys: Masculinity and Rural Life,* edited by Hugh Campbell et al., Pennsylvania State UP, 2006.

Barron, Hal S. *Mixed Harvest: The Second Great Transformation in the Rural North, 1870–1930.* U of North Carolina P, 1997.

Bassett, John E. *Sherwood Anderson: An American Career.* Susquehanna UP, 2006.

Bateman, Geoffrey W. "Horatio Alger's Queer Frontier." *Queering the Countryside: New Frontiers in Rural Queer Studies,* edited by Mary L. Gray et al., New York UP, 2016, pp. 49–68.

Beck, Thomas M. "Wand of Science Transforms the Ogre Coal." *Chicago Daily Tribune,* 30 Dec. 1934, p. D8.

Bederman, Gail. *Manliness & Civilization: A Cultural History of Gender and Race in the United States, 1880–1917.* U of Chicago P, 1995.

Bell, Bernard W. *The Afro-American Novel and Its Tradition.* U of Massachusetts P, 1987.

Bell, David. "Anti-Idyll: Rural Horror." *Contested Countryside Cultures: Otherness, Marginalisation, and Rurality,* edited by Paul J. Cloke and Jo Little, Routledge, 1997, pp. 91–104.

Benstock, Shari. *Women of the Left Bank: Paris, 1900–1940.* U of Texas P, 1986.

Berish, Andrew S. *Lonesome Roads and Streets of Dreams: Place, Mobility, and Race in Jazz of the 1930s and '40s.* U of Chicago P, 2012.

Berman, Marshall. *All That Is Solid Melts into Air: The Experience of Modernity.* 1982. Penguin, 1988.

Bessie, Alvah C. "In the American Idiom." Review of *The Green Corn Rebellion,* by William Cunningham. *The Saturday Review,* 26 Oct. 1935, pp. 10–11.

"Biggby Coffee Hits 100th Store Milestone." Biggby Coffee, 14 July 2008, https://www.biggby.com/biggby-coffee-hits-100th-store-milestone/. Accessed 5 June 2018.

"Biggby Coffee Ranks in Entrepreneur Franchise 500." Biggby Coffee, 15 Feb. 2018, https://www.biggby.com/biggby-coffee-ranks-entrepreneur-franchise-500/. Accessed 5 June 2018.

Bird, Sharon. "Masculinities in Rural Small Business Ownership: Between Community and Capitalism." *Country Boys: Masculinity and Rural Life,* edited by Hugh Campbell et al., Pennsylvania State UP, 2006, pp. 67–84.

Bissett, Jim. *Agrarian Socialism in America: Marx, Jefferson, and Jesus in the Oklahoma Countryside, 1904–1920.* U of Oklahoma P, 1999.

Blake, Linnie. *The Wounds of Nations: Horror Cinema, Historical Trauma and National Identity.* 2008. Manchester UP, 2012.

Bone, Robert A. *The Negro Novel in America.* Revised edition, Yale UP, 1965.

Bourne, Randolph. "A Mirror of the Middle West." *The Dial,* vol. 65, no. 778, 30 Nov. 1918, pp. 480–482.

Bownocker, John Adams. *The Occurrence and Exploitation of Petroleum and Natural Gas in Ohio.* Geological Survey of Ohio, Springfield Publishing, 1903.

Boym, Svetlana. *The Future of Nostalgia.* Basic Books, 2001.

Bridges, Tristan, and C. J. Pascoe. "Hybrid Masculinities: New Directions in the Sociology of Men and Masculinities." *Sociology Compass,* vol. 8, no. 3, 2014, pp. 246–258.

Brooker, Peter, and Andrew Thacker, editors. *Geographies of Modernism: Literatures, Cultures, Spaces.* Routledge, 2005.

Brooks, Tim, and Richard K. Spottswood. *Lost Sounds: Blacks and the Birth of the Recording Industry, 1890–1919.* U of Illinois P, 2004.

Brooks, Van Wyck. "America's Coming-of-Age." 1915. *Van Wyck Brooks, the Early Years: A Selection from His Works, 1908–1925,* edited by Claire Sprague, revised edition, Northeastern UP, 1993, pp. 79–158.

Brown, Bill. *A Sense of Things: The Object Matter of American Literature.* U of Chicago P, 2003.

Brown, D. Clayton. *Electricity for Rural America: The Fight for the REA.* Greenwood, 1980.

Brown, Judith. *Glamour in Six Dimensions: Modernism and the Radiance of Form.* Cornell UP, 2009.

Brown, Sterling. Review of *Not Without Laughter,* by Langston Hughes. 1930. *Critical Essays on Langston Hughes,* edited by Edward J. Mullen, G. K. Hall, 1986, pp. 60–63.

"Buffalo Bill Takes It Easy, but Cannot Keep Out of Saddle." *The Sandusky Star-Journal,* 14 Aug. 1916, p. 8.

Bunge, Nancy. "Women in Sherwood Anderson's Fiction." *Critical Essays on Sherwood Anderson,* edited by David D. Anderson, G. K. Hall, 1981, pp. 242–249.

Burbank, Garin. *When Farmers Voted Red: The Gospel of Socialism in the Oklahoma Countryside, 1910–1924.* Greenwood, 1976.

Burt, Stephen. "Lorine Niedecker: Raking Leaves in New Madrid." *Close Calls with Nonsense: Reading New Poetry,* edited by Stephen Burt, Graywolf P, 2009, pp. 317–327.

Butcher, Fanny. "Tabloid Book Review." Review of *Poor White,* by Sherwood Anderson. *Chicago Daily Tribune,* 5 Dec. 1920, p. 9.

"Buy a Fuller & Johnson Bemis Transplanter." Advertisement. *Dun's Review,* vol. 11, no. 2, 1908, p. 49.

Calt, Stephen. "The Anatomy of a Race Music Label." *R&B: Rhythm and Business—The Political Economy of Black Music,* edited by Norman Kelley, Akashic Books, 2002, pp. 86–111.

Calverton, V. F. Review of *Not Without Laughter,* by Langston Hughes. 1930. *Critical Essays on Langston Hughes,* edited by Edward J. Mullen, G. K. Hall, 1986, pp. 59–60.

Campbell, Bonnie Jo. "Boar Taint." *American Salvage,* Wayne State UP, 2009, pp. 151–167.

Campbell, Donna M. *Resisting Regionalism: Gender and Naturalism in American Fiction, 1885–1915.* Ohio UP, 1997.

Canby, Courtlandt. "Return to Boyhood with Lens and Pen." Review of *The Home Place,* by Wright Morris. *The Saturday Review,* 24 July 1948, p. 12.

Carby, Hazel V. *Race Men.* Harvard UP, 1998.

Cargill, Oscar. *Intellectual America: Ideas on the March.* Macmillan, 1941.

Casey, Janet Galligani. *A New Heartland: Women, Modernity, and the Agrarian Ideal in America.* Oxford UP, 2009.

Cathey, Ben. "Small Breweries Bubble Up in Small Towns." WTVG, 16 Jan. 2017, http://www.13abc.com/content/news/Small-breweries-bubble-up-in-small-towns--410863905.html. Accessed 23 May 2018.

Cawelti, John G. *Apostles of the Self-Made Man: Changing Concepts of Success in America.* U of Chicago P, 1965.

Cayton, Andrew R. L., and Susan E. Gray, editors. *The Identity of the American Midwest: Essays on Regional History.* Indiana UP, 2001.

Cayton, Andrew R. L., and Peter S. Onuf. *The Midwest and the Nation: Rethinking the History of an American Region.* Indiana UP, 1990.

Chang, David A. *The Color of the Land: Race, Nation, and the Politics of Landownership in Oklahoma, 1832–1929.* U of North Carolina P, 2010.

Chapman, Nathaniel G., et al. *Untapped: Exploring the Cultural Dimensions of Craft Beer.* West Virginia UP, 2017.

Chase, Cleveland. "In Retrospect." 1927. *Critical Essays on Sherwood Anderson,* edited by David D. Anderson, G. K. Hall, 1981, pp. 86–91.

Chauncey, George. *Gay New York: Gender, Urban Culture, and the Makings of the Gay Male World, 1890–1940.* Basic, 1994.

Ching, Barbara, and Gerald W. Creed, editors. *Knowing Your Place: Rural Identity and Cultural Hierarchy.* Routledge, 1997.

Chudacoff, Howard P. *The Age of the Bachelor: Creating an American Subculture.* Princeton UP, 1999.

Church, Forrest. "Wauseon Coffee Shop Celebrates New Location & New Craft Beer." *The Village Reporter,* 19 Oct. 2015, http://www.thevillagereporter.com/wauseon-coffee-shop-celebrates-new-location-new-craft-beer/. Accessed 24 May 2018.

"The Circus." *Fulton County Tribune,* 30 July 1915, p. 1.

"Circus Day." *Fulton County Tribune,* 8 June 1917, p. 5.

Clark, Suzanne. *Sentimental Modernism: Women Writers and the Revolution of the Word.* Indiana UP, 1991.

Clifford, Raymond. "The American and His Past." *Chicago Daily Tribune,* 30 Sep. 1928, p. G1.

Clover, Carol J. *Men, Women, and Chain Saws: Gender in the Modern Horror Film.* Princeton UP, 1992.

Clymer, Jeffory A. "Modeling, Diagramming, and Early Twentieth-Century Histories of Invention and Entrepreneurship: Henry Ford, Sherwood Anderson, Samuel Insull." *Journal of American Studies,* vol. 36, no. 3, 2002, pp. 491–512.

Cohen, Lizabeth. *Making a New Deal: Industrial Workers in Chicago, 1919–1939.* 2nd edition, Cambridge UP, 2008.

Comentale, Edward P. "'The Possibilities of Hard-Won Land': Midwestern Modernism and the Novel." *A Companion to The Modern American Novel, 1900–1950,* edited by John T. Matthews, Wiley-Blackwell, 2009, pp. 240–265.

Connell, Raewyn. *Masculinities.* 2nd edition, U of California P, 2005.

Cook, Sylvia Jenkins. *From Tobacco Road to Route 66: The Southern Poor White in Fiction.* U of North Carolina P, 1976.

Cowley, Malcolm. *Exile's Return: A Literary Odyssey of the 1920s.* Viking, 1934.

Cox, Kenneth. "The Poems of Lorine Niedecker." 1969. *The Full Note: Lorine Niedecker,* edited by Peter Dent, Interim, 1983, pp. 29–35.

Cronon, William. *Nature's Metropolis: Chicago and the Great West.* Norton, 1991.

Cunningham, Bob. "Crafty Move: Coffee Shop Owners Open Brewery in Wauseon." *The Blade,* 11 Oct. 2015, p. F1.

Cunningham, William. *The Green Corn Rebellion.* 1935. U of Oklahoma P, 2010.

——. "Okla. Farmers Plan No Pink Tea for Their Holiday." *Commonwealth College Fortnightly,* 15 Sept. 1932, p. 1+, https://libraries.uark.edu/SpecialCollections/commonwealth/fortnightly.asp. Accessed 13 Dec. 2017.

Cvetkovich, Ann. *An Archive of Feelings: Trauma, Sexuality, and Lesbian Public Cultures.* Duke UP, 2003.

Danbom, David B. *Born in the Country: A History of Rural America.* Johns Hopkins UP, 1995.

Davies, George C. Letter to George Geer, Postmaster, Wauseon, Ohio, 2 Sept. 1938. Case Files Concerning Embellishments of Federal Buildings, 1934–1943, Box 85, Folder Wauseon PO. Record Group 121, Records of the Public Buildings Service, 1801–2000. National Archives, College Park, MD.

Davis, Thadious M. *Southscapes: Geographies of Race, Region, and Literature.* U of North Carolina P, 2011.

Denning, Michael. *The Cultural Front: The Laboring of American Culture in the Twentieth Century.* Verso, 1998.

Derickson, Alan. *Dangerously Sleepy: Overworked Americans and the Cult of Manly Wakefulness.* U of Pennsylvania P, 2014.

Derleth, August. "New Morris Novel Lacks Simplicity." Review of *The World in the Attic,* by Wright Morris. *Chicago Daily Tribune,* 4 Sept. 1949, p. G6.

Doane, Mary Ann. *The Emergence of Cinematic Time: Modernity, Contingency, the Archive.* Harvard UP, 2002.

Donald, Miles. *The American Novel in the Twentieth Century.* Barnes & Noble, 1978.

Dooley, William Germain. "Old Homestead: A Lifelike Montage." Review of *The Home Place,* by Wright Morris. *New York Times,* 18 July 1948, p. BR5.

Dorman, Robert L. *Revolt of the Provinces: The Regionalist Movement in America, 1920–1945.* U of North Carolina P, 1993.

Dowell, Eldridge Foster. *A History of Criminal Syndicalism Legislation in the United States.* Johns Hopkins P, 1939.

Doyle, Laura, and Laura A. Winkiel, editors. *Geomodernisms: Race, Modernism, Modernity.* Indiana UP, 2005.

Du Bois, W. E. B. "The Negro Mind Reaches Out." 1925. *The New Negro: Voices of the Harlem Renaissance,* edited by Alain Locke, Simon & Schuster–Touchstone, 1997, pp. 385–414.

Dubofsky, Melvyn. *We Shall Be All: A History of the Industrial Workers of the World.* Edited by Joseph Anthony McCartin, abridged edition, U of Illinois P, 2000.

DuCille, Ann. *The Coupling Convention: Sex, Text, and Tradition in Black Women's Fiction.* Oxford UP, 1993.

Dudley, Kathryn Marie. *Debt and Dispossession: Farm Loss in America's Heartland.* U of Chicago P, 2000.

——. "The Entrepreneurial Self: Identity and Morality in a Midwestern Farming Community." *Fighting for the Farm: Rural America Transformed,* edited by Jane Adams, U of Pennsylvania P, 2003, pp. 175–191.

Dunne, Robert. *A New Book of the Grotesques: Contemporary Approaches to Sherwood Anderson's Early Fiction.* Kent State UP, 2005.

DuPlessis, Rachel Blau. "Lorine Niedecker's 'Paean to Place' and Its Fusion Poetics." *Contemporary Literature,* vol. 46, no. 3, 2005, pp. 393–421.

——. "Lorine Niedecker, the Anonymous: Gender, Class, Genre and Resistances." *The Kenyon Review,* vol. 14, no. 2, 1992, pp. 96–116.

Duvall, John N. "Regionalism in American Modernism." *The Cambridge Companion to American Modernism,* edited by Walter B. Kalaidjian, Cambridge UP, 2005, pp. 242–260.

Eaton, Walter Prichard. "House in the Cornfield." *New York Herald Tribune,* 18 July 1948, p. E4.

Eggan, Taylor A. "Revolutionary Temporality and Modernist Politics of Form: Reading Ngugi wa Thiong'o Reading Joseph Conrad." *Journal of Modern Literature,* vol. 38, no. 3, 2015, pp. 38–55.

"Elevator Calendar Prescribes Philosophers' Weekly Way of Life." *Columbia Daily Spectator,* 6 Feb. 1942, p. 1.

Ennis, Philip H. *The Seventh Stream: The Emergence of Rocknroll in American Popular Music.* Wesleyan UP, UP of New England, 1992.

Enniss, Stephen C. "Alienation and Affirmation: The Divided Self in Sherwood Anderson's 'Poor White.'" *South Atlantic Review,* vol. 55, no. 2, 1990, pp. 85–99.

Erdman, Andrew L. *Blue Vaudeville: Sex, Morals and the Mass Marketing of Amusement, 1895–1915.* McFarland, 2004.

Etcheson, Nicole. *The Emerging Midwest: Upland Southerners and the Political Culture of the Old Northwest, 1787–1861.* Indiana UP, 1996.

Evans, Arthur. "Making Rubber Helps to Raise Factory Cash; Du Pont Working Out of Hard Times." *Chicago Daily Tribune,* 1 Mar. 1934, p. 13.

Faludi, Susan. *Stiffed: The Betrayal of the American Man.* W. Morrow, 1999.

Farland, Maria. "Modernist Versions of Pastoral: Poetic Inspiration, Scientific Expertise, and the 'Degenerate' Farmer." *American Literary History,* vol. 19, no. 4, 2007, pp. 905–936.

Felski, Rita. *Doing Time: Feminist Theory and Postmodern Culture.* New York UP, 2000.

——. *The Gender of Modernity.* Harvard UP, 1995.

Ferguson, Richard, and Christer Olofsson. "The Development of New Ventures in Farm Businesses." *Handbook of Research on Entrepreneurship in Agriculture and Rural Development,* edited by Gry Agnete Alsos et al., Edward Elgar, 2011, pp. 21–37.

Ferrence, Matthew J. *All-American Redneck: Variations on an Icon, from James Fenimore Cooper to the Dixie Chicks.* U of Tennessee P, 2014.

Fetterley, Judith, and Marjorie Pryse. *Writing Out of Place: Regionalism, Women, and American Literary Culture.* U of Illinois P, 2003.

Fiedler, Leslie. *Love and Death in the American Novel.* Criterion, 1960.

Fine, Michelle, et al. "(In) Secure Times: Constructing White Working-Class Masculinities in the Late 20th Century." *Gender and Society,* vol. 11, no. 1, 1997, pp. 52–68.

Fink, Deborah. *Agrarian Women: Wives and Mothers in Rural Nebraska, 1880–1940.* U of North Carolina P, 1992.

"First Circus of the Season." *Goshen Democrat,* 28 Apr. 1911, p. 4.

Fitzgerald, Deborah Kay. *Every Farm a Factory: The Industrial Ideal in American Agriculture.* Yale UP, 2003.

Flatley, Jonathan. *Affective Mapping: Melancholia and the Politics of Modernism.* Harvard UP, 2008.

Fleissner, Jennifer. *Women, Compulsion, Modernity: The Moment of American Naturalism.* U of Chicago P, 2004.

Flournoy, Angela. Introduction. *Not Without Laughter,* by Langston Hughes, Penguin, 2018, pp. ix–xvii.

Foley, Barbara. *Radical Representations: Politics and Form in U.S. Proletarian Fiction, 1929–1941.* Duke UP, 1993.

Foote, Stephanie. *Regional Fictions: Culture and Identity in Nineteenth-Century American Literature.* U of Wisconsin P, 2001.

"Foreclosed Dairy Farms in SE Mich. Sold." *Morning Sun News,* 31 Aug. 2013, http://www.themorningsun.com/article/MS/20130831/NEWS03/130839953. Accessed 5 June 2018.

"'Fort' Theatre: The Home of Great Pictures!" *The Jefferson County Union,* 5 Jan. 1934, p. 2.

Frank, Waldo. *In the American Jungle [1925–1936].* Farrar & Rinehart, 1937.

Freeman, Elizabeth. *Time Binds: Queer Temporalities, Queer Histories.* Duke UP, 2010.

Freitag, Florian. *The Farm Novel in North America: Genre and Nation in the United States, English Canada, and French Canada, 1845–1945.* Camden House, 2013.

Fulton County Historical Society. *Fulton County, Ohio: A Collection of Historical*

*Sketches and Family Histories.* Higginson, 1976.

Garvey, Ellen Gruber. *Writing with Scissors: American Scrapbooks from the Civil War to the Harlem Renaissance.* Oxford UP, 2012.

Geer, George. Letter to Edward B. Rowan, Superintendent, Section of Painting and Sculpture, 6 Sept. 1938. Case Files Concerning Embellishments of Federal Buildings, 1934–1943, Box 85, Folder Wauseon PO. Record Group 121, Records of the Public Buildings Service, 1801–2000. National Archives, College Park, MD.

Gelfant, Blanche Housman. "A Novel of Becoming." 1954. *Sherwood Anderson: A Collection of Critical Essays,* edited by Walter B. Rideout, Prentice-Hall, 1974, pp. 59–64.

Gibbons, James. "The Novels of Dawn Powell." *Raritan,* vol. 20, no. 1, 2000, p. 142.

Gilbert, Sandra M., and Susan Gubar. *The Madwoman in the Attic: The Woman Writer and the Nineteenth-Century Literary Imagination.* Yale UP, 1979.

Golston, Michael. "Petalbent Devils: Louis Zukofsky, Lorine Niedecker, and the Surrealist Praying Mantis." *Modernism/Modernity,* vol. 13, no. 2, 2006, pp. 325–347.

Gramsci, Antonio. "Americanism and Fordism." 1971. *Selections from the Prison Notebooks of Antonio Gramsci,* edited by Quintin Hoare and Geoffrey Nowell Smith, International Publishers, 2005, pp. 277–318.

Grant, H. Roger. *Twilight Rails: The Final Era of Railroad Building in the Midwest.* U of Minnesota P, 2010.

Grant, Michael Johnston. *Down and Out on the Family Farm: Rural Rehabilitation in the Great Plains, 1929–1945.* U of Nebraska P, 2002.

Gray, Susan E. *The Yankee West: Community Life on the Michigan Frontier.* U of North Carolina P, 1996.

Green, James R. *Grass-Roots Socialism: Radical Movements in the Southwest, 1895–1943.* Louisiana State UP, 1978.

Greitzer, Jack J. *Cooperative Planning and Developing, Wauseon, Ohio (mural study, Wauseon, Ohio Post Office).* N.d., Smithsonian American Art Museum, http://americanart.si.edu/collections/search/artwork/?id=9590. Accessed 13 Dec. 2017.

———. *Cooperative Planning and Development of Wauseon.* 1938. Post Office, Wauseon, Ohio.

———. Letter to Edward B. Rowan, Superintendent, Section of Painting and Sculpture, 6 Dec. 1937. Case Files Concerning Embellishments of Federal Buildings, 1934–1943, Box 85, Folder Wauseon PO. Record Group 121, Records of the Public Buildings Service, 1801–2000. National Archives, College Park, MD.

———. Letter to Edward B. Rowan, Superintendent, Section of Painting and Sculpture, 13 Mar. 1938. Case Files Concerning Embellishments of Federal Buildings, 1934–1943, Box 85, Folder Wauseon PO. Record Group 121, Records of the Public Buildings Service, 1801–2000. National Archives, College Park, MD.

———. Letter to Edward B. Rowan, Superintendent, Section of Painting and Sculpture, 15 Sept. 1938. Case Files Concerning Embellishments of Federal Buildings, 1934–1943, Box 85, Folder Wauseon PO. Record Group 121, Records of the Public Buildings Service, 1801–2000. National Archives, College Park, MD.

Grieve, Victoria. *The Federal Art Project and the Creation of Middlebrow Culture.* U of Illinois P, 2009.

Grossman, James R. *Land of Hope: Chicago, Black Southerners, and the Great Migration.* U of Chicago P, 1989.

Grosz, Elizabeth. *The Nick of Time: Politics, Evolution, and the Untimely.* Duke UP, 2004.

Guilford, Russell H. *Official Souvenir Booklet in Celebration of 200 Years of National Freedom, 1776–1976, Emphasizing Fulton County, Ohio, 1850–1976.* Fulton County Bicentennial Committee, 1976.

Gupta-Carlson, Himanee. *Muncie, India(na): Middletown and Asian America.* U of Illinois P, 2018.

Halberstam, Judith. *In a Queer Time and Place: Transgender Bodies, Subcultural Lives.* New York UP, 2005.

Hamilton, Shane. *Trucking Country: The Road to America's Wal-Mart Economy.* Princeton UP, 2008.

Hampsten, Elizabeth. *Read This Only to Yourself: The Private Writings of Midwestern Women, 1880–1910.* Indiana UP, 1982.

Handy-Marchello, Barbara. "Gendered Boosterism: The 'Doctor's Wife' Writes from the New Northwest." *Regionalism and the Humanities,* edited by Timothy R. Mahoney and Wendy Jean Katz, U of Nebraska P, 2008, pp. 110–126.

Hansen, N. E. *Transplanting Alfalfa.* Agricultural Experiment Station, South Dakota State College of Agriculture and Mechanic Arts, Bulletin No. 167, Bowen, 1916.

Hapke, Laura. *Daughters of the Great Depression: Women, Work, and Fiction in the American 1930s.* U of Georgia P, 1995.

Harkins, Anthony. *Hillbilly: A Cultural History of an American Icon.* Oxford UP, 2004.

———. "The Midwest and the Evolution of 'Flyover Country.'" *Middle West Review,* vol. 3, no. 1, 2016, pp. 97–121.

Harp, Stephen L. *A World History of Rubber: Empire, Industry, and the Everyday.* Wiley Blackwell, 2016.

Hauser, Susan Carol. *Barn: Form and Function of an American Icon.* Voyageur, 2017.

Hayden, Karen E. "Inbred Horror Revisited: The Fear of the Rural in Twenty-First Century Backwoods Horror Films." *Reimagining Rural: Urbanormative Portrayals of Rural Life,* edited by Gregory M. Fulkerson and Alexander R. Thomas, Lexington, 2016, pp. 59–72.

Hegeman, Susan. *Patterns for America: Modernism and the Concept of Culture.* Princeton UP, 1999.

Henning, George F. *"Putting It All Together": A Collection of Historical Accounts of Ohio Cooperatives,* edited by Charles H. Ingraham, RG 40.129, Ohio State University Archives, Ohio State University, 1980.

Henry, Robin. "Queering the American Frontier: Finding Queerness and Sexual Difference in Late Nineteenth-Century and Early Twentieth-Century Colorado." *Queering the Countryside: New Frontiers in Rural Queer Studies,* edited by Mary L. Gray et al., New York UP, 2016, pp. 290–308.

Henry, Tom. "Mich. Fines Large Dairy $141,500." *The Blade,* 29 Sept. 2007, p. B1.

——. "New Owner Offers Tours at Revamped Milk Source Dairy." *The Blade,* 11 Aug. 2016, http://www.toledoblade.com/business/2016/08/11/New-owner-offers-tours-at-revamped-Milk-Source-dairy-Company-showcases-more-than-40-million-of-improvements.html. Accessed 5 June 2018.

Hensley, Kari. "Making Brooklyn Local: The Politics of Nostalgia in the Postindustrial City." Dissertation, New York University, 2013.

Herring, Scott. *Another Country: Queer Anti-Urbanism.* New York UP, 2010.

——. *Queering the Underworld: Slumming, Literature, and the Undoing of Lesbian and Gay History.* U of Chicago P, 2007.

——. "Regional Modernism: A Reintroduction." *MFS: Modern Fiction Studies,* vol. 55, no. 1, 2009, pp. 1–10.

Hicks, Granville. *The Great Tradition: An Interpretation of American Literature since the Civil War.* Revised edition, Quadrangle, 1969.

Higbie, Frank Tobias. "Heartland: The Politics of a Regional Signifier." *Middle West Review,* vol. 1, no. 1, 2014, pp. 81–90.

Hinrichs, C. Clare, and Thomas A. Lyson, editors. *Remaking the North American Food System: Strategies for Sustainability.* U of Nebraska P, 2007.

Hirsch, Jerrold. "Theorizing Regionalism and Folklore from the Left: B. A. Botkin, the Oklahoma Years, 1921–1939." *Regionalists on the Left: Radical Voices from the American West,* edited by Michael Steiner, U of Oklahoma P, 2013, pp. 135–156.

Hoffman, Frederick J. *The Modern Novel in America, 1900–1950.* Henry Regnery, 1951.

Hogue, Beverly J. "From Mulberries to Machines: Planting the Simulated Garden."

*Interdisciplinary Studies in Literature and Environment,* vol. 15, no. 1, 2008, pp. 101–110.

Holcomb, Gary Edward. "Langston Unashamed: Radical Mythmaking in Hughes's 1930s Short Fiction." *MFS: Modern Fiction Studies,* vol. 61, no. 3, 2015, pp. 423–445.

Holman, David Marion. *A Certain Slant of Light: Regionalism and the Form of Southern and Midwestern Fiction.* Louisiana State UP, 1995.

Holt, Douglas B., and Craig J. Thompson. "Man-of-Action Heroes: The Pursuit of Heroic Masculinity in Everyday Consumption." *Journal of Consumer Research,* vol. 31, no. 2, 2004, pp. 425–440.

Holt, Marilyn Irvin. *Linoleum, Better Babies, and the Modern Farm Woman, 1890–1930.* U of New Mexico P, 1995.

Holthaus, Gary H. *From the Farm to the Table: What All Americans Need to Know about Agriculture.* UP of Kentucky, 2006.

hooks, bell. *The Will to Change: Men, Masculinity, and Love.* Atria, 2004.

Horder, W. Garrett, editor. *The Sunlit Road: Readings in Verse & Prose for Every Day.* Dodge, 1908.

Howard, Gerald. "How Dawn Powell Can Save Your Life." *Salon.com.* 30 Sept. 1999, https://www.salon.com/1999/09/30/powell/. Accessed 13 Dec. 2017.

Howard, Leon. *Wright Morris.* University of Minnesota Pamphlets on American Writers, vol. 69. U of Minnesota P, 1968.

Howe, Irving. *Sherwood Anderson.* Sloane, 1951.

Hsu, Hsuan L. "Literature and Regional Production." *American Literary History,* vol. 17, no. 1, 2005, pp. 36–69.

Huggins, Nathan Irvin. *Harlem Renaissance.* Oxford UP, 1971.

Hughes, Langston. *The Big Sea: An Autobiography.* 2nd Hill and Wang edition, Hill and Wang, 1993.

——. *Not Without Laughter.* 1930. Scribner, 1995.

Hurt, R. Douglas. *Agricultural Technology in the Twentieth Century.* Sunflower UP, 1991.

——. *The Dust Bowl: An Agricultural and Social History.* Nelson-Hall, 1981.

Hutchinson, George. *The Harlem Renaissance in Black and White.* Harvard UP-Belknap, 1995.

"Ida Cox, 'Lawdy, Lawdy Blues.'" Advertisement. *Chicago Defender,* 15 Dec. 1923, p. A10.

Ikerd, John E. *Crisis & Opportunity: Sustainability in American Agriculture.* U of Nebraska P, 2008.

Inwood, Shoshanah M., and Jeff S. Sharp. "Farm Persistence and Adaptation at the

Rural-Urban Interface: Succession and Farm Adjustment." *Journal of Rural Studies,* vol. 28, no. 1, 2012, pp. 107–117.

Isenstadt, Sandy. "Auto-Specularity: Driving through the American Night." *Modernism/Modernity,* vol. 18, no. 2, 2011, pp. 213–231.

Jackson, Joseph Henry. "Bookman's Notebook: Pix of the Year." *Los Angeles Times,* 28 Dec. 1948, p. A5.

Jackson, Kenneth T. *Crabgrass Frontier: The Suburbanization of the United States.* Oxford UP, 1985.

Jackson, Robert. *Seeking the Region in American Literature and Culture: Modernity, Dissidence, Innovation.* Louisiana State UP, 2005.

Jackson, Virginia Walker. *Dickinson's Misery: A Theory of Lyric Reading.* Princeton UP, 2005.

Jameson, Fredric. *The Political Unconscious: Narrative as a Socially Symbolic Act.* Cornell UP, 1981.

Jellison, Katherine. *Entitled to Power: Farm Women and Technology, 1913–1963.* U of North Carolina P, 1993.

Jennison, Ruth. "Scrambling Narrative: Niedecker and the White Dome of Logic." *JNT: Journal of Narrative Theory,* vol. 41, no. 1, 2011, pp. 53–81.

——. "Waking into Ideology: Lorine Niedecker's Experiments in the Syntax of Consciousness." *Radical Vernacular: Lorine Niedecker and the Poetics of Place,* edited by Elizabeth Willis, U of Iowa P, 2008, pp. 130–150.

Johnson, Colin R. *Just Queer Folks: Gender and Sexuality in Rural America.* Temple UP, 2013.

Johnson, James Weldon. "Harlem: The Culture Capital." 1925. *The New Negro: Voices of the Harlem Renaissance,* edited by Alain Locke, Simon and Schuster–Touchstone, 1997, pp. 301–311.

Johnson, Michael K. *Black Masculinity and the Frontier Myth in American Literature.* U of Oklahoma P, 2002.

Joseph, Philip. *American Literary Regionalism in a Global Age.* Louisiana State UP, 2007.

Jurca, Catherine. *White Diaspora: The Suburb and the Twentieth-Century American Novel.* Princeton UP, 2001.

Kaplan, Amy. *The Social Construction of American Realism.* U of Chicago P, 1988.

Kazin, Alfred. *On Native Grounds: An Interpretation of Modern American Prose Literature.* Reynal & Hitchcock, 1942.

Kennedy, Rick. *Jelly Roll, Bix, and Hoagy: Gennett Studios and the Birth of Recorded Jazz.* Indiana UP, 1994.

Kennedy, Rick, and Randy McNutt. *Little Labels—Big Sound: Small Record Companies and the Rise of American Music.* Indiana UP, 1999.

Kennedy-Hendricks, Alene, et al. "Social Stigma toward Persons with Prescription Opioid Use Disorder: Associations with Public Support for Punitive and Public Health–Oriented Policies." *Psychiatric Services,* vol. 68, no. 5, 2017, pp. 462–469.

Kent, George E. "Hughes and the Afro-American Cultural Tradition." 1972. *Langston Hughes,* edited by Harold Bloom, Chelsea House, 1989, pp. 17–36.

Kerr, T. H. *Natural Gas in Ohio: A History.* Engineering Experiment Station, The Ohio State University, 1950.

Kimmel, Michael S. *Angry White Men: American Masculinity at the End of an Era.* Nation Books, 2013.

——. *Manhood in America: A Cultural History.* Free P, 1996.

Kirschner, Don S. *City and Country: Rural Responses to Urbanization in the 1920s.* Greenwood, 1970.

Kline, Ronald R. *Consumers in the Country: Technology and Social Change in Rural America.* Johns Hopkins UP, 2000.

Kolodny, Annette. *The Land before Her: Fantasy and Experience of the American Frontiers, 1630–1860.* U of North Carolina P, 1984.

Korsgaard, Steffen, et al. "Rural Entrepreneurship or Entrepreneurship in the Rural—Between Place and Space." *International Journal of Entrepreneurial Behaviour & Research,* vol. 21, no. 1, 2015, pp. 5–26.

Kosiba, Sara, editor. *A Scattering Time: How Modernism Met Midwestern Culture.* Hastings College P, 2018.

Kramer, Dale. *Chicago Renaissance: The Literary Life of the Midwest, 1900–1930.* Appleton-Century, 1966.

Kravatz, Jillian. "Craft-Beer Industry Coming to a Head in Ohio." *The Blade,* 16 Aug. 2015, p. D1.

Kroiz, Lauren. *Cultivating Citizens: The Regional Work of Art in the New Deal Era.* U of California P, 2018.

Krumm, Robert, editor. *Wauseon.* Arcadia, 2014.

Kubacki, Dave. "North River Brewing Company Brings Craft Beer to Wauseon." *Toledo City Paper,* 8 Mar. 2016, http://toledocitypaper.com/online/north-river-brewing-company-brings-craft-beer-to-wauseon/. Accessed 23 May 2018.

Kun, Josh. *Audiotopia: Music, Race, and America.* U of California P, 2005

"Latest Books Received." Review of *The Story of a Country Boy,* by Dawn Powell. *New York Times,* 18 Mar. 1934, BR23.

Lauck, Jon K. *From Warm Center to Ragged Edge: The Erosion of Midwestern Literary and Historical Regionalism, 1920–1965.* U of Iowa P, 2017.

——, ed. *The Midwestern Moment: The Forgotten World of Early-Twentieth-Century Midwestern Regionalism, 1880–1940.* Hastings College P, 2017.

Lears, T. J. Jackson. "Sherwood Anderson: Looking for the White Spot." *The Power of Culture: Critical Essays in American History,* edited by Richard Wightman Fox and T. J. Jackson Lears, U of Chicago P, 1993, pp. 13–37.

Lemke, Sieglinde. *Primitivist Modernism: Black Culture and the Origins of Transatlantic Modernism.* Oxford UP, 1998.

Leverenz, David. *Manhood and the American Renaissance.* Cornell UP, 1989.

Lewis, Robert. *Chicago Made: Factory Networks in the Industrial Metropolis.* U of Chicago P, 2008.

Lewis, Theophilus. "The Harlem Sketch Book." Review of *Not Without Laughter,* by Langston Hughes. *New York Amsterdam News,* 6 Aug. 1930, p. 9.

Lieberman, Jennifer L. *Power Lines: Electricity in American Life and Letters, 1882–1952.* MIT P, 2017.

Lindemann, Marilee. *Willa Cather, Queering America.* Columbia UP, 1999.

Litwack, Leon F. *Trouble in Mind: Black Southerners in the Age of Jim Crow.* Knopf, 1998.

Locke, Alain, editor. *The New Negro: Voices of the Harlem Renaissance.* 1925. New York: Simon and Schuster, 1992.

Lockwood, J. Samaine. *Archives of Desire: The Queer Historical Work of New England Regionalism.* U of North Carolina P, 2015.

Love, Glen A. "Horses or Men: Primitive and Pastoral Elements in Sherwood Anderson." *Sherwood Anderson: Centennial Studies,* edited by Hilbert H. Campbell and Charles E. Modin, 1976, pp. 235–248.

———. "Winesburg, Ohio and the Rhetoric of Silence." *American Literature,* vol. 40, no. 1, 1968, pp. 38–57.

Lovett, Robert Morss. "Mr. Sherwood Anderson's America." Review of *Poor White,* by Sherwood Anderson. 1921. *Critical Essays on Sherwood Anderson,* edited by David D. Anderson, G. K. Hall, 1981, pp. 35–37.

Lutz, Tom. *Cosmopolitan Vistas: American Regionalism and Literary Value.* Cornell UP, 2004.

Lynd, Robert S., and Helen Merrell Lynd. *Middletown: A Study in Contemporary American Culture.* 1927. Harvest/HBJ, 1957.

M.D.P. Review of *The Story of a Country Boy,* by Dawn Powell. *The Saturday Review of Literature,* vol. 10, 31 Mar. 1934, p. 596.

MacDougall, Robert. *The People's Network: The Political Economy of the Telephone in the Gilded Age.* U of Pennsylvania P, 2014.

MacKenzie, John K. *Gennettics.* John K. MacKenzie Gennett Record Company Collection, 8 Aug. 2012, Indiana Historical Society.

Madden, David. *Wright Morris.* Twayne, 1964.

Mahoney, Timothy R., and Wendy Jean Katz, editors. *Regionalism and the Humanities.* U of Nebraska P, 2008.

Marling, Karal Ann. *Wall-to-Wall America: A Cultural History of Post-Office Murals in the Great Depression.* U of Minnesota P, 1982.

Marx, Karl, and Friedrich Engels. *Manifesto of the Communist Party.* 1848. Translated by Samuel Moore. International Publishers, 1948.

Marx, Leo. *The Machine in the Garden: Technology and the Pastoral Ideal in America.* Oxford UP, 1964.

Maslowski, Andy. "Oil Technology." *The American Midwest: An Interpretive Encyclopedia,* edited by Richard Sisson et al. Indiana UP, 2007, pp. 1466–1467.

Matheny, Keith. "Stink Is Raised over Spraying and Lake Erie Algae Bloom." *Detroit Free Press,* 15 Dec. 2014, p. A1.

McClelland, Peter D. *Sowing Modernity: America's First Agricultural Revolution.* Cornell UP, 1997.

McCollum, Victoria. *Post-9/11 Heartland Horror: Rural Horror Films in an Era of Urban Terrorism.* Ashgate, 2017.

McGinty, Emma E., et al. "Criminal Activity or Treatable Health Condition? News Media Framing of Opioid Analgesic Abuse in the United States, 1998–2012." *Psychiatric Services,* vol. 67, no. 4, 2016, pp. 405–411.

McGurl, Mark. *The Novel Art: Elevations of American Fiction after Henry James.* Princeton UP, 2001.

McIlvaine-Newsad, Heather, et al. "Slow Food Lessons in the Fast Food Midwest." *Southern Rural Sociology,* vol. 23, no. 1, 2008, pp. 72–93.

McIlwaine, Shields. *The Southern Poor-White: From Lubberland to Tobacco Road.* U of Oklahoma P, 1939.

McNutt, Randy. *Guitar Towns: A Journey to the Crossroads of Rock 'n' Roll.* Indiana UP, 2002.

Meldrum, Marcia L. "The Ongoing Opioid Prescription Epidemic: Historical Context." *American Journal of Public Health,* vol. 106, no. 8, 2016, pp. 1365–1366.

Melosh, Barbara. *Engendering Culture: Manhood and Womanhood in New Deal Public Art and Theater.* Smithsonian, 1991.

Meyer, Roy Willard. *The Middle Western Farm Novel in the Twentieth Century.* U of Nebraska P, 1965.

Meyer, Stephen. *Manhood on the Line: Working-Class Masculinities in the American Heartland.* U of Illinois P, 2016.

Michaels, Walter Benn. *Our America: Nativism, Modernism, and Pluralism.* Duke UP, 1995.

Michelson, Jo. Personal interview, 31 May 2018.

Mikesell, Thomas, editor. *The County of Fulton: A History of Fulton County, Ohio, from the Earliest Days.* Northwestern Historical Association, 1905.

Miller, Karl Hagstrom. *Segregating Sound: Inventing Folk and Pop Music in the Age of Jim Crow.* Duke UP, 2010.

Miller, Nina. *Making Love Modern: The Intimate Public Worlds of New York's Literary Women.* Oxford UP, 1999.

Mitchell, David T., and Sharon L. Snyder. *Narrative Prosthesis: Disability and the Dependencies of Discourse.* U of Michigan P, 2001.

Moglen, Seth. *Mourning Modernity: Literary Modernism and the Injuries of American Capitalism.* Stanford UP, 2007.

Monagon, George P., and George M. Liscombe. *History of Fulton County, Ohio.* 1877. Fulton County Historical Society, 1970.

Morgan, Douglas N. "Review of *The Home Place.*" *College Art Journal,* vol. 8, no. 3, 1949, pp. 237–238.

Morris, Wright. *The Home Place.* 1948. U of Nebraska P, 1999.

Morris, Wright, and Wayne C. Booth. "The Writing of Organic Fiction." *Conversations with Wright Morris: Critical Views and Responses,* edited by Robert E. Knoll, U of Nebraska P, 1977, pp. 74–100.

Morris, Wright, and Peter C. Bunnell. "Photography and Reality." *Conversations with Wright Morris: Critical Views and Responses,* edited by Robert E. Knoll, U of Nebraska P, 1977, pp. 140–152.

Muñoz, José Esteban. *Cruising Utopia: The Then and There of Queer Futurity.* New York UP, 2009.

Murphy, Lucy Eldersveld. "Journeywoman Milliner: Emily Austin, Migration, and Women's Work in the Nineteenth-Century Midwest." *Midwestern Women: Work, Community, and Leadership at the Crossroads,* edited by Lucy Eldersveld Murphy and Wendy Hamand Venet, Indiana UP, 1997, pp. 38–59.

Murray, Douglas W., and Martin A. O'Neill. "Craft Beer: Penetrating a Niche Market." *British Food Journal,* vol. 114, no. 7, 2012, pp. 899–909.

Musher, Sharon Ann. *Democratic Art: The New Deal's Influence on American Culture.* U of Chicago P, 2015.

Muyumba, Walton M. *The Shadow and the Act: Black Intellectual Practice, Jazz Improvisation, and Philosophical Pragmatism.* U of Chicago P, 2009.

Myers, Richard L. *The 100 Most Important Chemical Compounds: A Reference Guide.* Greenwood P, 2007.

Nelson, Dana D. *National Manhood: Capitalist Citizenship and the Imagined Fraternity of White Men.* Duke UP, 1998.

Neth, Mary. *Preserving the Family Farm: Women, Community, and the Foundations of Agribusiness in the Midwest, 1900–1940.* Johns Hopkins UP, 1995.

Neville, Helen. "Two Proletarian Novels." *The Nation,* 9 Oct. 1935, p. 417.

"New Goods from Dodge Co." *Walden's Stationer and Printer,* vol. 40, no. 1, 1917, p. 84.

"New Post Office Mural Draws Praise of Critics." *Fulton County Expositor,* 15 Sept. 1938, p. 1.

"New Wauseon Industry." *Fulton County Tribune,* 4 Apr. 1919, p. 1.

Nicholls, Peter. "Lorine Niedecker: Rural Surreal." *Lorine Niedecker: Woman and Poet,* edited by Jenny Penberthy, National Poetry Foundation, 1996, pp. 193–217.

Nicolaisen, William F. H. "Time in Folk-Narrative." *Folklore Studies in the Twentieth Century,* edited by Venetia J. Newall, Rowman & Littlefield, 1980, pp. 314–319.

Niedecker, Lorine. *Collected Works.* Edited by Jenny Penberthy, U of California P, 2002.

Nieland, Justus. *Feeling Modern: The Eccentricities of Public Life.* U of Illinois P, 2008.

Noble, Allen G., and Hubert G. H. Wilhelm. *Barns of the Midwest.* Ohio UP, 1995.

Nordin, Dennis S., and Roy Vernon Scott. *From Prairie Farmer to Entrepreneur: The Transformation of Midwestern Agriculture.* Indiana UP, 2005.

North, Michael. *The Dialect of Modernism: Race, Language, and Twentieth-Century Literature.* Oxford UP, 1994.

"'Not Without Laughter' and Other Recent Fiction." Review of *Not Without Laughter,* by Langston Hughes. *New York Times,* 3 Aug. 1930, p. 56.

"A Note or Two." *Chicago Defender,* 31 Jan. 1925, p. 7.

O'Connor, William Van. *The Grotesque: An Amercan Genre and Other Essays.* Southern Illinois UP, 1962.

O'Dell, Larry. "William Meredith Cunningham: An Oklahoma Proletarian Novelist." *Chronicles of Oklahoma,* vol. 86, no. 3, 2008, pp. 316–327.

Odum, Howard W., and Harry Estill Moore. *American Regionalism: A Cultural-Historical Approach to National Integration.* Peter Smith, 1966.

*Official Publication of the Wauseon Centennial.* Wauseon Homecoming Board and Centennial Committee, 1954.

Oliver, Paul. *Barrelhouse Blues: Location Recording and the Early Traditions of the Blues.* Basic, 2009.

Olsen, Bjørnar. *In Defense of Things: Archaeology and the Ontology of Objects.* AltaMira P, 2010.

Olson, Liesl. *Chicago Renaissance: Literature and Art in the Midwest Metropolis.* Yale UP, 2017.

Oman, Patricia. "'He Who Walks behind the Rows': Agricultural Horror Films and the American Farm Crisis of the 1980s." *MidAmerica,* vol. 39, no. 1, 2012, pp. 82–99.

——. "Publishing from Flyover Country: The Rejection of Heartland Iconography by Contemporary Midwestern Literary Magazines." *Midwestern Miscellany,* vol. 45, no. 1, 2017, pp. 52–69.

Ovington, Mary White. "Hughes: Novelist." Review of *Not Without Laughter,* by Langston Hughes. *Chicago Defender,* 4 Oct. 1930, p. 13.

Ownby, Ted. *Subduing Satan: Religion, Recreation, and Manhood in the Rural South, 1865–1920.* U of North Carolina P, 1990.

Page, Tim. *Dawn Powell: A Biography.* Henry Holt, 1998.

Park, Marlene, and Gerald E. Markowitz. *Democratic Vistas: Post Offices and Public Art in the New Deal.* Temple UP, 1984.

Parrington, Vernon Louis. *Main Currents in American Thought: An Interpretation of American Literature from the Beginnings to 1920.* Vol. 3, *1860–1920: The Beginnings of Critical Realism in America,* Harcourt, Brace, 1930.

Pascoe, C. J. *Dude, You're a Fag: Masculinity and Sexuality in High School.* U of California P, 2007.

Peiss, Kathy Lee. *Cheap Amusements: Working Women and Leisure in Turn-of-the-Century New York.* Temple UP, 1986.

Penberthy, Jenny. *Niedecker and the Correspondence with Zukofsky, 1931–1970.* Cambridge UP, 1993.

Pereira, Kim. *August Wilson and the African-American Odyssey.* U of Illinois P, 1995.

Perlman, Selig, and Philip Taft. *History of Labour in the United States, 1896–1932.* Vol. 4, *Labor Movements,* Macmillan, 1935.

Peters, Margot. *Lorine Niedecker: A Poet's Life.* Terrace, 2011.

Peterson, Jeffrey. "Lorine Niedecker: 'Before Machines.'" *Lorine Niedecker: Woman and Poet,* edited by Jenny Penberthy, National Poetry Foundation, 1996, pp. 245–279.

Pichaske, David R. *Rooted: Seven Midwest Writers of Place.* U of Iowa P, 2006.

——. "Where Now 'Midwestern Literature'?" *Midwest Quarterly: A Journal of Contemporary Thought,* vol. 48, no. 1, 2006, pp. 100–119.

Pinard, Mary. "Niedecker's Grammar of Flooding." *Radical Vernacular: Lorine Niedecker and the Poetics of Place,* edited by Elizabeth Willis, U of Iowa P, 2008, pp. 21–30.

Pinkerton, Steve. "'New Negro' v. 'Niggeratti': Defining and Defiling the Black Messiah." *Modernism/Modernity,* vol. 20, no. 3, 2013, pp. 539–556.

Pizer, Donald. *Twentieth-Century Literary Naturalism: An Interpretation.* Southern Illinois UP, 1982.

Poore, Charles. "Books of the Times." Review of *The Home Place,* by Wright Morris. *New York Times,* 31 July 1948, p. 13.

Potter, Marion E., and Emma L. Teich, editors. *The Cumulative Book Index.* H. W. Wilson, 1914.

Powell, Dawn. *The Story of a Country Boy.* 1934. Steerforth, 2001.

Power, Richard Lyle. *Planting Corn Belt Culture: The Impress of the Upland Southerner and Yankee in the Old Northwest.* Indiana Historical Society, 1953.

Pretshold, Karl. "Farmers in Rebellion." Review of *The Green Corn Rebellion,* by William Cunningham. *The New Masses,* 26 Nov. 1935, pp. 23–24.

Rabinowitz, Paula. "'Between the Outhouse and the Garbage Dump': Locating Collapse in Depression Literature." *American Literary History,* vol. 23, no. 1, 2011, pp. 32–55.

———. *Black & White & Noir: America's Pulp Modernism.* Columbia UP, 2002.

———. *Labor & Desire: Women's Revolutionary Fiction in Depression America.* U of North Carolina P, 1991.

Ramsey, Frederic, and Charles Edward Smith, editors. *Jazzmen.* Harper & Row–Limelight, 1985.

Rauchway, Eric. "An Economic History of the United States 1900–1950." *A Companion to the Modern American Novel, 1900–1950,* edited by John T. Matthews, Wiley-Blackwell, 2009, pp. 1–12.

Ray, Bradley, et al. "Examining Fatal Opioid Overdoses in Marion County, Indiana." *Journal of Urban Health,* vol. 94, no. 2, 2017, p. 301.

Reichert Powell, Douglas. *Critical Regionalism: Connecting Politics and Culture in the American Landscape.* U of North Carolina P, 2007.

Reighard, Frank H., editor. *A Standard History of Fulton County, Ohio, an Authentic Narrative of the Past.* Vol. 1, Lewis, 1920.

Reisman, Jerry. "Lorine: Some Memories of a Friend." *Lorine Niedecker: Woman and Poet,* edited by Jenny Penberthy, National Poetry Foundation, 1996, pp. 35–38.

Ribeiro, Oscar, et al. "Real Men, Real Husbands: Caregiving and Masculinities in Later Life." *Journal of Aging Studies,* vol. 21, no. 4, 2007, pp. 302–313.

Rice, Marcelle Smith. *Dawn Powell.* Twayne, 2000.

Rideout, Walter B. Introduction. *Poor White,* by Sherwood Anderson, Viking, 1966.

———. *The Radical Novel in the United States, 1900–1954: Some Interrelations of Literature and Society.* 1956. Columbia UP, 1992.

———. *Sherwood Anderson: A Writer in America.* U of Wisconsin P, 2006–2007. 2 vols.

*River View, South—Starr Piano Factory in Distance, Richmond, Ind.* N.d., Wayne County Historical Museum, Richmond, IN.

Robin, Leo, and Ralph Rainger. "Turn That Frown Upside Down." *The Way to Love,* Paramount, 1933.

Robinson, Elizabeth. "Music Becomes Story: Lyric and Narrative Patterning in the

Work of Lorine Niedecker." *Radical Vernacular: Lorine Niedecker and the Poetics of Place,* edited by Elizabeth Willis, U of Iowa P, 2008, pp. 112–130.

Rochberg-Halton, Eugene. "Life, Literature, and Sociology in Turn-of-the-Century Chicago." *Consuming Visions: Accumulation and Display of Goods in America, 1880–1920,* edited by Simon J. Bronner, Norton, 1989, pp. 311–338.

Rohy, Valerie. *Anachronism and Its Others : Sexuality, Race, Temporality.* SUNY P, 2009.

Rosenberg, Gabriel N. *The 4-H Harvest: Sexuality and the State in Rural America.* U of Pennsylvania P, 2016.

Rosenblatt, Roger. "Not without Laughter." 1974. *Langston Hughes,* edited by Harold Bloom, Chelsea House, 1989, pp. 37–43.

Rosenfeld, Paul. "Sherwood Anderson." *The Dial,* vol. 72, Jan. 1922, pp. 29–42.

Ross, Marlon Bryan. *Manning the Race: Reforming Black Men in the Jim Crow Era.* New York UP, 2004.

Ross, Mary. "A Little Colored Boy Grows Up." Review of *Not Without Laughter,* by Langston Hughes. *New York Herald Tribune,* 27 July 1930, p. 5.

Rothstein, Arthur. *Fighting the Drought and Dust with Irrigation. Cimarron County, Oklahoma.* 1936. Library of Congress, https://www.loc.gov/item/2017760368/. Accessed 15 June 2018.

Rotundo, E. Anthony. *American Manhood: Transformations in Masculinity from the Revolution to the Modern Era.* Basic, 1993.

Rovit, Earl. "A Memorable Reality." *The Sewanee Review,* vol. 110, no. 2, 2002, pp. 285–289, aph.

Rowan, Edward B. Letter to Jack J. Greitzer, 18 Oct. 1937. Case Files Concerning Embellishments of Federal Buildings, 1934–1943, Box 85, Folder Wauseon PO. Record Group 121, Records of the Public Buildings Service, 1801–2000. National Archives, College Park, MD.

——. Letter to Jack J. Greitzer, 6 Apr. 1938. Case Files Concerning Embellishments of Federal Buildings, 1934–1943, Box 85, Folder Wauseon PO. Record Group 121, Records of the Public Buildings Service, 1801–2000. National Archives, College Park, MD.

Rubin, Joan Shelley. *The Making of Middle/Brow Culture.* U of North Carolina P, 1992.

Sanborn Map Company. "Wauseon, Fulton Co., Ohio." 1905. Ohio Web Library, https://sanborn.ohioweblibrary.org/viewer/?id=33834. Accessed 30 May 2018.

——. "Wauseon, Fulton Co., Ohio." 1923. Ohio Web Library, https://sanborn.ohioweblibrary.org/viewer/?id=33870. Accessed 30 May 2018.

——. "Wauseon, Fulton Co., Ohio." 1910. Ohio Web Library, https://sanborn.ohioweblibrary.org/viewer/?id=33845. Accessed 30 May 2018.

——. "Wauseon, Fulton Co., Ohio—New Report, October, 1937." 1923. Ohio Web Library, https://sanborn.ohioweblibrary.org/viewer/?id=33883. Accessed 30 May 2018.

Sanborn-Perris Map Company. "Wauseon, Fulton Co., Ohio." 1893. Ohio Web Library, https://sanborn.ohioweblibrary.org/viewer/?id=33822. Accessed 30 May 2018.

——. "Wauseon, Fulton Co., Ohio." 1899. Ohio Web Library, https://sanborn.ohioweblibrary.org/viewer/?id=33827. Accessed 30 May 2018.

Scandura, Jani. *Down in the Dumps: Place, Modernity, American Depression.* Duke UP, 2008.

Schivelbusch, Wolfgang. *The Railway Journey: The Industrialization of Time and Space in the 19th Century.* U of California P, 1986.

Schlereth, Thomas J. "Country Stores, County Fairs, and Mail-Order Catalogues: Consumption in Rural America." *Consuming Visions: Accumulation and Display of Goods in America, 1880–1920,* edited by Simon J. Bronner, Norton, 1989, pp. 339–375.

Schorer, Mark. *The World We Imagine: Selected Essays by Mark Schorer.* Farrar, Strauss & Giroux, 1968.

Schwall, Harry E. Letter to George Geer, Postmaster, Wauseon, Ohio, 23 Aug. 1938. Case Files Concerning Embellishments of Federal Buildings, 1934–1943, Box 85, Folder Wauseon PO. Record Group 121, Records of the Public Buildings Service, 1801–2000. National Archives, College Park, MD.

Scroggins, Mark. *The Poem of a Life: A Biography of Louis Zukofsky.* Shoemaker & Hoard, 2007.

Sedgwick, Eve Kosofsky. *Between Men: English Literature and Male Homosocial Desire.* Columbia UP, 1985.

——. *Epistemology of the Closet.* U of California P, 1990.

Seguin, Robert. "Cosmic Upset: Cultural Revolution and the Contradictions of Zora Neale Hurston." *Modernism/Modernity,* vol. 16, no. 2, 2009, pp. 229–253.

Sellars, Nigel Anthony. *Oil, Wheat & Wobblies: The Industrial Workers of the World in Oklahoma, 1905–1930.* U of Oklahoma P, 1998.

Seymour, John S. "Annual Report of the Commissioner of Patents for the Year 1894." GPO, 1895.

Shortridge, James R. *The Middle West: Its Meaning in American Culture.* UP of Kansas, 1989.

Slotkin, Richard. *The Fatal Environment: The Myth of the Frontier in the Age of Industrialization, 1800–1890.* U of Oklahoma P, 1998.

Smith, Adam. *An Inquiry into the Nature and Causes of the Wealth of Nations.* 1776. Vol. 2, Oxford UP, 1909.

Smith, Henry Nash. *Virgin Land: The American West as Symbol and Myth.* Harvard UP, 1950.

Spears, Timothy B. *Chicago Dreaming: Midwesterners and the City, 1871–1919.* U of Chicago P, 2005.

"Starr Piano Co., Richmond, Indiana, 1909." Hoosier Recollections, http://www.flickr.com/photos/hoosier_recollections/5229988275/in/set-72157625398561485. Accessed 21 Sept. 2012.

"Starr Piano Co., Richmond, Indiana, 1910." Hoosier Recollections, http://www.flickr.com/photos/hoosier_recollections/5229988275/in/set-72157625398561485. Accessed 21 Sept. 2012.

*Starr Piano Factory, Aerial View from the South.* N.d., Wayne County Historical Museum, Richmond, IN.

*Starr Piano Factory, View from the North.* N.d., Wayne County Historical Museum, Richmond, IN.

"Stationery and Novelties." *The Bookseller, Newsdealer and Stationer,* vol. 52, no. 1, 1920, pp. 440–447.

"Stationery, Novelties and Toys." *The Bookseller, Newsdealer and Stationer,* vol. 45, no. 1, 1916, pp. 762–773.

Steinbeck, John. *The Grapes of Wrath.* 1939. Penguin, 1992.

Steiner, Michael, editor. *Regionalists on the Left: Radical Voices from the American West.* U of Oklahoma P, 2013.

Stone, Geoffrey. "Novels of Three Nations." *Commonweal,* vol. 20, 1934, pp. 222–223.

Stong, Phil. "The Country Boy Who Came to the City." Review of *The Story of a Country Boy,* by Dawn Powell. *New York Herald Tribune,* 25 Mar. 1934, p. 4.

Stover, John F. *The Life and Decline of the American Railroad.* Oxford UP, 1970.

Stradal, J. Ryan. *Kitchens of the Great Midwest.* Pamela Dorman Books/Viking, 2015.

Strauss, Harold. "Farmers' Rising." *New York Times,* 1 Sept. 1935, p. BR6.

*The Sunlit Road Calendar: Favorite Edition.* Dodge, 1934.

Sutton, Robert P. *Heartland Utopias.* Northern Illinois UP, 2009.

Swensen, James R. *Picturing Migrants: "The Grapes of Wrath" and New Deal Documentary Photography.* U of Oklahoma P, 2015.

Szalay, Michael. *New Deal Modernism: American Literature and the Invention of the Welfare State.* Duke UP, 2000.

Tarlo, Harriet. "Lorine Niedecker on and off the Margins: A Radical Poetics Out of Objectivism." *Kicking Daffodils: Twentieth-Century Women Poets,* edited by Vicki Bertram, Edinburgh UP, 1997, pp. 191–209.

Teaford, Jon C. *Cities of the Heartland: The Rise and Fall of the Industrial Midwest.* Indiana UP, 1993.

Thurman, Wallace. "Books in Review." Review of *Not Without Laughter,* by

Langston Hughes. 1930. *Langston Hughes: The Contemporary Reviews,* edited by Tish Dace, Cambridge UP, 1997, pp. 142–144.

"The Tiger Automatic Plant Setter." Advertisement. *Farm Implement News Buyer's Guide,* vol. 30, 1920, p. 312.

Tilden, David. "Review 3." Review of *The Green Corn Rebellion,* by William Cunningham. *New York Herald Tribune,* 1 Sept. 1935, p. F8.

Tischleder, Babette Bärbel, and Sarah L. Wasserman. "Thinking Out of Sync: A Theory of Obsolescence." *Cultures of Obsolescence: History, Materiality, and the Digital Age,* edited by Babette Bärbel Tischleder and Sarah L. Wasserman, Palgrave Macmillan, 2015, pp. 1–17.

Tomlinson, Charles. "A Rich Sitter." Introduction. *The Full Note: Lorine Niedecker,* edited by Peter Dent, Interim, 1983, pp. 7–10.

Trachtenberg, Alan. "The Craft of Vision." *Critique,* vol. 4, no. 3, 1961, p. 41.

——. "Home Place." *Raritan,* vol. 26, no. 1, 2006, pp. 64–87+.

——. *The Incorporation of America: Culture and Society in the Gilded Age.* 1982. Hill and Wang, 2007.

Tracy, Steven C. "Langston Hughes and Aunt Hager's Children's Blues Performance: 'Six-Bit Blues.'" *Montage of a Dream: The Art and Life of Langston Hughes,* edited by John Edgar Tidwell and Cheryl R. Ragar, U of Missouri P, 2007, pp. 19–31.

Trine, Ralph Waldo. *Along the Sunlit Road: Reprinted from the Sunlit Road Calendar.* Dodge, 1915.

Turnepseed, E. B. Letter to George Geer, Postmaster, Wauseon, Ohio, 29 Nov. 1938. Case Files Concerning Embellishments of Federal Buildings, 1934–1943, Box 85, Folder Wauseon PO. Record Group 121, Records of the Public Buildings Service, 1801–2000. National Archives, College Park, MD.

Turner, Frederick Jackson. *The Frontier in American History.* Henry Holt, 1921.

Upton, Lee. *Defensive Measures: The Poetry of Niedecker, Bishop, Glück, and Carson.* Bucknell UP, 2005.

"Urban Pitfalls." Review of *The Story of a Country Boy,* by Dawn Powell. *New York Times,* 25 Mar. 1934, BR9.

US Census Bureau. *1920 Census of Population and Housing.* GPO, 1921.

——. *1940 Census of Agriculture.* GPO, 1942.

——. *1940 Census of Population.* GPO, 1942.

——. "Census Regions and Divisions of the United States." N.d., https://www2.census.gov/geo/pdfs/maps-data/maps/reference/us_regdiv.pdf. Accessed 27 July 2017.

——. *Negro Population 1790–1915.* GPO, 1918.

Vacher, Peter. *Soloists and Sidemen: American Jazz Stories.* Northway, 2004.

Vandello, Joseph A., et al. "Precarious Manhood." *Journal of Personality and Social Psychology,* vol. 95, no. 6, 2008, pp. 1325–1339.

Van Doren, Carl. *Contemporary American Novelists, 1900–1920.* 1922. Macmillan, 1923.

Van Willigen, John, and Susan C. Eastwood. *Tobacco Culture: Farming Kentucky's Burley Belt.* UP of Kentucky, 1998.

Vega, Sujey. *Latino Heartland: Of Borders and Belonging in the Midwest.* New York UP, 2015.

Vellequette, Larry P. "Lender Gets Title to Big Vreba-Hoff Farms in Michigan." *The Blade,* 19 Nov. 2010, http://www.toledoblade.com/news/local/2010/11/19/Lender-gets-title-to-big-Vreba-Hoff-farms-in-Michigan.html. Accessed 5 June 2018.

Vidal, Gore. "Dawn Powell, the American Writer." *New York Review of Books,* vol. 34, no. 17, 5 Nov. 1987, pp. 52–60.

Vogel, Shane. *The Scene of Harlem Cabaret: Race, Sexuality, Performance.* U of Chicago P, 2009.

Walker, Kenneth Roland. *A History of the Middle West from the Beginning to 1970.* Pioneer, 1972.

Walker, Kevin. "Vreba Hoff Dairy Faces State Litigation, May Close Business." *Farm World,* 5 Jan. 2011, http://www.farmworldonline.com/news/ArchiveArticle.asp?newsid=11731. Accessed 5 June 2018.

Wall, Cheryl A. "Whose Sweet Angel Child? Blues Women, Langston Hughes, and Writing during the Harlem Renaissance." *Langston Hughes: The Man, His Art, and His Continuing Influence,* edited by C. James Trotman, Garland, 1995, pp. 37–50.

Walzer, Norman C., and Andrew Scott Blanke. "Business Starts in the Midwest: Potential Entrepreneurial Groups." *Community Development,* vol. 44, no. 3, 2013, pp. 336–349.

Watts, Edward. *An American Colony: Regionalism and the Roots of Midwestern Culture.* Ohio UP, 2002.

Weaks-Baxter, Mary. *Reclaiming the American Farmer: The Reinvention of a Regional Mythology in Twentieth-Century Southern Writing.* Louisiana State UP, 2006.

Weber, Brom. "Anderson and 'The Essence of Things.'" *The Sewanee Review,* vol. 59, no. 4, 1951, pp. 678–692.

——. *Sherwood Anderson.* U of Minnesota P, 1964.

Weber, Max. *The Protestant Ethic and the Spirit of Capitalism.* 1904–1905. Translated by Talcott Parsons, Scribner, 1958.

Weber, Ronald. *The Midwestern Ascendancy in American Writing.* Indiana UP, 1992.

Weems, Jason. *Barnstorming the Prairies: How Aerial Vision Shaped the Midwest.* U of Minnesota P, 2015.

Weiner, Lauren. "Dawn Powell: The Fruits of Revival." *New Criterion,* vol. 17, no. 10, 1999, p. 23.

Wendel, Charles H. *Encyclopedia of American Farm Implements & Antiques.* 2nd edition, Krause, 2004.

Wertheim, Arthur Frank. *Vaudeville Wars: How the Keith-Albee and Orpheum Circuits Controlled the Big-Time and Its Performers.* Palgrave Macmillan, 2006.

Whalan, Mark. *Race, Manhood, and Modernism in America: The Short Story Cycles of Sherwood Anderson and Jean Toomer.* U of Tennessee P, 2007.

Whipple, T. K. "Sherwood Anderson." *Sherwood Anderson: A Collection of Critical Essays,* edited by Walter B. Rideout, Prentice-Hall, 1974, pp. 87–100.

White, Ahmed A. "The Crime of Economic Radicalism: Criminal Syndicalism Laws and the Industrial Workers of the World, 1917–1927." *Oregon Law Review,* vol. 85, no. 3, 2007, pp. 649–769.

White, Ed. *The Backcountry and the City: Colonization and Conflict in Early America.* U of Minnesota P, 2005.

Wickramatilake, Shalini, et al. "How States Are Tackling the Opioid Crisis." *Public Health Reports,* vol. 132, no. 2, 2017, pp. 171–179.

Wilhite, Keith. "Contested Terrain: The Suburbs as Region." *American Literature: A Journal of Literary History, Criticism, and Bibliography,* vol. 84, no. 3, 2012, pp. 617–644.

Wilkerson, Richard Gentry, et al. "The Opioid Epidemic in the United States." *Emergency Medicine Clinics of North America,* vol. 34, no. 2, 2016, pp. e1–e23.

Williams, Raymond. *The Country and the City.* Oxford UP, 1973.

Willis, Elizabeth. "The Poetics of Affinity: Niedecker, Morris, and the Art of Work." *Radical Vernacular: Lorine Niedecker and the Poetics of Place,* edited by Elizabeth Willis, U of Iowa P, 2008, pp. 223–246.

Wilson, Brian C. *Yankees in Michigan.* Michigan State UP, 2008.

Winkiel, Laura A. "Nancy Cunard's *Negro* and the Transnational Politics of Race." *Modernism/Modernity,* vol. 13, no. 3, 2006, pp. 507–530.

Winters, Joseph Richard. *Hope Draped in Black: Race, Melancholy, and the Agony of Progress.* Duke UP, 2016.

Wixson, Douglas. *Worker-Writer in America: Jack Conroy and the Tradition of Midwestern Literary Radicalism, 1898–1990.* U of Illinois P, 1994.

Womack, John Jr., and Roxanne Dunbar-Ortiz. "Dreams of Revolution: Oklahoma, 1917." *Monthly Review,* vol. 62, no. 6, 2010, pp. 42–56.

Worden, Daniel. *Masculine Style: The American West and Literary Modernism.* Palgrave Macmillan, 2011.

Wray, Matt. *Not Quite White: White Trash and the Boundaries of Whiteness.* Duke UP, 2006.

Wray, Matt, and Annalee Newitz, editors. *White Trash: Race and Class in America.* Routledge, 1997.

"Writes First Novel." *New York Amsterdam News,* 9 July 1930, p. 20.

Wydeven, Joseph J. *Wright Morris Revisited.* Simon & Schuster Macmillan-Twayne, 1998.

Yaeger, Patricia. *Dirt and Desire: Reconstructing Southern Women's Writing, 1930–1990.* U of Chicago P, 2000.

"You Can't Resist These Gennett Records." Advertisement. *Chicago Defender,* 20 Oct. 1923, p. 7.

Zerubavel, Eviatar. *Hidden Rhythms: Schedules and Calendars in Social Life.* U of Chicago P, 1981.

——. *Time Maps: Collective Memory and the Social Shape of the Past.* U of Chicago P, 2003.

Zieger, Robert H. *American Workers, American Unions, 1920–1985.* Johns Hopkins UP, 1986.

Zukin, Sharon. "Consuming Authenticity: From Outposts of Difference to Means of Exclusion." *Cultural Studies,* vol. 22, no. 5, 2008, pp. 724–748.

# INDEX

*Page numbers in italics refer to illustrations.*